Tribal Development and its Paradoxes

Tribal Development and its Paradoxes

Ashutosh Thakur

AUTHORSPRESS

First Published 2001
by Authorspress

E-35/103, Jawahar Park (Shree Ganesh Complex),
Laxmi Nagar, Delhi-110 092
e-mail: authorspress@yahoo.com

Typeset in NewCenturySchlbk by Chitra Computers

Tribal Development and its Paradoxes
ISBN 81-7273-050-0

Printed in India at Tarun Offset, Delhi.

Preface

The tribals are social groups, usually with a definite area, dialect, cultural homogeneity and unifying social organisation. Their identity and culture are closely linked to the natural resources and the environment amidst which they live. India has the largest concentration of tribal population in the world. The tribals are the indigenous people of the land. They are generally called as *adivasis*, which literary means earliest settlers. Under the Constitution of India they have been specified as Scheduled Tribes and are given special treatment and facilities for socioeconomic development.

Today, the identity of the tribals and their continuity are threatened due to neo-colonial and national vehicles of oppression. They are systematically and methodologically being dispossessed of the ownership of their means of production, of the product of their labour and of the very means of human existence. The tribals are continuing their long-standing struggle to re-establish their traditional rights, and for the right develop their culture, religion and social institutions. Through various indigenous people's organisations they are at present reasserting their right for sustainable development and progress.

Indian Constitution has provided many special provisions for the tribal communities with a view to ensure social justice and further their upliftment. Tribal administration has gained momentum since the fifth five year plan, and to ensure a coordinated and integrated approach for the amelioration of the tribal people, an area development approach known as Tribal Sub-Plan area approach has been adopted. The government as well as non-governmental organisations are trying to enhance the welfare of the tribal people by providing a package of services to them and thereby help in reducing development gaps.

The success achieved in the past in transforming the tribal population for sustainable development is far from any satisfactory level. Time has now come to make a realistic assessment so that the welfare and development activities targeted for this vulnerable sections of the society may ensure satisfaction of minimum needs, control and management of productive resources, productive employment generation, maximum participation of the people in development process and the required national integration of tribals with other sections of the society.

The strategy for tribal development has to take into account the basic characteristic of tribal areas. The developmental approach should be based on the principle of making the tribal mass aware and eager for their own development. The increased involvement of more and more elevated tribals for planning and implementing developmental programmes for the tribal area may be advocated as such attempts can be more realistic, productive and feasible. The tribal based sociocultural milieu should assimilate the desirable changes to adjust harmoniously with the changes in the process of development.

The present work attempts to focus on the developmental strategies of tribal communities and emphasis on the need for viable development programmes to accomplish their wide-range developmental needs. It will be valuable not only to academicians, but also to administrators and policy makers.

Ashutosh Thakur

Contents

Contents

1

Introduction

The tribal population of India is comprising 257 communities according to the 1991 census. These tribal communities belong to different racial stocks, speak languages of different families and show considerable variation in basic economy. Madhya Pradesh, Orissa, Bihar and Rajasthan account for more than 60 per cent of the entire tribal population in the country. A tribe which is scheduled in one place may not be scheduled in another place and the list of the scheduled tribes maintained by the State Government often varies to that of the Central Government.

Most of the tribal communities of India are autogenous excepting those in Himalayan and northeastern region of the country, who were latter immigrants to the Indian subcontinent. Nevertheless, in the long history of Indian civilisation all have mingled together borrowing culture extensively from each other. No doubt the process of acculturation has been slow and accommodative; the dividing lines between different groups in terms of cultural and economic systems is not clear, though social stratification has been almost complete. However, some of the tribal communities articulated and got assimilated with the greater society, whereas some of them preferred to recede into the remoter hilly and inaccessible forest areas.

The tribal people maintain their livelihood by undertaking a number of occupations such as forestry and food-gathering, shifting cultivation, settled agriculture, industrial and agricultural labour, animal husbandry, fishing, trade and commerce of which household industry including handicrafts is of prime importance.

The four major geographical divisions of tribal population in India are:

i) *North-eastern zone*: Tribes like the Abor, Garo, Khasi, Kuki, Lepcha, Mismi, Naga, Rabha, etc., who mostly belong to the mountain valleys and other areas of North-east India.

ii) *Central zone*: Tribal communities like the Bhumij, Gond, Ho, Oraon, Munda, Santal, Bhil, etc., are living in the older hills and Chhotanagpur plateau, along the dividing line between peninsular India and Indo-Gangetic basin.

iii) *South-western zone*: In the hills and converging line of the Ghats live the Chenchu, Irula, Kadar, Kota, Kurumba, Toda, etc.

iv) *Others*: This group includes various scattered tribal groups like the Andamanese and such other tribes of Andaman and Nicobar Islands.

The tribes of North-eastern India follow shifting cultivation; those of central zone are engaged in agriculture; and the economy of a number of tribes of South-western zone is based on food-gathering. The most interesting aspect of tribal economy is that, they rarely follow one occupation exclusively.

Development has become an enemy of some tribal groups, particularly small tribal groups, which have remained outside national political systems. In their greed, the national majorities or the larger groups have been grabbing tribal land through legislation or even illegally, without even the formalities for acquiring oil, mining and timber. Some tribal farmers elsewhere have to see their lands flooded by dams or other kinds of developmental activities with the help of administrators.

In the worldwide western offensive against the rearguard of primitive societies, extermination, eviction or subjugation has been the rule and conversion the exception; most fold societies of the pre-civilised times are no more and if some of them persist in their primary condition, they are a mere handful and objects of anthropological curiosity and enquiry. Viewed in this perspective, theoretically the general approach adopted towards tribal development in this country has been characterised by sensitivity and humaneness. Yet, in the midst of engrossing national public and private affairs, little notice is taken of some small groups of people in this country who live marginally. Even the existence of such groups seldom comes to light, except when some quirk of circumstance forces it on public consciousness.

From the demographical point of view, out of the over 257 different scheduled tribes communities, about 72 have been treated as primitive groups by the government of India. Perhaps it is easier to recognise weak tribal groups one comes across than lay down diacritical marks for their identification. Nevertheless, different authorities have attempted to introduce systems in the matter of identification.

The tribes are so many and so rapidly changing as to defy analysis; however, there can be noticed some traits which could be of help e.g., distinctiveness in the matter of where the community begins and where it ends expressed in group consciousness of the people of the community, quality of compactness, a unit of personal observation becoming fully representative of the whole, a quality of homogeneity rendering activities and state of mind much alike for persons in corresponding sex, age groups etc.

The status of members of a group is perceived by each acting towards one another; and if towards outsiders, the group may form a segment of a wider system. Social scientists have also categorised such groups into a few classes like the hunter and the food-gatherer, the shifting cultivator, the primitive agriculturist, etc.

There is no general agreement as to what constitutes diacritical marks of distinction of tribal groups. There are some parameters like numerical size, rate of reproduction, state of ecological equilibrium, degree of isolation, extent of interaction with outside communities which can be thought of as desirable criteria to be made use of for identification purposes. But, by and large, these parameters elude precise quantification and bristle with difficulties in their application. The four practical salient characteristics which have emerged are: numerical smallness, low level of literacy, use of simple technology, and pre-agricultural or primitive agricultural pursuits.

These marginal communities need fostering, nursing and care. The most crucial issue is of their demographic stability i.e., their extinction or continued survival. Some of the groups are very small. The forces which have operated to reduce these groups to their present diminutive status, if allowed to continue uninterruptedly and indefinitely, would lead them towards total extinction. The health and nutrition status of some groups is appealingly low. This may be due to the impoverished natural resource environment or on account of failure to harness the extant natural resources. In fact, a number of factors might operate to create the sociocultural situation in which the group might be placed.

Tribal communities have their autonomous culture and they are proud about it, they would no longer like to be treated as museum specimen tucked away in hills and jungles to be visited occasionally by the city-bred intellectuals. They would like to derive the benefits of changing economic developments sweeping the country. They would like to share in the national mainstream. There is no doubt a problem is here and it is how to bring about socioeconomic development and integration without sacrificing the cultural excellence that has marked many of these communities. In planning the development of these areas, it is essential to take into account the special characteristics of each of the tribes; its level of socioeconomic development, its system of values and the present stage of its material culture.

The present approach on development of the tribal areas lays emphasis on area development. This approach looks upon an area predominantly inhabited by tribals as a unit with given resources endowments. The objective becomes the development of the entire population inhabiting that area and not merely the tribals. Tribal Development Agencies were created as societies under the Societies Registration Act, 1860. Later, Intensive Tribal Development Projects as government agencies were created as the concept of a Sub-Plan within the framework of the State Plan came into being. The Sub-Plan for tribal area is basically a plan with an area-approach emphasising the development of the tribals. Emphasis is put in the Sub-Plan on agriculture, including land, reclamation and land development, group demonstration and provision of input assistance.

Small irrigation projects including dug-wells and lift irrigation wells, horticulture, and backyard plantation are taken up on priority basis. Large scale afforestation is also taken up. Animal husbandry, poultry and beekeeping are encouraged as subsidiary income-earning employment. With a view to providing integrated credit-cum-marketing structure a new co-operative pattern popularly known as LAMPS has been organised and they provide a package of services like purchase of surplus agricultural and minor forest produce from the tribals at reasonable prices and supply provision of adequate credit.

The development process should also evolve a mechanism through which the emergent aspirations and the felt-needs of the tribals are gathered, processed and taken to decision-making levels so that the plans and programmes which are eventually drawn up for development, incorporate those aspirations. Because of the language difficulty, there is very little communication between the tribal world and the political and administrative leaders. Well-formulated plans and availability of funds are no guarantee that the plans would be executed properly.

The communication barrier between the tribal societies and the larger society around them is broken. For this the first important step would be to formulate a well-thought person policy for the development of tribal areas. This policy should be able to work out a tenure system for carefully chosen officers having a flair for development work who are suitably equipped for the purpose. Tribals are very sensitive and proud, straight forward, impulsive and dignified people.

They have a sense of innate self-respect and are imbued with a strong sense of community. As a matter of fact, the non-tribal world stands to learn from their sense of community living and their intense commitment to life even in the face of great tragedies and economic deprivations. As the development efforts go on it is essential that we try to maintain these valuable aspects of their culture so that small communities of the tribal world do not become carbon copy of more complex and urbanised societies with their problems of atomised individuals suffering from a loss of the sense of belonging, ennui and boredom.

The small community makes possible the expressions of creativity and joy of living to be preserved in a unique and authentic way. The distortions are less, the genuineness and true-to-life character still predominate. This makes preservation of the authenticity of culture and its transmission a simpler and natural task, which in turn makes it all the more important because we, who believe in unity in diversity, should emphasise the need for maintaining small communities and their cultures, allowing them to develop in their own unique ways.

Development implies creating conditions in a given society for wholesome living of its members. It stands for the rise in the standard of living of the weaker sections, greater participation in the affairs of the larger society and the state, freedom from poverty, unconstrained development of individual's personality and a congenial relationship among the various constituents of the social fabric. But great challenges do persist in the process of development, particularly in a vast and complex country like India, where per capita income is Rs. 1484 and 76.27 per cent of people live in half a million of villages situated in rural interiors.

The British Government in India made attempts to comprehend the diverse tribal societies in the country and this endeavour of their for studying the exotic cultures brought in anthropology to the subcontinent. Pace of economic change was accelerated as people from the plains, being pushed by the increasing pressure of population, migrated to tribal areas in search of new opportunities. The hitherto isolated tribal communities now came into face-to-face interaction with non-tribals as well as with a strong central power, which was not satisfied only with exercising sovereignty over the tribals but had genuine economic interests as well.

The economic interests of the British led to the development of communication facility in inaccessible tribal areas and rapid monetisation of the tribal economy, but it adversely affected the tribes; firstly, in most of the areas a somewhat wanton and unplanned exploitation of forest and other resources gradually tended to upset the age-old ecological balance; secondly, it brought out tribal land to the open market; and thirdly, it made tribals more susceptible to exploitative loans.

The past two centuries witnessed soothing discontent all over the tribal regions as they were confronted with acute problems relating to land and forest, the two vital props of tribal economy. Some of the tribal communities did neither appreciate nor relish extraneous interference in the management of their own affairs—social, economic, religious and political.

A commonly accepted policy in British India was that of isolation or segregation of the tribal population. Isolation is a phenomenon wherein a group of people or a community was disconnected from other communities and resided in remote pockets having their own distinct way of life. The force behind this policy gathered strength from the uni-dimensional thinking of the foreign rulers and some others. One of the units of this thinking was the realisation that the administration would be difficult in far flung and interior tribal areas. Another support was the feeling that isolation would help keep separate the tribal people from political infection. The third was the assumption that the tribals were better and happier in their natural surrounding and traditional sociocultural milieus.

As isolationists, the then rulers declared certain contiguous and thickly populated tribal belts as the excluded and partially excluded areas. The policy of isolation was supported by the then separatist anthropologists who even advocated for tribal reserves. They sought support from the explanation that in colonial countries many tribals could not withstand the impact of aggressive western culture and became extinct.

India being characterised by multiplicity of races and cultures, flourishing together the phenomenon of isolation would not be able to run counter to the facts of Indian situation. The Christian missionaries, the Hindu social workers and reformers and other engaged in risk of tribal development and uplift thought of another solution, altogether different from that of isolation. They started their campaign for assimilation of the broad social matrix. The terms assimilation or missionary solution could be applied to any attempt to deal with aboriginals not by solving their own problems from inside and on the basis of their own life and culture but by changing them or assimilating them into a new community. Considering tribal social customs as inferior, the missionaries started making efforts to substitute them by their respective ones, regarding the latter as superior.

Though some kind of assimilation continued for decades together and even now some of the agencies are practically actively involved in it, the approach was not accepted by a large number of anthropologists, nor by the government. The charges made against assimilation were quite a few. One thinking in regard to assimilation has been that it would simply help poor tribals to become poor converts. Then a complete assimilation did noτ conform to the trends of Indian history. Another defect brought to the surface was that the assimilation would lead to a break with the past, and will not be an evolution from it.

The greatest psychological handicap in assimilation is the element of inferiority complex which gets created among the tribal people towards their religion and culture. At the same time assimilation creates conditions wherein chances of rapid acquisition of vices of civilisation and loss in their earlier values can be prominent and sharp. Simultaneously, the loss of arts and crafts, music and dance, cooperate life and discipline is also done.

The missionaries were anxious to see the primitives civilised, their inferior social customs and ideas eliminated, and their identity assimilated into the Christian church. They succeeded in many ways. But because of their feelings of cultural and religious superiority, they are responsible for disturbing their cultural integration and incuicating a feeling of inferiority among the *Adivasis*. Some missionaries and social workers did lead to the establishment of schools, hospitals, boardings and cooperative societies among various tribes. But at the same time, some of them are also responsible for the creation of separatist and anti-national tendencies. Behind whatever they have done was their chief mission of proselytisation of the members of the native population. Their approach was always tinged with the motive of evangelisation.

Likewise, Bhagat movement has created socially divisive tendencies. At the same time some non-official workers, because of their direct or indirect association or link with the wider political parties, have already started doing harm to the tribal people. Under the reform movements, many of them, infact, serve as the political links at the tribe or village level. Within this vicious circle, or even independently, some politicians approach the tribals for their own ends. Such politicians' approach is characterised by certain serious defects. They create trends and tendencies to exploit position and the increasing discontent of the tribals, they use them as spring boards for achieving their targets. The act is preceded by false assurances, and if needed, by the injection of anti-national sentiments and perverted communal feeling.

Situation took a turn in the post-independence years when at one stage, it was commonly agreed to adopt the policy of integration of the tribal people into the general social matrix of India and the national democratic set up. The government and most of the anthropologists and social workers approved of the integration policy.

In the year 1953 the social scientists, welfare workers, the leaders of the political party in power and government officials met in Lohardaga to participate in a Conference of Tribal Workers. Discussions were held to devise line of action for the integration and uplift of the tribal population. It was an outcome of the realisation that complete assimilation and isolation were unpracticable in the fight of dynamics and historical processes of Indian social life.

In the past there had been coexistence of all kinds of intercommunicating societies with their respective cultural configurations. In the light of the genius of Indian social life the various ethnic groups, with their multi-cultural fact, have been brought together and integrated. It was laid down that as an important part of policy, the introduction is to be attempted without damaging tribe's distinctive socio-cultural entity. Another realisation of the framers of integration policy was that by isolating and neglecting the large population of the tribes, the country would not progress. With integration, India, as a vast mosaic would then contain numerous ethnic and cultural groups as its components with diverse cultural patterns.

After independence the nation constitutionally committed to bring about comprehensive and integrated development of this weaker section of the Indian society. The founding fathers of the Constitution indeed realised the technoeconomic and educational backwardness of the tribal communities, and inserted special provisions in it for their protection, upliftment and participation in the affairs of the nation with a view to ensuring that they do not go down in unequal competitions with the advanced sections.

The Constitutional provision has two important features; firstly, the tribal affairs are sought to be kept about considerations of political parties, and outside the purview of the state legislatures and the Parliament with regard to grants for welfare; and secondly, the fact that then tribal situation in the country is diverse has been paid due attention by making specific provisions for the northeastern and scheduled tribal areas.

The tribals are not to be uprooted from their traditional cultural moorings. The policy framers also agreed on the point that if right approach is cultivated, the integration of the tribals would not and presuppose assimilation. It was resolved that for integration, the economic and educational standard of the tribal groups should be brought on par with the rest of people. In support of integration of the tribes, columns were provided in the Indian Constitution.

Artical-46 of the Constitution states that

> "The State shall promote with special care the educational and economic interests of the weaker sections of the people, and, in particular of the Scheduled Castes and Scheduled Tribes, and shall protect them from social injustice and all forms of exploitation".

To give an immediate start to the matter, Special Multi-purpose Tribal Blocks were started in various states of the country. To remain more concerned and particular, it was further laid down in Article 339 that

> "The President may at any time and shall at the expiration of ten years from the commencement of this Constitution by order appoint a commission to report on the administration of the Scheduled Areas and the welfare of the Scheduled Tribes in the States".

Article 244 empowers the President to declare any area, where there is a substantial population of tribal people, as a Scheduled Area under the 5th Schedule or in Assam as a Tribal Area under the 6th Schedule. Under 5th Schedule, the executive power of a state extends to the Scheduled Areas but the Governor is vested with the authority to modify state and central laws and to make regulations for their peace and good government.

In all states having Scheduled Areas, a Tribes, Advisory Council has to be set up. The 5th Schedule also provides that the executive powers of the Union shall extend to the giving of directions to the state as to the administration of the said areas.

Article 339 lays down that

> "The executive power of the Union extends to the giving of directions to a State as to the drawing up and execution of schemes specified in the directions to be essential for the welfare of the Schedule Tribes in the State".

Article 275 reads that

> "There shall be paid out of the Consolidated Fund of India as grant-in-aid of the revenues of a State such

> capital and recurring sums as may be necessary to enable that State to meet the costs of such schemes of development as may be undertaken by the State with the approval of Government of India for the purpose of promoting the welfare of the Scheduled Tribes in that State, or raising the level of administration of the Scheduled Areas therein to that of the administration of the rest of that State".

Articles 330, 332 and 334 provide for reservation of seats in the State Legislatures and House of people for Scheduled tribes.

In regard to the establishment of the Tribes, Advisory Council, it has been included that

> "There shall be established in each State having Scheduled Areas therein and if the President so directs, also in any state having Scheduled Tribes but no scheduled Areas therein, a Tribes, Advisory Council consisting of not more than twenty members of whom, as nearly as may be, three-fourth shall be the representatives of the Scheduled Tribes in the Legislative Assembly of the State. It shall be the duty of Tribes, Advisory Council to advise on such matters pertaining to the welfare and advancement of the Scheduled Tribes in the State as may be referred to them by the Governor".

The approach has also been pinpointed under Articles 15,16 and 17 which "make it possible while legislating on any matter to take into consideration the special conditions of the tribals in the matter of enforcing the provisions relating to the equality of all citizens. The object is to safeguard their interest and their way of life".

Gandhiji once said "We must approach the poor with the mind of the poor". 'Approach the tribesman with the mind of the tribesman.' In Gandhian method of welfare programme, everything was based on local economy, works were undertaken through local institutions, unwanted innovations were avoided and fundamental needs were concentrated upon.

What Nehru said about the tribal people and about the solution of their problems also points to the approach in the context of integration. He states, "they possess a variety of culture and are in many ways certainly not backward.

There is no point in trying to make them a second rate copy of ourselves. Schemes for welfare, education, communication, medical relief were no doubt essential but one must always remember, however, that we do not mean to interfere with their way of life, but to help them to live it. The tribal people should be helped to grow according to their genius and tradition. He introduced Panch Sheel policy for tribal development.

Developmental strategies started with ameliorative programmes in the First Five-Year Plan when the community development movement was launched in the country. Within the community development framework special projects were taken up for tribal areas. During the Second Plan the concept of tribal area development along with welfare was introduced. The community development frame was accepted for the tribal areas with reduced geographical size and higher quantum of financial outlays. The Tribal Development Blocks, a less intensive version of Multipurpose Tribal Development Projects, converted all areas with more than two-thirds tribal concentration by the end of the Third Plan. During the Fourth Plan there was no additional geographical coverage although the Scheduled Areas and Tribes Commission had recommended extension of Tribal Development Blocks to all areas with more than fifty per cent tribal population. Comprehensive area development approach was conceived of in the Fifth Five-Year Plan and integrated Sub-Plan was drawn up with direct linkages with a state's economy and total Plan. The concept has been further defined in the Sixth Plan to include individual tribal family development. This new strategy undoubtedly has ushered in a new phase in tribal development in the country. There has been significant breakthrough, if not a spectacular achievement, in the field of tribal development.

The Tribals are socially and culturally very strong, and during the recent decades some of them have developed a radical ethnocentric attitude. This sort of attitude, which is normally whipped up and steered by the elites within a tribe, has more often than not, given rise to sociopolitical movements. Self-centric elites have emerged, who now constitute the advanced section in a tribe, but there is a general lack of development-oriented and committed leadership among the tribes.

In spite of their virgin potentialities for development they continue to be technoeconomically backward and are behind the main stream living in areas around them. An important issue which relates to this is that the development effort has made no more than a marginal impact on them barring a few instances; as a result they continue to live in an idyllic situation being content with whatever they get in their respective habitats. In the past tribal habitats were exclusively being exploited by the tribals themselves; but now a days these are exploited by government and other agencies, too. Outside agencies exploit natural resources comparatively recklessly as they do not have a sense of belonging whereas every tribe has its cultural norms of exploitation; and hence they do not do it in a pernicious manner.

The development process has widened the gap between the poor and the rich. This is also true now among the tribes, who were once egalitarian and homogeneous. None expected the same degree of achievement, in spite of equal economic inputs in different tribal communities, because of cultural, racial, demographic and ecological differences which exist among them.

However, people at the helm of affairs never probably imagined that the development process would make the poor poorer. Five reasons can possibly be enlisted for this sad and gloomy picture; firstly, planning was centralised; secondly, planning was mostly done by economists and bureaucrats who did not pay any attention to the cultural factors in the development process; thirdly, people's participation was not envisaged as an integral part of development; fourthly, inadequacy of the administrative machinery to cope up with the paramount task of development; and fifthly, lack of a separate development cadre composed of various specialists and experts to execute development programmes in an integrated manner.

There are many sociocultural barriers to the acceptance of development schemes, and consequently, to social change.

In simpler societies social structure, in some situations, operates as a barrier. Mutual obligations and expectations within the framework of family, lineage and kin-groups are social imperatives and not optional. Reciprocal obligations, which contribute to the solidarity of group/society, constitute obstacles to the acceptance of economic programmes that are not in conformity with the values of the target population. Before launching a welfare programme it is essential to study the motivation and survey the proclivities of the target population.

In each society there are always some change-inhibiting factors, which preclude of foil implementation of welfare programmes. No, society is free from vested interests. Likewise, there are conservatists in every society who adhere to traditionalism and resist change. Technological and economic development cannot successfully be undertaken in a society without necessary changes in the value-attitude system. Transformation of value-attitude system is basic and fundamental to economic development of a society. And existence of value-attitude system is equally fundamental to the continuance and smooth functioning of a society. Planners and executors of development programmes do not pay any attention to these problems; and this is one of the causes that widens the hiatus between the development target and achievement.

The tribal groups are of wide variations in psychological, cultural, social, economic and political backgrounds. The diversity lends richness to the national mosaic; simultaneously, it poses a challenge to planners, administrators, social scientists and other thinkers. Sometimes cultural constraints impede dissemination of technology. But rashness in introduction and undue insistence on adoption of improved technology are liable to offend their psychological, cultural and religious susceptibilities. Proper care has, therefore, to be observed in ensuring that the pace of innovation is in step with their assimilative capacity and that the contents of development plans accord with their genius. This imposes an onerous responsibility, making it incumbent on the administration to be tuned sensitively to the ethos of each group, based on prior, intense surroundings. For careful advancement of tribal people careful planning is needed. A primary requirement is to study and understand the existing practices, including norms and taboos guiding the social network of the tribals. This will give a fairly comprehensive idea of the cultural or other conditions and the problems. Such a study of individual tribe and tribal groups would also take into account the various areas of economic organisation, especially the needs and necessary part of it.

In the interest of right kind of integration, the formation of plan should be preceded by the scientific study of the culture of a tribe. Careful planning is to be based on the specific problems and needs of the tribe or even its groups. During the course of planning, nature of the attitude of the tribe or its group members towards the agencies of change is to be considered. Such a necessity has claim, under the phenomenon that social change is never independent of human will and purpose.

There is a growing consciousness that the prevailing socioeconomic and political systems are more homogenising than humanising and that the dominant worldview is more fallacious than realistic and holistic. The fact of the fast depletion of resources has become a threat to the consumerist society. This has challenged the very uneconomic thinking and the mindless pursuit of wealth. As such people have started talking about sustainable practices for better living, sound economic behaviour for people's greater well being and judicious political governance for equality and justice in society.

The pedagogy of the tribals is meant the knowledge and wisdom of the tribal people who can teach us how to live better. This pedagogy is the value system of the tribals who are different from those of the stratified and caste ridden societies. It is looking at life from the tribal perspective.

The myths and stories of tribal forms the basis of the tribal ideology. It provides legitimation to tribal life and work. The tribal ideology also includes a more or less clear analysis and understanding of tribal society, a vision for the future and a choice of approaches and strategies. The tribal ideology is thus, a sum total of the tribal values on which are constructed the various social, economic and political systems.

God, the human person, spirits and nature are the four elements that construct the tribal worldview. God, according to the tribals is the creator of everything. He is omnipotent and omnipresent. He is also a benevolent and all caring God. He is the invisible sovereign spirit. He has created the spirits, humans and nature in the world. Each has a function to play in life. Humans have to till the earth to feed themselves. They also have to tend and harness nature which in turn sustains them.

The spirits are God's messengers and agents. They are the guardians of other created beings. They dwell on hills and mountains, on groves and plantations and on water bodies and village boundaries. Everything on earth is under their guardianship. Thus they watch over nature as the allies of human beings. In return they get respect and sustenance from them who offer libations and propitiations to them from time to time. This inextricable mutual symbiosis among humans, nature and spirits is the foundational principle of the tribal worldview. These beliefs and precepts come to the tribal people from God Himself through myths and stories. Myths for the tribal people hold the absolute truth.

The events of the myths which tell the stories of creation, fall and restoration, narrate the events as actually happened not in history but in some primordial time. The myths have aetiological function in that they have a symbolic value. The creed of the tribals posits the existence of certain spiritual causes which account for the empirical world. The myths and stories themselves are however simple and always carry a message. The tribe or the community is God's own making. He created man and woman and ordered them to procreate for His own sake. Thus all are God's children.

The tribes live in clans which are symbolically grouped after animate and inanimate totems. Since the tribe is a link between God and humans, living in the tribe is heaven and living outside it is hell as in the case of social ostracism as punishment. Similarly, after birth a child is initiated into the tribe through rites and rituals and after death the deceased is restored to the ancestors.

A tribal feels intensely the sense of the holy or the unholy in the world. And from this deep religious conviction he/she regulates his/her life. The temporal life too is governed by mutually accepted rules and regulations, always mindful of the fact that God dwells in the tribe and that no one must be unfair towards others. Such a sacrosanct picture of tribal worldview might look too good to be true. But the fact is that the tribal life and belief system is not free from aberrations which, however, must be countered.

The tribal ideology gives legitimation to tribals as a social group. It articulates first of all the tribal identity in terms of geographical, historical, ethnological, linguistic arid socio-cultural features. These give the tribals their distinct character and distinguish them from other peoples of the country. The tribal ideology contains in itself emotional elements which are capable of moving its men and women and giving them a feeling of security simply because they contain a summary of the past, explain the present and foresee the future. These aspects will be explained more clearly through the socio-economic and political systems of tribals. On the socio-cultural sphere, the tribal ideology is rooted in the principle of equality and their sense of balance in the man-woman relationship in their respective social rights.

There is no rigid social stratification among tribals on the basis of caste and class, nor is there discrimination on the basis of name, sex or place of birth. Elders are respected and people relate with one another on kinship and friendship lines. Religion and culture are woven around monotheistic beliefs and spirit and nature related rites of passage. The tribal priest offers sacrifices to God at the sacred grove on behalf of the community.

Land is in the trusteeship of the tribal community and the different households have only usufructory rights. Even when the families own the landed properties, they are understood to be only the caretakers. In fact, land is not a commodity to be sold and purchased as it has a spiritual and emotional value. Tribal lands and forests have been the source of people's livelihood satisfying their basic needs of food, shelter, clothing and health care. Most of the agricultural operations are carried out on the basis of mutual self-help and cooperation. The village is ruled by the council of elders constituted of all the adult members of the community. The village leader is elected on the basis of consensus and the functions as the 'first among equals'. Decisions at village meetings are also arrived at through consensus after all those present have been heard. Many villages make a federation and many federations make a confederation, ruled by the respective elders.

Their business is to deal with the temporal administration of the communities. The customary law developed through their history provides regulatory principles for organising, administering and maintaining the socio-economic and political relationships in the tribal societies.

The ideology of the tribal people has also been shaped by their constant struggle for existence as a different cultural entity against the civilisation of the colonisers. Thus the ideology of their present struggles in different parts of the country is to rejuvenate the dying roots of their cultural identity. This entails first of all the identification of the forces of oppression and cultural erosion and then to supplant the tribal roots in society through the revolutionary movement. In fact the tribals in many places have adopted the values and systems of other societies. But the point that is being made here is to look at the tribal perspective and draw inferences for our times.

There are competing systems and thoughts, more often than not dominating and regulating human societies. These dichotomies and conflicts are variously termed as the 'mainstream ideology vs. 'the 'subaltern ideology', organised religions' vs. 'popular religions' or the orthodox paradigm' vs. 'the political-economy paradigm' in their respective spheres to mention a few. A comparative analysis of these perspectives reveals their dynamics and implications as well as presents a choice of models in today's context. The economic thinking too is determined by the society's worldview and ideology. For the formal economics land, forests and natural resources are both capital and means of production. Wealth is put to multiply wealth for higher standards of life. According to the principle of comparative advantage and division of labour, a few are the owners of means of production and the majority sell their labour. The scale and intensity of production also determines the use of resources.

While large scale, heavy technology based and resource depleting development approach is the hallmark of the capitalist economic system, small scale, labour intensive and resource regenerating approach is the characteristic of the informal economic system. While the former is in clear favour of gigantism, the latter abides by the principle of sustainability and "small is beautiful". Similarly, while capitalist monopolism or even competitive capitalism aim at high economic growth for high mass consumption, informal economics go for the need based production. In the former, the owners earn profit and the labourers get wages, but in the latter each receives according to his/her need and gives according to his/her capacity. According to the capitalist ecological principle, nature is to be subjugated and conquered. The human-nature relationship is thus dichotomous. The eco-friendly tribal principle, on the other hand, promotes sustainable approaches of resources use. The human-nature relationship is thus symbiotic and holistic.

The caste and class systems of the Hindu and the capitalist society respectively, stand in direct opposition to the casteless and the classless society of the tribals. And just as the former get their origin and legitimation from the sacred scriptures or the economic doctrine, the latter obtain their significance from the religious myths and their day to day living. Needless to say, the organised traditions want to maintain the status quo whereas the indigenous cultures provide sufficient scope for liberal mobility like greater equality of men and women in society and greater economic freedom to women.

Structures of the mainstream society are more hierarchical and pyramidal but those of the smaller societies are circular and horizontal. Accordingly individualism or collective fellow-feeling is fostered among the people. Another characteristic of the established societies is that the structures and services get formalised as institutions like the government, the trade unions or the schools and hospitals.

A society takes recourse to its religion and culture in seeking answers to the basic questions of human life-birth, death, suffering after-life etc. Though profound religious experience is the genesis of the great religious like Christianity, Islam, Hinduism, Buddhism etc., in the course of time ritualism tends to take precedence over religious experience and pictism over the prophetic content.

But in popular traditions like tribal religious, the awareness and the experience of the hold is pervasive. The stress is not on teaching and preaching, but on moral living and community fellowship. The organised religious and cultures also try to reach out to others. The adherents of these faiths want to share their religious experience with other people. In so far as this sharing of religious experience is not liberating the people—socially, economically and culturally—it must be censored as irreligious and dehumanising. Religion and culture must enhance people's self-respect and identities.

Election, majority decision and centralised authority are some of the features of the organised political systems. People's participation in these systems is indirect. The polity and authority of governance is written down in constitutions which also contain people's rights and responsibilities. The executive, legislative and judicial systems are specified and are regulated by different bodies. In the tribal societies however, there are no formal governments, nor is there a written code of conduct. The polity and authority is vested in the whole community as such because even the council of elders is not the supreme body but has only functional powers. The whole community has a say in the assignment of leaders. Decisions are taken by the people themselves in a consensus and justice is also dispensed ultimately by the whole community.

The vast majority of true forest cultures still alive in India call only be found inside the sanctuaries and national parks that many human rights groups mistakenly denounce. The enemy of both biodiversity and traditional cultures is the much-vaunted market that urban investors use to appropriate forest wealth.

The many Chief Wildlife Wardens are under no obligation to displace traditional communities as their meagre needs can indeed be met by the productivity of the forest with some adjustment in terms of reducing the impact of livestock on forest regeneration and cooperation with wildlife authorities in countering those indulging in poaching, or the illegal extraction of forest wealth for sale in nearby urban markets. Clearly, it is crucial that such forest communities not be allowed to become pawns in the hands of the urban or rural rich.

Iron ore mining and rampant government-sponsored deforestation has already crippled the fabulous forests that gave rise to a biodiversity that has still not been tabulated and to cultures that have been eroded faster than they could be documented. Bastar is the very quintessence of natural India. In Bastar, the tiger and its associated life forms depend almost entirely on the forests that clothe the catchment of the Indravati River. A series of proposed dams threaten the Indravati valley and though some of these projects have been abandoned, others continue to be pushed despite evidence to suggest that they would cost the nation more than they can ever hope to produce. Official and illegal timber and mineral extraction also wounds this fragile area, its wildlife and its people. The Indravati river rises from the highlands of Jorhmal and drains the slopes of the Chandgiri peak in the Eastern Ghats of Orissa, before flowing westwards to Madhya Pradesh. It flows for 400 km before emptying into the Godavari. A true mountain current, it is fed through its left and right banks by several lesser rivers such as the Nibra, Kotri, Bandia and Berudi. The entire system was once thickly forested and despite years of criminal desecration by the timber lobby, miners and sundry developers, parts still support a bewildering diversity of animal life largely within the confines of the Indravati Tiger Reserve.

In those parts of Bastar where the forests have not been devastated, cut off from so-called development, tribal communities such as the Dorlas continue to access roots, tubers, forest fruit, fish, crabs and small game to supplement a diet of pulse, and grains obtained through marginal agriculture. Thousands of their compatriots have not been so fortunate. Their forests were stolen from them and they have consequently been converted to the State of, bonded labour, rural destitutes, and urban migrants. Timber felling and mining was however terminated with the declaration of the 1,950 sq. km. Indravati Tiger Reserve several years ago, just as it was terminated in and around hundreds of wildlife sanctuaries and parks across India.

Wildlife protection laws, without ever once meaning to, have proved to be the lifeline of traditional adivasi forest cultures in India. By contrast, the Tribal Welfare Department and several social activist groups that share its vision have by acts of commission or commission helped developers to rob adivasi communities of dignity and self-sufficiency while attempting to improve their lot.

Tragically the displacement of tribal communities and the loot of their lands, forests, rivers and ancestral properties continues unabated. However, with a no-forced-displacement policy having been officially placed on record by government bodies Such as the Indian Board for Wildlife and Project Tiger, forest communities are able to practice their traditional lifestyles in. and around the over 550 protected forests set aside for wildlife protection. There can be no denying however that the Wildlife (Protection) Act 1972 and the Forest (Conservation) Act, 1980, like all other Indian laws, also had their genesis in colonial legislation. Human rights activists are never tired of pointing this out at every opportunity. What they do not point out, however, is that the same legislation effectively keeps most market forces at bay, thus allowing nature to be nature and adivasis to be adivasis.

Wildlife and forest laws did not violate many legitimate rights of adivasi communities. They did. And minor changes in the law that prevents the exploitation of adivasi communities at the hands of irresponsible and sometimes corrupt forest staff are indeed called for. It is vital, however, that in trying to deliver justice to adivasis, we do not loosen the provisions of the Acts to the point where Chief Ministers, businessmen and contractors, thus far prevented from consuming wildlife areas, are able to usurp the wealth of wildlife India. This, after all, is precisely what they have done outside wildlife protection zones.

Tribal communities know their forests better than any forest department staff and are therefore able to use hidden forest trails and ancient technologies for survival to access life-support resources. Meanwhile Chief Ministers, miners and dam builders are effectively denied access to wildlife reserves. Human rights groups and social activists need to drum up the humility to accept that they have failed to prevent such powerful forces from wiping out adivasi cultures.

Howsoever, distasteful the thought, they will also have to admit that in the surviving forests set aside to protect tigers, elephants, deer and birds, a relatively small but significantly percentage of scheduled tribes such as the Adis, Bhils, Baigas, Bhumias, Chenchus, Garos, Korku, Mannans, Maria Gonds, Nagas, Santals, and Warlis, have been able to hold on to many of their ancient traditions. Here they have been able to follow their own genius for survival with a dignity denied them elsewhere. As anthropologists, and ethnographers will themselves confirm, outside the protected area (PA) network, quite apart from the wounds inflicted by economic domination, adivasi communities have actually been irreparably harmed by legions of intellectuals mid bureaucrats who saw to it that adivasis conformed to their own visions of development, language and customs.

A Juggernaut of mines, dams, roads, thermal plants, copper smelters, forestry schemes literally extirpated tribal lands displacing millions and killing lakhs. For all their utterances, not one human rights or social activist group was able to prevent this human tragedy. Without resort to wildlife laws, not even one single 1,000 sq. km. forest has been saved in the past 50 years by social activists to enable adivasi communities to sustain their traditional survival techniques and customs.

Politicians are trying to turn the tragedy of starvation deaths in Vidharba to their advantage by asking for the denotification of the Melghat Tiger Reserve. Here is what will follow the denotification: far roads will quickly replace the dirt tracks, two and three star hotels, luxury farm houses and other such distractions for the rich will be built. A long-standing proposal to construct a major dam across the Tapi river will be pushed through, displacing still more villagers and usurping the forest that feed their children. This is precisely what has happened. A sum of Rs. 90 crores was allocated for tarring, strengthening and widening roads that adivasis would never use as they prefer their own shaded forest path that get them where they wish to go quicker. Tourism has seen a rise. So has poaching and illegal timber felling.

The communities that lived inside the Tiger Reserve boundary survived pinch periods and their children were saved not on account of any help from human rights activists, or the government. On the contrary, because strict protection had encouraged wild plant species to flourish, they knew how and where to access wild fruit, roots, tubers, vines and leaves. Now the infrastructure for the exploitation of the forest and its tribal communities has tragically been laid. Though they acknowledge the fact that communities inside the protected forest were dramatically better off than those outside, no human rights groups have yet been able to counter the tragedy of the road building which provides access for illegal timber operations and commercialisation of the habitat of both the Korku and the tiger. It takes a touch of humility to accept the veracity of an opposing point of view. It also takes a degree of self-confidence to admit to a mistake.

Wildlifers have largely accepted that past policies involving forced displacements were wrong. Why one wonders do human rights activists seem unwilling to recognise the chauvinism inherent in their position that any and all actions that benefits humans are justified even if rivers, soils and unpopulated (by humans) forests die in the process. Such attitudes are of course equally matched by the foolishness of some wildlifers who yowl about the need to move all humans out of wilderness areas at the point of guns if necessary. Such short-sightedness on both sides of a false divide merely serves to benefit the exploiters. The only real resistance to such violence comes from social activists, who may not really demonstrate any real understanding or caring for wildlife protection, or species diversity.

Instead of joining hands to strengthen the battle against the World Bank, several well-known wildlifers have actually chosen to become consultants to the World Bank. In one fell swoop, from defenders of the wilderness they have thus become collaborators in its destruction. The result of such betrayals is far reaching. By dividing natural allies (tribal activists and wildlifers) the World Kink mid its camp followers hope to rule the forest and plunder its wealth.

An identical situation has emerged in Andhra Pradesh where reports suggest that forest officers and bureaucrats have been induced to certify that the root stock of natural forests is diseased. This paved the way to bulldoze the forests to make way for monoculture plantations of clonal eucalyptus. The ones to suffer most from such steps apart from the wildlife and the forest itself are the many chenchu adivasi communities whose culture and genius emerged from the diversity that is being assassinated. Something similar is taking place in Nagarhole, Karnataka, where social activists and wildlifers are at each other's throats instead of fighting shoulder to shoulder against commercial forestry proponents and those who would mine, dam or otherwise kill our sanctuaries and national parks through five star tourism and tea and coffee plantations.

The largest single financial input into tiger habitats anywhere in the world comes from the offices of the World Bank at 1818 H Street Washington. This money has been unthinkingly welcomed by many myopic conservationists in

India and overseas. They are singularly unaware that for every dollar that the Bank pours into what it terms as biodiversity enhancement it allocates at least another $100 to destroy the natural ecosystems of India.

With conservation groups unable to muster the courage or political acumen to light the terrible troika of politicians, businessmen and bureaucrats whose avarice has led them to the very heart of our most precious forests, mines operate with impunity in tiger forests. Five star tourism is being promoted in Ranthambhor, Nagarhole, Bandhavgarh, Corbett and Periyar. Timber extraction has been increased in and around Melghat and Srisailam and, for that matter, around almost every known tiger habitat in India. Insurgency is destabilising the Manas, Palamau, Valmiki and Indravati Tiger Reserves.

Deforestation hits led to devastating flood in Kaziranga, which is now awash in pesticides leached down from surrounding tea estates. Hundreds of licenses have been issued for commercial fishing in the Pench Tiger Reserve. In this tragic situation we hear of shallow social activists almost gleefully asking: Why save wildlife in a country where people are starving? Unlike their counterparts in large cities, those living in close proximity with forest dwellers however already know the answer to this meaningless question.

TRANSFORMATION OF SOCIETY

A radical change is required in our worldviews and working styles in order to bring about a transformation of society. The tribal ideology can help us in this context. The first principle that ought to direct our lives should be the realisation that we cannot treat ourselves as masters of the resources any more. And because we are human persons, we have the responsibility of seeing that resources are allowed to regenerate. If nature is taken care of, it will take care of us. Harming nature in any way—resource depletion, environmental degradation, pollution etc.—would ultimately mean risking resource scarcity, elimatic disorders and health hazards. It is for this reason that tribals took at nature with awe and reverence.

The tribals were the first to accommodate other people in their land. And it is the tribals who first developed indigenous systems of health care and nurturing of the flora and fauna. All their contribution to human civilisation must be taken into account. They are thus one of the first peoples to shape and shine the human society. But tribals have been made to be the last by other people. They were conquered and subjugated by alien intruders. Their lands were taken away by those whom the tribals accommodated when they came. Sons and daughters of the soil were also made slaves and servants of the invading outsiders. This process of dispossession even continues today through all kinds of land alienation either for development projects or for housing, government and commercial colonies.

Socially, economically and politically, they have been dispossessed and dehumanised. The benefits of development too have been siphoned off from them. It is for these reasons that the tribals must be empowered first. Whatever has been taken away from them must be restored to them. They become the reference point of development today. In this process, any aberration in their socio-cultural system must be corrected. They must be enabled to develop according to their own pace and pattern. Tribals continue to occupy the first position both in terms of human settlement and ascendancy and as target groups of human liberation.

The economic systems of today need to be reoriented according to the principle of sustainability. The earth and its resources are finite. The tribals have long lived and taught the principle of sustainability. We must use them but allow them to regenerate themselves. Resources are also means of livelihood for the tribals. Hence the priority of resource use ought to be the protection of people's livelihood and then only for industrial and commercial purposes. In the pluralistic society of India, each and every race, culture, tradition and people have equal rights to live freely and justiciably. The great social and religious intolerance seen today, is a gross violation of human rights and against any prospects of a sustainable society. If the various traditions cannot live in peaceful co-existence, no amount of harping on sustainable development can bring about any real good.

The great socio-economic disparities and politico-cultural convolutions as well as psycho-ethical turmoils in society present a distressing record of human progress indeed. At the root of this disturbing situation lie conflicting motives and systems of human life. The material-immaterial relationship or the human-universe connection is perceived and constituted differently by different cultures and societies. The dominant systems are more homocentric in their world-view's than the subaltern traditions which are more holistic and universal, though not without some shortcomings.

In the interaction of the diverging perspectives, there is little true synthesis emerging worth the name, as the bigger systems and cultures tend to impinge upon the smaller ones. It is in this sense that greater openness and sensitivity to smaller systems is called for. It is envisaged that this will make the different perspectives more reciprocal and viable to bring about a sustainable society.

2

Tribal Development

Development means change plus growth. It results in a sense of well-being among the members of the society. Although non-materialistic aspects may enter into the picture for a sense of well-being, but it is the material aspects that have to be given greater consideration. The total well-being of a community is often measured in terms of the facilities and services that are available. Whatever be the agency for achieving development, it must be aware of the nature of development in order to achieve the same. The main aim of development is to increase national as well as per capita income and to raise the standard of living of the people and to secure justice, freedom, equality and security for them in the society.

For achieving the goals and tasks of development public administration has been considered an important instrument. There is a great pressure on governments to accelerate national development, make use of up-to-date and relevant technological innovations, adopt and facilitate necessary institutional changes, increase national production, make full use of human and other resources and improve the standard of living. Public administration consists of management of men and material engaged in the service of the state.

Development administration would be public administration with a special purpose. The strategies and goals of change may vary but there are always generic processes through which agreement on goals is reached and plans, policies, programmes and projects are formulated and implemented. Development administration, therefore, is concerned primarily with the tasks and processes of formulating and implementing plans, policies, programmes and projects, in respect to whatever mixture of goals and objectives may be determined.

The development administration in tribal areas is likely to disturb the existing equilibrium between the tribals and their environment. The economic and social development demands introduction of better agricultural practices, better irrigation facilities, introduction of industry, facilities for health and education, etc. All these would require an influx of outsiders in the area. The introduction of developmental programmes is likely to change or at least affect the tribal norms and values.

Though there are a number of developmental models and theories, they are reducible to what is commonly known as vicious circle theory. Alternative versions of the theory may sometimes stress the scarcity of factors other than capital but it is always the inadequate availability of one or the other crucial input which is identified as the binding constraints on development.

However, in the present conjuncture of forces it is not always so much the inadequacy of resources as the inadequacy of demand which is the operative constraint on the rate of capital accumulation. In order to be effective, any strategy of intervention must, therefore, not only ensure the growth of physical stock in a backward area but also the expansion of effective demand for goods produced in that area. It, therefore, appears necessary to identify the economic base of the area and concentrate on the growth of these sectors. The export sector of a backward area can serve as an effective basis for development.

A surplus balance of trade need not always lead to the development of the area as it may coincide with a deficit on capital account and even when the balance of payment is so balanced that there is no net outflow of capital in the accounting sense, there may still be a leakage of surplus from an under-developed area because of a fundamental under-valuation of its products by more developed areas.

As the modern theory of under-development points out, it is this leakage of the investable surplus which constitutes the very basis of the phenomenon of under-development. It is also argued that private investment considerations might siphon away resources from a backward area rather than attract resources from outside.

Administrators and planners are coming to realise that their previous models have slighted some critical elements, namely the cultures and societies of the people for whom and on whom development plans were enacted. Anthropologists not only come to development problems from the perspective of the people, they also tend to try to understand particular projects as part of a longer system. It is the system of social relations and cultural understandings that is critical for the success or failure of projects. Development consists of purposive efforts by people, led by public figures and planners, to organise themselves in new technical, cultural and social ways. These are ways that will enable them to achieve the style and quality of life to which they aspire.

Anthropological influences on administration in the tribal areas is generally accepted. Social anthropology studies the total social behaviour of communities, different kinds of social relationships of people within and without a group in a community, the cultural contents of society and the total society as an integrated whole.

Because of its scope, nature and methods of studying the society as such, the knowledge of social anthropology is likely to be useful to the administrators engaged in the development of the tribal areas. The development programmes involve socio-cultural and economic change in the life of the tribal people.

The administrators must know the existing ways of life of the tribal people and the theories of social change. It is to be realised that though economic changes are often faster, in the long run, both economic and social changes have to go together. The need for being careful with regard to the hard core of culture and the utility of anthropological approach rather than bureaucratic method of dealing with the tribal people has to be realised.

In early periods, tribal communities are in ecological equilibrium with their environment. The equilibrium may get disturbed due to natural and socio-economical reasons. The intensity of contact of small tribal groups with other groups varies considerably. The small tribal groups can be classified on the basis of four characteristics, viz., size, isolation, confrontation and ecological equilibrium.

Ecological disequilibrium arises generally because a community had not been able to keep pace with the changing environment, both physical and human. This would require faster pace of change in the community so that it can catch up with the rest of the society by freeing self from the dependence on a narrow ecological field with the rest of the community but while planning for the initial phases of development, the fact of the loss of nerve in many cases has to be fully taken into account. In this period, a benevolent outside contact may help them in getting over the confrontation complex and establish new communication channels. The steps for removing the causes of ecological disequilibrium have to be as swift as possible.

The main four stages in development of tribal communities in a state of ecological disequilibrium can be envisaged as follows:

Stage 1: State of confrontation.

Stage 2: State of countering external forces, institutionalising measures for countering individual or group forces, effective attention to problems of health, and recognition of the native skills, restoration of self confidence and citizen education.

Stage 3: State of first-aid to the traditional economy, breaking the communication barriers and education, and gradual upgradation of native skills and introduction of new element time perspective.

Stage 4: Confrontation ceases.

The environment of an area has its impact on the administration of the area. The tribal culture, its economy, social custom and political system also influences the administrative set up and practices in that area. The complexities arising out of the tribal ecology is quite different from those of other areas and hence requires a different approach. In order to administer development, the knowledge of the tribal social system, customs and socio-economic conditions are of great relevance. The development administration in the tribal areas has its own problems.

GOALS OF TRIBAL DEVELOPMENT

Nehru's foreword to Verrier Elwin's book on North East Frontier Agency (NEFA) demonstrates the goals of tribal development in India as follows:

i) People should develop along the lines of their own genius and we should avoid imposing anything on them. We should try to encourage in every way their own traditional arts and culture.

ii) Tribal rights in land and forest should be respected.

iii) We should try to train and build up a team or their own people to do the work of administration and development. Some technical people from outside unit no doubt be needed, especially in the beginning but we should avoid introducing too many outsiders into tribal territory.

iv) We should not over-administer these areas or overwhelm them with multiplicity of schemes. We should rather work through and not in rivalry to their own social and cultural institutions.

v) We should guide results not by statistics or the amount of money spent, but by the quality of human character that is involved.

The goals of tribal development can be summarised as economic, social and political.

Economic growth means more output and economic development implies both more output and change in the technical and institutional arrangements by which it is produced. It entails the diversion of a nation's scarce resources and productive powers to the augmentation of its stocks of productive wealth and to the progressive enlargement of its gross and net national product of goods and services. The objective is in aggregate or in per capita terms.

Economic development is an increase in real per capita income of a country. In the context of tribal development, it aims at increasing the incomes and strengthening the material aspects of tribal culture through better utilisation of the environmental resources, i.e., forests, minerals, flora and fauna, agriculture, horticulture, animal husbandry and industrial potentials. The problem of equitable distribution of income and wealth within the tribal culture vis-a-vis Indian society as a whole, needs further enquiry.

Social development means bringing about improvement in the social being of the people and as such lays stress on provision of health services, education, housing, cultural amenities, protection of children, a change in the status of women, regulation of labour and improved status for workers and reduction of disease, poverty and other social ailments. All the tribal groups are not in the same stage of social development. There are some groups in remote and inaccessible tribal villages. There are some groups which have had the benefit of sufficient interaction with rural and urban population. There may be a third group of people, who have made adjustments with the rural-cum-urban social environment and who are already on the way of assimilation into the larger complex. The fourth group comprises of those who have become a part of the urban and rural complex and as such are indistinguishable from the other population.

Sufficient time should be given to the first three groups to get them oriented to the Indian social life as a whole, there is a great deal to be said in favour of some of the important forms of tribal culture. It is evident that changes are bound to make inroads even into the hard-core of the tribal culture as a whole. It may be useful to outline criterion of cultural development for the four groups mentioned above on the basis of a differential approach. The main question then boils down to the comprehensiveness rather than rate of change itself. Provided the proper approach is found, it may be possible for level-jumping in case of many tribal groups, so that the culture complex can undergo a rapid transformation as a whole.

The problem of value-orientation of tribal development is inextricably linked with the value framework of the emergent society in India as a whole. Otherwise there may be a lot of economic prosperity brought to the tribal groups, Panchayati Raj system may be introduced, efforts may be made to keep up the older forms of non-material culture of non-tribal groups but serious problems of adjustment and assimilation are likely to arise in future, e.g., i) the tribal group may get absorbed in the highly complex caste structure of the society, which they do not have at present. In case they are placed at the lowest, it would be regression for them than progress, and ii) the tribal groups may be drafted into the highly complex and philosophically oriented religious system, which might undermine, the very roots of tribal culture.

The concern for political development is said to have resulted from the failure of economic development programmes which is attributed to political imperfections in the society. Political development refers to the process of politicisation, that is increasing participation or involvement of the citizen in the state activities and in power calculations and consequences. The political goals of development imply evolution towards, democratic process and forms of government. The approach to different tribal groups would, however, depend upon the existing social organisation and the tribal Panchayats/councils, if any. Each tribal group would have to be worked on an individual basis.

Evolution of the political structure of democracy in tribal areas would mean that ultimately it would have to be linked with the larger framework of power politics in Indian society as a whole. While in some areas, independent political parties from the tribal groups have emerged, it may be useful to draw up and abide by healthy communication among different political parties; not to exploit the tribal groups politically. At the same time, interest orientation and politicisation of tribal groups is essential.

The goals of tribal development can be grouped into the following two objectives, i) long term objectives, and ii) short term objectives. The long term objectives are: a) to narrow the gap between the levels of development of the tribals and the others, and b) to improve the quality of life of the tribal communities. The short term objectives are: a) elimination of exploitation in all forms, b) speeding up the process of socio-economic development, c) improving organisational capabilities, and d) building up inner strength of the people, etc.

The development of tribal communities is one special aspect of this general process as the socio-economic situation of these communities is somewhat different from the general socio-economic situation in India. The tribal economy can be said to be at one end of the spectrum of India's general socio-economic scene.

Tribal development poses a special challenge to the development administration due to two reasons. Firstly, administration itself in the tribal areas emerges as a very strong group in comparison to the local community. Secondly, the constitution has placed a special responsibility for development of these regions on the administration. The powers of administration increase because of this special responsibility, and in the context of imbalance of power between administration and local community in these areas, the responsibility of administration further increases. Though all the tribal areas are not at the same stage of socio-economic development, nevertheless, it can be said that there are sonic basic similarities in all these areas on the basis of which certain common policy issues can be formulated.

The tribal areas are characterised by their aloofness, a lower level of economic activity and a closed social structure. In a determined effort for economic development in tribal areas during the second half of the 20th century, these areas got special attention as they were the most backward areas and had a great potential for forest, mineral and agricultural development. The natural barriers were overcome; roads got built, mineral explorations started, forest potential exploited and a bigger stream of administrators, contractors, traders and other fortune-seekers started. As the new climate emphasises achievement, ignores the means and sanctifies competition, the articulate outsider has, therefore, one motivation-quick acquisition. The tribals become defensive, they are not able to meet this group on terms of equality.

The development programmes are carried out by the government machinery. So far as the general Indian scene is concerned, the level of specialisation of the socio-economic system is supposed to be higher. The process of development and the nature of the programmes are designed according to the needs of this system with considerable specialisation. Whenever the need of a particular sector outgrows the limited means of the concerned institution and it is no longer possible for it to satisfy that need, another institution is born. In this way, economic development and institutional specialisation continue to reinforce each other.

The organisational structure designed at the state headquarters have same pattern for the tribal and non-tribal areas as a result of which there is a tendency of over specialisation in the tribal areas. The specialisation arises from the needs of a specific situation and stipulates full co-ordination amongst all institutions for achieving the central objective. Synchronisation of all services require a good communication system and duty-conscious personnel. The socio-economic situation of the tribal areas is extremely simple. When the over specialised system of administration is superimposed on these areas, the simple tribal community sees it from a distance as a strange phenomenon. The second important aspect in these areas is sectoral programme in the context of the integrated life of the tribal. The simple tribal community leads a whole life, it has no sectors, hence individual oriented programmes might not succeed here. Thus, the problems of development administration of the tribal areas in this country are multifarious and complicated.

ADMINISTRATION STRATEGY

The problem of developmental administration in the tribal

areas can be grouped as organisational problems, and personnel problems. There is a considerable diffusion of authority, inadequate control, lack of coordination and from the point of view of the tribals, difficulty in identifying persons concerned with specific programmes because of the growing complexity and multiplicity of the institutions. The problem of personnel is also equally acute and even the educated tribals migrate from their own areas and gravitate to towns and cities. In addition, much distinction cannot be made between regulatory and developmental administration in these areas in the context of the fact that elimination of exploitation has been given the highest priority.

The tribal communities on the international borders were frequently involved in the circulation of goods and services through non-monetised exchange system from one country to another. They were living bridges, as it were, between countries and civilisations. Inside the country also, many tribal communities played the same role. Before the development of road, sea and air transport, many of the areas inhabited by the tribals were nature's highways, as it were. When an ethnic group serves as a bridge or performs the buffer role, it is in the interests of the dominant contact groups that they should maintain their distinct identity.

There is a point of view that until recently the tribes lived in isolation. There is an opposite point of view that the tribal communities have always have been a part of the Indian society. Isolation of the tribals is a by-product of the development of modern transport. Prior to that, the tribals had contact with different cultures and politico-social entities; but they considered themselves to be different.

In many areas, the tribals were politically and administratively isolated from the rest of the countrymen. But at the same time, during the same period, the benefits of modern technology and science began to penetrate into the tribal areas. Gradually a sense of inadequacy to cope with the modern world dawned on them.

The primitive complex, did not, however, overwhelm the tribals. They were shielded by another complex, namely, majority complex. At the taluk level, about half of the tribal population lives in areas where they are in the majority. In the context of their low literacy and simple technology, their political and cultural aspirations did not ordinarily go beyond the taluk level. The fact that they were a majority at this level was a greater social reality to them than the fact that they were a minority at the state or the national level. But the situation is rapidly changing. The special rights and concessions provided in the Constitution have enabled many of the tribals to take to higher education and go in for higher administrative and political positions. The primitive complex, sugar-coated by a majority complex, is giving place to a minority complex.

The minority complex brings in its train an acute identity crisis, and not unoften nemesis complex. The latter frequently drives the tribals to the destruction of goods and property for inhering in a millennium and to take recourse to various cult movements. The identity crisis also often results in various types of revivalistic movements. If in some fields, in the field of technology to wit, there is acceptance of the modern way of life to some extent, in some others there is reinforcement of tribalism as a value. Thus, the present digs a tunnel into the past and buries itself inside it.

Regionalism is a co-brother of modernism in tribal areas. It is the outcome of the interplay of a number of forces. First, the tribals are becoming conscious of the fact that to reap the benefits of modern technology, they require to become viable in human and physical resources. This stimulates various processes of expansion of identity. More frequently, small and mutually district local groups try to discover elements of commonness in their culture traits, myths and legends, and adopt a common appellation as an addition name. At a later stage, common elites and common institutions come into existence. They try to establish unified control over the resources and over certain aspects of the social organisations. These phases of identity expansion and spatial linkage of the same can be described as infra-nationalism and proto-nationalism. Proto-nationalism also tends to fuse with regionalism.

The tribals find that when an improved technology is introduced in the areas inhabited by them, they cannot reap the benefits of the same. They lack the requisite skill to operate in the context of the new technology; on the other hand, land, forest and other resources on which they traditionally depend, are put to new use and, as a result, their economy suffers a setback. Regional sentiments grow.

Territories with which the tribal communities were associated in one way or the other, come to be considered to be potential regions of their influence. Sometimes, they tend to be politically organised for establishing their control over such regions.

The infra-national and proto-national processes, flanked by revivalistic and also frequently revitalistic movements, bring in a qualitative change in the traditional tribes. They cease to be tribes in the orthodox sense of the term, they emerge as tribals. The term Scheduled Tribe covers the primitive tribes, the post-primitive tribals, and even the post-tribal special historical categories. Tribe is a historical social-type; Scheduled Tribe is a social category envisaged by the Constitution for a certain type of social engineering.

The Constitution has committed the nation to two courses of action in respect of the Scheduled Tribes, viz., i) giving protection to their distinctive way of life and ii) bringing them on par with the rest of the nation so that they may be integrated with the national life. There are many communities which cannot be considered to be tribes today according to anthropological definition, but are entitled to the above dual courses of action. Obviously, they should continue to be considered as Scheduled Tribes. The rationale for this approach is derived from two facts, viz., i) historical image of the communities concerned, and ii) social dynamics of the modern post-primitive communities.

Most of the communities which are at present included in the list of the Scheduled Tribes have two important characteristics. Whatever may be their objective condition today, they were considered to be primitive in economy and social organisation till the recent past; they were also considered to be different from the rest of the population. It is beside the point whether they are really different or not. In other words, the most important dimension of the Scheduled Tribes is their historical image. The purpose of declaring communities as Scheduled Tribes is not, however, to perpetuate this historical image. The purpose is to efface the legacy of the historical image.

In the ancient world, from, the womb of the primitive community came out the peasant. But in giving birth to the child, the mother died. That was the era when maternity death rate was quite high. In the modern world, the transformation of the primitive communities takes place in an entirely different milieu. First, agriculture is not the only advanced technology available to them, they also see industrialisation taking place all around. Second, agriculture is frequently dominated by world productive forces governed by the industrial ethos. Third, they live in a world where inter-ethnic relations are conditioned by at least minimal humanism. They do not require to accept a relationship of subjugation for survival. Fourth, welfare democracy tends to create one elite culture in all institutions starting from the family which is simultaneously universalistic and individualistic in its orientation.

The post-primitive tribes tends to become bi-nuclear-one, oriented towards the surrounding peasant society, the other towards the urban-industrial communication network. The tribe gives birth to the tribal. But the child does not eat up the mother. Only she is put to a perpetual slumber in the ancestral shrine. The post-tribal society is multi-nuclear; one oriented to the universalistic elements of the primitive past; one to the peasant culture of the region one oriented to the universalistic elements, even transcending the nation society, whose commitment to the nation-state depends on a number of geopolitical factors.

After independence, the colonial policy of maintaining the *status quo* was replaced by a policy of development and integration. The makers of the Constitution of India were, however, conscious of the fact that due to historical reasons, certain amount of mental barrier prevailed between the tribal and the non-tribal population in some parts of the country. It required a deft and phased approach to remove the barrier. They also recognised that unless the material conditions of the life of the tribals were improved so as to bring them on par with the rest of the nation, the tribals would remain as weaklings in the social structure of the country.

The salient features of these provisions are: i) special responsibility of the state to bring about all-round advancement; ii) promotion of their educational and economic interests, and protection from injustice and all forms of exploitation; iii) reservation in services, iv) reservation of seats in Parliament and State legislatures; and v) appointment of a special officer to investigate all matters relating to the safeguards provided for the Scheduled Tribes and Scheduled Castes.

The new approaches are being underlined by two guiding principles i) protection of the tribal population, and ii) their integration with the national society through development. It may appear to many that the two principles are mutually incompatible. They may be sceptical about the possibility of integrating the tribals with the national life through a policy of protection. But this scepticism is in fact the outcome of a narrow interpretation of the terms 'protection of the tribals', 'national integration', and 'development'. Protection of the tribals in the real sense of the term does not mean artificial maintenance of the status quo; it means creation of the conditions in which natural growth of the tribal societies can take place without imposition from outside and also without inhibition from inside.

Social integration is the same as cultural assimilation. But this is not correct. Social integration means acceptance of common goals and symbols by different parts of a whole; basically it is a dimension of political relationship and not cultural relationship. People with diverse cultural traits may foster common goals and symbols.

There are at least four models of social integration in a pluralistic society.

i) Identification with the dominant group,

ii) Mutual give and take of the different parts to constitute a new whole,

iii) Coexistence of different parts as autonomous systems and simultaneous acceptance of common group goals and group symbols, and

iv) Organisation of individuals whose basic commitments are to the values of cosmopolitan humanism and who consciously and freely accept membership of different reference groups the sake of deepening and diversifying.

All the four processes are in existence in varying degrees in different parts of the country. A fundamental change is taking place in the world-view of the tribals as well as other folk societies.

Until recently, the main focus of their world-view was ritual order through which they tried to keep the supernatural powers in good humour and ensure their own welfare. Now they are, by and large, aware that technology is the god; they have little motivation left for adopting Hindu Gods and Goddesses or for being incorporated in the Hindu ritual order.

In implementing the national strategy of development for the tribal societies it is also necessary to attend to the indicators of social development with particular reference to the following cardinal points:

i) Minimal harmony with the physical environment.

ii) Minimal harmony with the social environment.

iii) Minimal incorporation of modern technology and science.

iv) Communication and participation in wider network.

v) Cultural resilience.

vi) Identity crystallisation.

vii) Social mobilisation and distributive justice.

viii) Integration and autonomy.

ix) Universalisation and sovereignty of the individual.

When the specific indicators are worked out in detail with reference to these dimensions, they will reflect and also reinforce a synthesis of the two basic approaches, viz., protection and integration. It will be mistake to consider India's national strategy to the problems of the tribals in isolation. India is a signatory to an International Labour Organisation (ILO) convention on the indigenous population, and the provisions of India's Constitution anticipate many of the important features of this convention. Though there are some highly specific formulations, for instance the 6th Schedule of the Constitution, which reflect the politico-social history of the country, broadly the Indian constitutional provisions represent the spirit of the contemporary age. There are similar provisions and postulates in the constitutions and the national strategies of many other countries.

In the matter of identification of the indigenous population, different and often contradictory criteria tend to be used by administrators, lawyers and sociologists. Every country has tackled the problem of definition in its own way, according to its own traditions, history, social organisation and policies. As regards the legal and administrative approaches to the tribal population, citing examples from some countries would be appropriate.

In Latin America, the descendants of the aboriginal inhabitants are considered to be citizens, enjoying the rights and subject to the obligations laid down in the constitution. Only in order to protect them, and because of the primitive state of some groups of aboriginal descent, do the laws of some countries make a practical distinction between Indians and non-Indians.

In Equador, for instance, Article 185 of the Constitution provides that agricultural work, particularly that performed by Indians, shall be subject to special regulations with regard to the working day, and that the government shall give priority to promoting the moral, individual, economic and social improvement of the indigenous population.

In Panama, Article 6 of the 1946 Constitution lays down that the state shall afford special protection to the Indian communities, with the object of effecting their economic, political and intellectual integration into national life and of their living standards in general.

In Brazil, the Indians or forest dwellers are subject to a special system of law; this places them under the protection of the state and restricts their civil rights in some respects until they have acquired the cultural and economic development which will enable them effectively to enjoy the rights conferred by law on citizens in general.

In US, with the adoption in 1887 of the General Allotment Act, a new policy was instituted whereby possession of the tribal lands, previously held in common was to be ceded to the individual Indians. The Indian Reorganisation Act of 1934 recognises the Indian tribes as political bodies having sovereign powers of self-government except to the extent that such powers may be limited by special treaties or laws. The Indian Affairs Bureau was set up in 1824 to conserve the economic assets of the tribes, train the adults to adopt modern ways of making a living, and render services in education, medical and other fields. During 1952, a Division of Programme was established in the Bureau of Indian Affairs to stimulate, guide and assist the development of joint planning by tribal leaders and the staff of the Bureau for the improvement of the basic economic status of the Indians, and the gradual withdrawal of the Bureau from their affairs.

Canada adopted a revised Indian Act in 1951. The Act deals with the political and legal status of the Indians, the management of their lands and trust funds, welfare and other social services, education, the organisation and administration of land administration and other matters affecting conditions among Indians. The ultimate object of the public policy concerning Indians, is to encourage and assist them to become economically independent and voluntarily to merge into the general population by adopting the predominant culture of the country.

Many of the Asian countries also adopted special provisions for tribal population. In Burma, the aborigines, particularly the forest-dwelling population, are governed by special regulations, concerning the hill tracts of the Kachin, Shan and Kayah states, and the frontier areas. The aims of the Chin Special Division Act of 1948 are to make the aborigines in that area self-governing and to assist them in improving their standards of public health and education and their economic conditions. In Pakistan, the tribal areas of North-West Frontier Province are the responsibility of the Governor of the North-West Frontier Province, in the capacity of agent of the central government, they have a large measure of autonomy.

There are important similarities and differences between India and many other countries in different Continents in dealing with the tribal population. The need of a special approach is, however, recognised almost everywhere as a strategy of nation-building. Some countries identify the tribal population in a flexible manner and aim at creating conditions when more and more people can be removed from the category requiring special treatment.

Scheduling of tribals

Scheduled Tribes has been a special category in India's polity for several decades. The social meaning of Scheduled Tribes is to be abstracted primarily from this empirical reality of today and only secondarily from the conceptual framework of tribe as a social type in a particular phase of human history. According to India's Constitution, the first notification of the tribes in a state is to be made by the President. The first list of the Scheduled Castes and Scheduled Tribes was notified by the President in 1950. It was amended by the Parliament in 1956 on the recommendations of the Backward Classes Commission. Since then there have been several proposals for fresh inclusion and deletion from the lists of the Scheduled Castes and Scheduled Tribes.

One way of dealing with any fresh proposal for inclusion in the list of the Scheduled Tribes is by comparing its social organisation, economy and cultural traits with the central tendencies of the existing Scheduled Tribes of the concerned sociocultural region in these fields. The problem of delineating the cultural regions of India in a manner which is relevant for the present purpose, is yet to be taken up. Pending that, by the large, the central tendencies are to be determined with reference to the states as units after taking into consideration the existing ethnographic information.

The Indian Council of Social Science Research has taken up the task of preparing ethnographic profiles in respect of all the Scheduled Castes and Scheduled Tribes of the country. A code structure has been prepared for computerisation of the data available in these profiles. It is now being further examined in collaboration with the anthropological survey of India. After the data have been computerised it will be possible to proceed further in the direction of identification of the central tendencies.

Whether the inclusion of a community in the list of the Scheduled Tribes was originally justified or not, descheduling cannot be done after a lapse of time, like writing on a clean slate. The fact that the community has been treated as a Scheduled Tribes for sometime, has by itself caused certain social-ecological adaptive processes to take place in varying degrees of intensity. One should consider i) what has been the role of the community in providing leadership from within the Scheduled Tribe category, particularly in the matter of asserting their constitutional rights, and serving as a bridge between the more primitive communities and the rest of the population; ii) to what extent the legacies of historical relationships continue to influence the self-image and others image and iii) what is the geopolitical context. Besides the all-India and regional comparability, internal compatibility with reference to the other Scheduled Tribes as well as the Scheduled Castes of the region is also to be considered.

Another important point to be mentioned in this context is on the ground of change of religion. What is really change of religion? This is a hazardous approach as the labels go on fluctuating quite frequently. While the parents in the villages returned themselves as Hindus, the sons who also considered themselves to be Hindus before coming to the city, returned themselves as followers of tribal religion after receiving higher education and settling down in the city. It is also found that in many cases even adults who returned themselves to be Hindus, are now claiming to practise tribal religion. Now who should be left out? The question holds good also for those who have adopted the labels of Christianity or Buddhism or Islam. In fact, one may go further and ask whether identification of religion by label is Indian mode of thought at all.

The Scheduled Tribes and Scheduled Areas Commission, set up under Article 339 of the Constitution, have, in their report submitted in 1961, suggested the following four criteria for declaration of an area as scheduled area:

i) Preponderance of the tribals in the population,

ii) Compact and reasonable size of the area,

iii) Underdeveloped nature of the area, and

iv) Marked disparity in the standard of the people.

The Scheduled area had been constituted with a view to developing them and promoting the economic, educational and social progress of the Scheduled Tribes living therein and assisting them in enjoying their rights unhindered and undisturbed.

The commission had received a large number of representations for declaring 58,877 square miles in the states of Gujarat, Kerala, Madhya Pradesh, Orissa, erstwhile Punjab. Rajasthan, Himachal Pradesh, Manipur and Andaman and Nicobar Islands as scheduled areas. The commission, however, suggested that instead of declaring more areas as scheduled areas, it would be better to adopt an alternative approach to protect the Scheduled Tribes and ensure development of scheduled areas within a stated period. This plan envisaged that the state government would undertake general legislation applicable throughout the scheduled and non-scheduled areas for protection of the rights of the tribals in lands and in forests, and their protection from exploitation by the money lenders.

At the same time, the Commission suggested that all the tribal areas should be grouped under tribal development blocks so that bulk of the tribal population is brought under tribal development blocks under intensive development programmes. This recommendation of the commission was discussed at a conference of state ministers held in July 1962, and it was decided to accept the alternative recommended by the commission.

There is certainly much to say in favour of reversion to the scheduled area approach. Apart from the fact that the Government of India or the state governments have failed to implement fully the recommendations of the Scheduled Tribes and Scheduled Area Commission, one is to give serious thought to the changes that have taken place in the tribal situation in the sixties. The analytical perspective of infra and proto-national movement with implied shift from mere welfare approach or development approach to a composite sociocultural and politico-economic approach lends support to the point of view that the constitutional device of declaring scheduled areas should not be perpetually shelved.

The limitations of the scheduled areas approach are given below:

i) Underlying this approach is the overdependence on the wise dispensation of the administrative elite.
ii) It is likely to accentuate the social distance between the tribals and the non-tribals in the scheduled areas and also outside, in the states where such areas are situated.
iii) It is likely to orient the political process in a direction in the entire tribal belt, whose long-term geopolitical implications are to be carefully sorted out.

In view of the serious limitation of the reversion to the scheduled area approach, it is to be examined seriously whether a new initiative cannot be taken in a different direction. The cardinal points of the new initiative should be the formation as well as mobilisation of social capital, the salient features of which are:

i) A sense of moral propriety of the system,
ii) Participation in the decision-making process at every level,
iii) Conviction of having rational control over the implementing agencies at every relevant level, and

iv) Perception of an epochal goal not only concerning the immediate community but also the wider interactional network.

The task of creating appropriated legislative and administrative setup is not that of merely enacting the right laws or establishing a network of administrative and executive agencies. It is also a task of building up a system of communication between the people and the authority. The Constitution of India vests a special authority in the Commissioner for Scheduled Castes and Scheduled Tribes to keep the nation informed of the working of the Constitution.

It is to be examined whether the present arrangements by which the Director General of the Backward Classes Welfare is considered to be the controlling authority even of the staff placed at the disposal of the Commissioner, is compatible with his much wider responsibility.

For the last few years, Parliamentary Committee on Scheduled Castes and Scheduled Tribes is carrying on useful probe into a number of matters. It, however, appears that the committee can make greater use of the Commissioner's organisation without giving up its prerogative of making observations on its own. It also seems desirable that the Commissioner should have adequate field and technical personnel. He should also have at his disposal funds to initiate research, organises seminars and conferences at various levels, to bring out the correct position in respect of a number of problems and to assess the aspirations and motivations of the Scheduled Tribes and Scheduled Castes as well as the moral, intellectual and political climate of the country in respect of these people.

Institutions are to be built into the system to ensure participation of the tribals in the decision-making process and in the implementation of the various programmes. There should be a statutory central tribes' advisory council, with representation from the Scheduled Tribe members of Parliament, social workers, social scientists and planners.

It would be advisable to constitute the council with the representatives from among the members of Parliament at the first stage, the other categories of members may be co-opted by them at the second stage. The rules in regard to the formation and functioning of these councils may be reviewed to make them more effective. Similar statutory councils may be formed in all the districts, taluks and project areas where the tribals are in majority.

According to specific contexts, it may also be reviewed whether at those levels separate organs of democratic decentralisation should continue to exist; and if they exist what should be the relation with the statutory-constituted tribes' advisory councils. The advisory councils at various levels should be involved in the formulation of plans, review of the relevant legislations and scrutiny of the various reports including those prepared by the Tribal Research Institutes at the instance of the various organisations and also on their own. The relevant aspects of the report of the Commissioner for Scheduled Castes and Scheduled Tribes should also be discussed in the councils.

Departments of tribal welfare

In multi-level planning and implementation, the Directorate-General of Backward Classes Welfare can play a useful role by conducting a number of pilot projects to serve as models for the states and public-sector bodies. Running of training and orientation-programmes for the officials and non-officials concerned with the tribals, coordination of the activities of voluntary organisations at the national level, promotion of development-oriented community organisations among the tribals themselves should be the other major functions of the Directorate-General.

In several states, departments of Tribal Welfare and Administration implement some of the programmes directly. But more frequently the state Tribal Welfare departments are expected to coordinate the activities of the various other departments. However, there is no uniform model of coordination. Sometimes, it only means that the schemes of the different departments meant for the tribals are assembled together by the Tribal Welfare department for obtaining clearance from the Planning Commission and the state Finance department. In some cases, the Tribal Welfare department is involved in evolving the norms of operation for the different schemes meant for the tribals, but it has no authority to check in the field whether or not the norms are being implemented. There are, however, instances, where, in some states, the Tribal Welfare departments exercise considerable prerogative in ensuring that the activities of the various department in the tribal areas are adapted to the special needs of the tribals.

In most states, the funds from the tribal sector are released by the Tribal Welfare department to the various implementing departments which disburse them at the district and other levels. In some cases, after the amount to be allocated to the different districts is decided in consultation with the implementing department, the Tribal Welfare department releases the fund to the district-level officials of the former with intimation to the state-level authorities and directly obtains progress reports from the district-level.

Organisation structure of the Tribal Welfare department differs from state to state. In some states the secretariat and the directorate are separate, in others, there are no separate directorates. In several states the district-level officials can directly communicate with the directorate, but in many cases they are to communicate only through the collector. Exact information on the role of the Tribal Welfare departments as the organs of specialisation in respect of the tribals, their organisational structure and the prerogatives that they enjoy in planning, financing evaluating and reorienting the functions of the different departments, are not available for many states. These require to be systematically collected and analysed so that the optimum combination of the organisational structure, communication structure, communication structure and specialisation function can be determined.

The personnel policy and research support for building up specialised roles of the tribal department require to be carefully examined. The personnel policy will be considered in due course. As regards research support, it is to be noted that currently there are tribal research institutes in several states. But frequently they remain marginal both to the academic system and the tribal administration system and at the same time they fail to inspire much confidence of the tribals themselves. More frequently than not, they suffer from all round credibility gap. In policy formulation, their research findings will have little impact unless they are helped to make up the credibility gap. It seems that, of late, there is some recognition of this problem.

It has been suggested that one of the ways of mitigating it is to give sufficient status to the heads of the research institutes. But this will not mean much. In one state, an ex-Vice Chancellor was appointed as the head of the research body. But he does not appear to have been particularly effective. In this context, the following aspects need special consideration.

i) Automatic flow of information about the activities of the various departments in respect of the tribals;
ii) Right to ask for information on specified subjects;
iii) Participation in the meetings of tribes' advisory councils at various levels as observers;
iv) Right to take up at least 25 per cent of the studies on own initiative;
v) Right to communicate results of research to outside scholars and other except for a limited number of classified subjects;
vi) When they take up studies at the instance of tribes-, advisory councils or Government of India, right to communicate directly to the sponsoring body the results of the studies;
vii) Right of direct academic contact with universities and other academic bodies; and
viii) Facility for participating in refresher and reorientation course.

There should be a research coordination body at the centre which will serve as the clearing house of information regarding various aspects of the research activities in respect of the tribals; help the research institutes to frame research problems and research designs with an all-India perspective; and provide technical information and advice to the Commissioner for Scheduled Castes and Scheduled Tribes and other concerned agencies.

The autonomous functioning of this body should be ensured. It should not be a part of the Backward Classes Welfare. Its area of interests should be much wider. If it is under the administrative control of any of these agencies, its activities are not unlikely to be circumscribed to serve their immediate short-range interests. One of the tasks that the central body should take up on a priority basis, is a comprehensive review of the various legislations pertaining to the tribals and predominantly tribals and tribal areas.

Administrative measures to tribal lands

The land problem of the tribals is with much complexity and it is due to the nature of association of the tribal population with their lands; frequent loss of control of the communities over their resources on the introduction of new land-use pattern; self-image of the tribal elites and their perception of their actual or potential role in the decision-making process at various levels of the national life; conflict between the traditional and the modern elite in the perception of the goal of economic and social development; and absence of political preparation for changing production relations, stalemate in productive resources, production technology, but rapid change in consumption norms.

In many areas, the association of the tribal communities with the land around them does not belong to the purely economic category. Frequently, it belongs to the twilight zone of political and economic categories and can be described as proto-political. Proto-political nature of the relationship of the tribals in some areas raises a number of complex policy issues, to wit: whether such relationship is conducive to efficient land-use pattern; whether the relationship is in conformity with the objective of social justice, and whether such relationship can be changed by state action without transgressing the constitutional safeguards for the tribal population. In respect of each of these issues the conditions differ from area to area and the actual action will require considerable research support.

There are areas where the tribals enjoy special prerogative in utilisation of the land resources. Such special rights have been specifically recognised under the 6th Schedule of the Constitution. Then again there are as of historical association, and lastly is the land which belongs to the purely economic category in the sense the term is understood among the non-tribals. The policy implications of different types of relations with land are diverse. Where the relationship is of proto-political nature, full participation of the tribal elite is to be ensured at every level in the decision making process relating to the land system. Where the tribals enjoy special prerogative, complex social engineering is called for, so that in the wake of economic development, the position of the community in the local power and prestige structure is not adversely affected until it is effectively and voluntarily integrated with a power and prestige structure of higher order. Where it is a question of pure historical association, a vigorous programme is to be undertaken for diversification of economic activities.

The framework for a positive policy in respect of tribal land is to be based on,

i) an understanding of the structure and organisation of customary rights;

ii) changes under the impact of contact, technological change, government policy, growth of ideology, and other measures;

iii) review of the legislative and executive measures with reference to recognition of the customary rights in land and forests, survey and settlement operations and preparation of records of rights; protection against alienation of alienated land priority in settlement of land; elimination of exploitation including exactions by middlemen, collecting agents etc.

Customary rights need not be sustained by newly created sanctions if they are not in consonance with the broad public policy. At the same time, they should be recognised in such a flexible manner that dynamic adjustment of old rights is not inhibited or impeded.

Survey and settlement operation

In the matter of survey and settlement operations, there should be adequate preparation by generating consciousness about its significance, creating special agency and taking political action against crypto-rights and obligations that came into existence during the predatory wards.

In 1894, the traditional rights of the tribals over forests were converted into rights and privileges. But in 1952, these became rights and concessions to be transformed into simple concessions later on. While laying down a viable forest policy, it is to be kept in view that in a democratic society no right can be extinguished; democracy grows by growth and transformation of rights and integration of the same with the structure of rights of a higher order.

Legislative measures to tribal lands

There are three types of legislations for regulating transfer of tribal lands. They place restrictions on,

i) Transfer by sale or mortgage from tribals to non-tribals;

ii) Transfer to any person with flexible approach in respect of persons belonging to the same tribe;

iii) Transfer to any person, non-tribal or tribal;

iv) Sale to other non-Scheduled Tribe, Scheduled Caste or other Backward Classes; and

v) Reserved area.

The significance of the legislations differs according to the nature of economic stratification, ethnic diversity, level of technology and cultural differentiation.

Dynamic context of land transfer is to be visualised with reference to:

i) Expansion of infrastructure of growth without growth preparation;

ii) Diversification of economy;

iii) Shifts in the productive function of land;

iv) Emergence of a new class of commercial and industrial entrepreneurs from among the tribals, and

v) Improvement in the working conditions of the tribals through exagenous intervention.

Sometimes, in the dynamic context of interplay of the various forces, transfer of land means shift of capital from one sector of economy to another and also augmentation of the production function of the capital at the disposal of the tribals. All transfer is not necessarily alienation, but beyond a threshold point, depending on the level of technology and intensity of social integration, any transfer may become alienation. A legislative programme relating to the lands of the tribals will require administrative and political planning keeping these aspects in view.

The problems of rehabilitation of the tribals, who are displaced as a sequel to the setting up of industrial projects or acquisition of land for other public purposes cannot be considered without reference to the total socio-economic structure. The policy of paying off the tribals, particularly when the development of their resources is taking place, is a negative approach. As a development strategy, their rights to the fruits of enhanced economic return, derived out of the resources under their control, should he continued till a minimum proportion of technical manpower, as well as of persons capable of taking entrepreneurial or policy-making role comes up from among them.

There has been un-uniform progress in the allotment of cultivable waste lands to the tribals. Again, in many cases, the tribals have passed out the lands to others. It is to be examined whether the allottees should be persuaded to form labour cooperatives, which will be entitled to massive state support in various forms.

Land colonisation schemes for the tribals have not been successful, in most of the states. The schemes fail to recognise that grant of land, provision of houses and supply of bullocks are not enough. Building up the fertility of virgin land takes time and its productivity, immediately after reclamation, is not always adequate to maintain a tribal family. Greater emphasis is also to be given to irrigation linked up with land colonisation; besides, the beneficiaries should be given wages during the period of reclamation, and subsidiary occupation during the off-agricultural season. A major drawback of the scheme is that the colonies are planned without reference to the total economy and the social structures of the tribes as well as of the region.

Indebtedness reflects imbalance in the relationships of four factors:

i) Resource deterioration, stagnation in technology and consumption leading to a productive relation marked by intensive exploitation:

ii) Rapid technological change without change in the quantum of total resources and the consumption pattern,

iii) Stagnation in production relations as well as resources and the consumption pattern;

iv) Stagnation in production relations as well as resource position, but rapid change in technology and consumption pattern leading to a vulnerable social structure marked by progressive pauperisation or displacement of large segments of population, and

v) Stagnation in resource position, technology and productive relations, but rapid change in consumption pattern.

There are legislations for moneylending, enforcing debt redemption and abolishing debt bondage labour. But rules for enforcement of the legislation do not appear to have been framed in all cases. Besides, the specific provisions of these legislations require careful review.

Mobilisation of social capital

Instruments for mobilisation of social capital include constitutional provisions of reservation in legislative bodies, setting up of advisory bodies with representation of tribal elites at various levels, and reservation in services. Among other measures aiming towards the same end, mention may be made of reservation in the organs of panchayati raj and encouragement to the voluntary organisations to take up welfare and development activities among the tribals.

Reservation in legislation bodies

Social base of the representatives of the tribals in the

reserved seats in the Lok Sabha and the Vidhan Sabha is changing. How these changes are linked up with changes or stagnation in the economic structure in the tribal areas, are to be analysed. Besides, the implications of the changes are to be examined in terms of: a) more effective participation in the national policies and in the decision-making process at different levels; b) deconcentration of political power and prestige within the tribal societies; c) wider diffusion of political consciousness; d) broad-based and informed political participation eschewing sterile populism; e) optimum balancing of traditional elite and elite of modernisation; f) optimum consolidation of democratic forces both on ethnic and socio-economic platforms; and g) consolidation of forward-looking elite.

Organs of democratic decentralisation

It is necessary to specify the democratic forces at the various levels in the regional context to make the panchayats the real organs of democratic decentralisation. At every level there should be political planning to ensure that such forces are adequately represented and oriented to harness the support of modern technology and the sciences, including the social sciences.

Tribes' advisory councils

The tribes advisory councils have strengthen the bureaucratic approach to the problems of development rather than generate a broader understanding of the epochal change of the tribal societies. If there are periodical meetings of the members of the councils of different states, they may, by comparison of experiences, see things in a wider perspective. With these periodical meetings of tribal leaders, social scientists, social workers and other knowledgeable persons may also be associated in limited numbers.

Reservation in services

To effectively implement the constitutional provision of reservation in services, mere administrative measures will not be adequate. A stage has come for detailed manpower planning, taking into consideration the existing and the prospective manpower requirements, the social and cultural inhibitions and motivations, the economic incentives and the training facilities. Simultaneously, the impact of reservation in services, on the overall development of the tribal societies requires to be continuously reviewed. There is a point of view that due to reservation, the best minds' are sucked into the administrative machine, preventing the emergence of effective political elite or competent entrepreneurs in the fields of trade, commerce and industries.

Voluntary organisations

The voluntary organisations have a crucial role to play in democratic planning. The tendency in most area has been to ignore the social organisation of the tribals themselves. The exogenous social service organisations functioning in the tribal areas, should carefully review their organisational and operational strategies, recruitment policies, arrangements for the training and reorientation of their workers and functionaries, and also the methods adopted by them in the formulation of long-range and short-range programmes.

A servicing organisation is not necessarily a voluntary organisation it may be a mere non-official organisation. When a tribal society is extremely backward in technology and education, a philanthropic social service organisation certainly reflects the voluntariness of the wider society. But when the tribal community concerned advances in the scale of technology and education, unless the social service organisation can harness the social idealism of the tribal youth, it tends to loose its voluntary character.

The role of the voluntary organisations in the tribal areas can be envisaged as follows:

i) Impact a sense of participation among the diverse communities in the decision-making process at the appropriate levels, keeping in view their dispersal profile, productive resources, productive relations, manpower position and sociocultural orientation;
ii) Ensure that the special angle of the tribals is kept in view;
iii) Ensure that economic planning is appropriately linked up with social planning; and

iv) Ensure that the necessary structural changes are brought about as a strategy of development, and also as an essential goal of development.

PLANNING STRATEGIES

Planning strategies inform the foregoing formulations, viz., multi-level planning and participant development, requiring participation both in planning and implementation. The dichotomy of good planning and bad implementation is a false dichotomy. Planned development of the tribals is frequently hemmed by a number of dilemmas. Two of the more important ones are first man first or last man first; and historical ethos or twists and turns of complex social engineering.

The tribal educated elites represent the classes and not the masses, that they are the worst exploiters of the co-tribals, and that in the development planning highest priority is to be given to the interests of the weaker sections among the tribals. The irony is that frequently the accusing fingers against the exploiters among the tribals themselves are raised by those who are riding roughshod over the tribal societies as a whole. When the Indian society as a whole is class-ridden and when exploitation marks the social relations in almost every field, can the emerging tribal elites be very much different? The social scientists, planners and administrators should examine whether they are not betraying their ethnic bias in accusing the tribal elites. They should examine what is the historical role of such elites. They should also appreciate that historical role is not identical with empirical role.

To create aggregation of functions and to generate a system of linkages is the first historical step towards breaking the barrier between the tribals and the nation society. If there is occasional retardation, reversal or slowing down of the process, the responsibility may belong as much to the tribal elites as to the elites belonging to the rest of the nation. It is to be appreciated that the tribals as a whole are weak; and except for a few, none of the tribal communities comes anywhere near the rest of the nation. A strategy of nation-building will, in some context, require that the rate of advancement of the advanced sections among the tribals should be accelerated so that the process of creation of one national elite is completed. This is indispensable for reducing the inter-ethnic distances within the national polity.

There are weaker sections both among the tribals and the non-tribals and the minimum-needs programme is envisaged to meet their urgent requirement on the basis of highest priority. So far as the minimum-needs programme is concerned, there should not be any separate tribal sector. There should be only one national sector. But this again does not rule out separate programmes for the weaker sections among the tribals as a part of the programme of their planned development. There are a large number of minor tribes without much political pull. There are again the nomadic tribes. Their problems require special study.

As the tribal societies have egalitarian ethos inherent in them, and as India is moving towards a socialistic pattern of society, social stratification or the growth of a private sector should not be encouraged in tribal areas. It is overlooked that the egalitarian ethos of the tribals and the relative absence of stratification among them have enabled their rapacious exploitation by the non-tribals. So long as the private sector plays any important role in the country's productive system, it will be iniquitous to discourage private sector among the tribals.

The so-called egalitarian ethos and relative homogeneity of the tribals was a function of low level of technology, rather than of socialisation of production in the context of a high level of technology. The question of a limited private sector from among the tribals is, therefore, to be considered with reference to three historical tasks, viz., introduction of improved technology and modern market relationship, elimination of the exogenous forces of exploitation which simultaneously take the character of economic drainage and cultural imposition, and social mobilisation in terms of the common social and cultural heritage of mankind which will facilitate the socialisation of the production system and creation of the conditions of egalitarianism and distributive justice in the present day's setting.

Tribal development blocks

During the Second Plan, a development orientation was more clearly introduced in the tribal programme and Special Multipurpose Tribal Development (SMPT) blocks were introduced in a few areas predominantly inhabited by the tribals. After reviewing the working of these blocks, a composite team headed by Verrier Elwin recommended a more flexible approach and a more conscious effort to give tribal orientation to these blocks while spelling out the techniques and strategies of operation. The SMPT blocks were renamed as tribal development blocks. In the states of West Bengal, Mysore and Kerala, where there are only tribal pockets, sub-blocks were introduced during the Third Plan.

Hundred per cent assistance for the T.D. blocks was provided by the central government. Other centrally sponsored schemes till the end of the Fourth Plan period were cooperation, girl's hostels, post-matric scholarships, coaching and pre-examination, research, training and special projects. There were also state plan projects where block grants and loans were given. These covered education, economic development, health, housing and others. Though there was a plethora of schemes, broadly the emphasis was on T.D. blocks, underlying which is the assumption that the development of the tribals is critically linked up with the territories inhabited by them. The rantionale behind this assumption appears to be that the spatial mobility among the Scheduled Tribes is low. The bulk of them will spend their life in their existing habitats. Unless the conditions of life in the areas inhabited by the tribes are improved, it will not be possible to sustain the improvements that will be brought about through isolated schemes in different areas.

Though the T.D. block has brought about change in the out look of the tribals it has certain major limitations. Some of them are the following:

i) Limitation due to the smallness of the area.

ii) Fragmented approach to development planning,

iii) Application of a large number of standardised schemes in tribal areas,

iv) Neglect of the employment aspect of development,

v) Failure to take up settlement of land disputes in the pre-extension state,

vi) Investment of as much as 20 per cent in construction in productive schemes like agriculture, animal husbandry, etc.,

vii) They were in most cases the exclusive efforts of the tribal sector and the general sector programme failed to catch the tribal areas, and

viii) The benefits of development did not percolate beyond the upper crust of the tribal community in most of the areas.

Fifth Plan approach

The Fifth Plan approach to tribal development as adopted by the National Development Council are:

i) The main thrust of development will be provided by the general sector.

ii) The problem of development of tribal communities will be considered in three parts:

a) Areas with more than 50 per cent tribal concentration,

b) Areas with dispersed tribal population,

c) Isolated groups facing special problems at the pre-agricultural level of economic development.

iii) a) The states will prepare sub-plans for all areas with more than 50 per cent tribal concentration.

b) The sub-plans will represent the totality of effort of the and other organisations like the Khadi and Village Industries Commission or voluntary organisations.

c) The Sub-plan areas will be divided into viable projects.

d) Each project is expected to have three to five lakh population, and will be conterminous with the existing administrative boundaries of a tehsil, talk or district.

e) There will be a three-tier structure of planning: Micro-region will be conterminous with a development block. Macro-region will be a continuous block, etc. of comparable level of social and economic-development with three to five lakh population.

f) In many states there will be one macro economic region while in others, there will be two or more.

g) The state-sector outlay for the sub-plan should take into account: the total population in the areas of tribal concentration; the total geographical area of the region and comparative level of economic development, and the state of social services.

h) There would be weightage for lower level of social and economic development and sparseness of population.

i) The actual weightage is to be decided by each state in the context of its own circumstances.

j) Investments in sectors like heavy industry in tribal areas should have counter balancing investment in social services for the regions concerned.

k) Each central ministry will supplement corresponding state sector effort by adopting general central sector schemes and taking up special centrally-sponsored schemes.

l) Special attention of the central sector will be needed to bridge the gap between the outlay which will be necessary to reach a minimum level of economic development by the end of the Fifth Five Year Plan and the total resources which can be mobilised in the state sector, central ministries and financial institutions. The outlays of the central sector will get concretised only after the first draft sub-plan is examined at the national level and discussed within the overall national frame for development of tribal areas.

iii) The sub-plan is to be prepared in two parts, which are complementary.

Part I will bring out the salient features of basic problems of tribal areas and key issues of development; identify the development potential of each region; define the broad perspective in a time dimension; and attempt to bridge the gulf between tribal areas and advanced areas in a period of 15-20 years. By the end of the Sixth Plan, the level of development of the tribal areas should be equal to the level of the neighbouring areas at the beginning of the Sixth Plan and the financial resources necessary to achieve these objectives should emerge.

Part II will deal with sectoral programmes. Higher priority is to be given to the protective measures and the programmes which are time-bound in nature. The sectoral programme should start with this most important administrative-cum-economic activity. The next priority is to be given to programmes covering the maximum number of persons in the shortest time, obviously agricultural and allied activities, irrigation, cottage industries, determined by considerations of feasibility. The sectoral programmes in the sub-plans will, however, be supplemental to state sectoral plan and hence should take note of only the special features in respect of the tribal areas. The sub-plan should also review the functioning of the various organisations and their inter-relationship in the tribal areas. It is visualised that multiplicity of organisations, resulting in diffusion of responsibility, lack of control and coordination, and also presenting difficulty to the people to identify the concerned agencies is the cause of much ineffectiveness of developmental programmes.

In the Fifth Plan approach, the regional framework, the plan target and the concept of single-line administration are of crucial importance.

Regionalisation is very much different from regionalism. It is a process of functional specialisation of space and of flow of commodities and services as a sequel to this specialisation. In a publication brought out as a part of the 1961 Census, the country has been divided into a number of macro, meso and micro regions. This classification is primarily based on the assessment of the economic resources and the existing and potential territorial linkages that may exist or that may come into existence through the utilisation and exploitation of these resources. For the classification of the regions as macro, meso and micro, the various functions have been hierarchically arranged as functions of first order, second order and so on. One of the criticisms levelled against this classification is that it has considered mainly the physical and human resources to the neglect of the political forces and social structural factors.

In a subsequent publication of the Census, the validity of this criticism has been recognised. Any regionalisation programme, in respect of the areas predominantly inhabited by the tribals, should take note of the theoretical and empirical studies already made in this field.

In the outline of the Fifth Plan approach to the sub-plan in respect of the tribals, the functions at the micro, meso and macro levels are:

i) Micro level:
   a) education up to higher secondary level
   b) elementary health services
   c) agricultural extension
   d) supply of agricultural inputs
   e) minor irrigation schemes
   f) elementary veterinary service
   g) multipurpose cooperative
   h) local panchayat
   i) household industry
   j) village approach road

ii) Meso level:
   a) higher general education
   b) technical and vocational training
   c) manpower planning and employment services
   d) advanced health services with referred facilities

e) agricultural research extension
f) seed multiplication farms
g) soil conservation and land management
h) apex integrated credit marketing structure with adequate godowning and buffer stock facilities
i) development of road and communication infrastructure connecting market with state/district highways
j) distribution of network of power, rural electrification, etc.
k) local resource based industries with adequate market linkages
l) forest management
m) horticulture development
n) complementary development programme in the hinterland, and of bigger industries
o) minor and medium irrigation projects
p) research statistics and evaluation.

iii) Macro level

a) coordination of activities in tribal development projects
b) agricultural research on a regional basis
c) direction of the various sectoral programmes in the project
d) major irrigation projects
e) river valley development
f) industrial and mineral development of the region to ensure complementarity of the project level development programme.
g) marketing support projects
h) evaluation.

One of the first steps towards regionalisation is the categorisation of the tribal areas in terms of growth potential. Categorisation of tribal areas in terms of growth potential is given below.

i) Problem area

— *Type I*: Primitive agriculture and forestry are predominant; infrastructure of growth is lacking-the bulk of the tribals are in acute poverty and are not inclined to seasonal or long-term migration for work.

— *Type II*: Primitive agriculture and forestry are predominant; infrastructure of growth is in rudimentary stage; the bulk of the tribals are poor but have tradition of seasonal or long-term migration for work.

ii) Prospective area

— *Type I*: Economy is tending to be diversified, infrastructure of growth is considerably built up; but the tribals are being disassociated from the control of the resources and from decision-making in resource utilisation pattern, and tend to migrate outside the area for work.

— *Type II:* Economy is tending to be diversified, infrastructure of growth is considerably built up; the tribals continue to control the resources and are effectively associated with decision-making in respect of the utilisation of the resources, particularly where alternative choices are available.

iii) Dynamic area

— *Type I*: Economy is highly diversified, productive relations are tending to be freed from the survival of feudalism, infrastructure of growth has been built up at high level technological transformation is rapidly taking place, but the tribals are losing control over the resources and in decision-making process about the utilisation of the resources.

— *Type II*: Economy is highly diversified; productive relations are tending to be freed from the survival of feudalism, infrastructure of growth has been built up at a high level; technological transformation is rapidly taking place, but the tribals are retaining control over the resources; they have high political participation and are having a dominant voice in decision-making about resource utilisation.

For regional planning, the region as a whole should also be classified with particular reference to the type of linkages that subsist between the tribal area and the rest of the region, it is to be appreciated that regional planning more importantly involves spatial planning and social planning, though administrative planning has its own place as well. In the Fifth Plan outline for the tribals, it has been visualised that the objective should be to bring the tribal areas on par with the adjoining non-tribal areas by the end of the Sixth Plan; and it has been visualised that the dimension of the capital outlay will be determined by this. One may wonder if such an approach may not lead to the evasion of detailed spatial planning and social planning.

As the scheduled tribes belong to the economically weaker and deprived classes of the society, special provisions have been made in the Constitution of India for safeguarding rights and interests of this vulnerable group of the society. The accelerated rate of development of tribal population was targeted in our planned development strategy with a view to bring them up to the level of the general population within a time frame. The benefits of job reservation and other statutory protection have not been uniformly availed by the tribals. As a result the plight of the tribals is far behind the non-tribal population in most part of the country. The lack of basic education and awareness about their own legitimate rights stand in the way of asserting on the areas of their direct and indirect benefits by a vast majority of the tribals.

The Fifth Five Year Plan emerged as a watershed in the history of tribal development in the country. In order to streamline more and more need-based and result-oriented programmes, a Task Force on "Development of Tribal Areas" was set up in 1972 with the following terms of reference:

— to review the nature and level of development that had taken place.

— to suggest a perspective of development for a fifteen-year period.

— to formulate proposals for Fifth Plan indicating priorities, policies, programmes and outlays in the light of the perspectives.

The five working groups set-up under the Task Force observed that the problem of development of tribal areas was primarily linked to the general backwardness of the areas, the poverty of the people and the integration of tribals with rest of the population. It was observed that the tribes of different areas faced different problems. In the northern zones the remoteness of the habitat and hard climatic conditions; in the north-east zone the disrupted economy following the formation of Bangladesh; in the east, central and western zones the pressure of population on land, land tenure, indebtedness, low productivity of forests; and in the southern zone shifting cultivation were identified as the major constraints limiting the scope for desired rate of development.

The areas with high concentration of tribal population should be identified and a combination of ecological, occupational and social parameters be properly assessed for required policy formulation. It was emphasised by the Task Force to give more importance to primary sector as a means for tribal development. In the same year an Expert Committee on tribal development was constituted by the Department of Social Welfare which submitted the strategy for tribal development to be pursued in the Fifth Five Year Plan.

The tribal development agencies in tribal dominant states aimed to make massive investment exclusively for tribals from central funds while making use of state outlays for development of both tribals and non-tribals. The Five Year Plan made it possible to evolve the concept of a sub-plan for the tribal regions of a state within the overall frame of the state plan. The main objective of the tribal sub-plan has been spelt out as development of the area with focus on the scheduled tribes within the sub-plan area. This concept consisted of identification of development blocks within a state having more than 50 per cent scheduled tribe population and launching of massive efforts for tribal development within that 'Sub-plan Aréa'.

The financial resources available was required to be channelised as investment in the tribal areas so as to translate the investment into concrete benefits for the tribal families. The unit of planning for an Integrated Tribal Development Project (ITDP) in a state, comprised a set of Development blocks within a district. The concept of tribal sub-plan conceived in Fifth Five Year Plan period continued till the end of Eighth Five Year Plan. The outlay during annual plan 1997-98 under tribal sub-plan did include provisions for items like crop husbandry, horticulture, sericulture, animal husbandry, cattle development, fisheries, Cooperations run by State Tribal Area Development Corporations, irrigation, power, transport, education, sports, research, medical and health, employment and training etc.

By all yardsticks, it is unfair to believe that the benefits have been evenly distributed to all sections across the regions. In some areas, no doubt, the benefits meant for tribals were realised to some extent by the tribals whereas in some other areas the benefits meant through investment programmes for tribals were realised disproportionately by the non-tribal population. In the traditional tribal belt of Rajasthan, the employment scenario could not be changed over the years. Despite enormous investments made for the development of agriculture and non-agriculture sector, the burden of employment of the tribal population is still on agriculture and allied activities in this area, mostly as agricultural labourers.

With the tiny resource-constrained holdings, it has become a harder task for the tribal farmers to make use of the latest advancements in agriculture production including the adoption of modem technologies. The farm mechanisation is still a distant reality for a large majority of tribal farmers. As the self-generated capital is going to become a major constraint for the tribal farmers, it has become necessary to have more labour intensive farm activities so that the return to labour and subsequently the size of family labour income through farming activities becomes a viable option for the tribals.

The evolution of agricultural technologies meant for efficient use of draught animal power has not been given adequate attention in the past. The rainfall situation in southern Rajasthan is relatively better over other regions and the area is blessed with abundant natural vegetation. As a result, this region is a cattle-dense region in the state. There is a great potential to evolve organic farming on a scientific basis in this region. Large quantities of compost can be developed by the local inhabitants by making use of plant/tree residuals and other organic materials locally available. There is abundant scope to popularise the production and marketing of compost as a viable economic activity in this region.

The potential for required raw materials coupled with high labour supply when augmented with adequate marketing set-up may facilitate to take compost making as a means of income generating economic activity for the tribals in southern Rajasthan. The organic farming is gaining overwhelming importance as a means for sustainable agriculture keeping the soil health as a matter of primary concern.

The popularisation of Neem trees in the tribal areas can be another option to make use of the products for biological control of crops from diseases and pests and to minimise post-harvest losses using the Neem based grain preservation techniques in traditional 'Kothis' used for grain storages. The tribal belt in most parts of the country has strong forest base. The economic use of medicinal plants, both for curing the ailments and for generating part of household income, is a potential means for any tribal belt.

Whenever the problem of rehabilitation arises as a result of taking up of major irrigation projects and other developmental works in tribal areas, generally the tribals do not get adequate justice for their resettlement. When they are uprooted once from their land base, it becomes a serious hindrance for their re-establishment and the situation becomes worse when appropriate alternative land is not made available to them. The facilitators/leaders for implementation of developmental programmes are to be chosen from the tribals hailing from that area, so that the local inhabitants can be mobilised for their participatory role in developing, implementing and maintaining such infrastructure and facilities for the sustainable development of the tribals.

Many of the tribal areas are remote, forested, hilly or sloppy. The natural resource endowment is vastly different from that of other parts. Besides, as a result of age-long seclusion, the tribal communities have been cut-off from the main stream and technological advancement has turned out to be a slow process for them. The culture and psyche developed by the tribals to combat with the environment also stand in the way of any rapid change in their socio-economic development. These factors make it necessary to set up planning strategy for tribal people and area on a specially designed pattern. The formulation of the programmes/projects for tribal development requires a clear methodology of approach by taking into account the socio-cultural base of the people and physical environment of the area.

The efforts made in the past for tribal development resulted in evolving a set of tribal institutions, statutory bodies and voluntary organisations. The success achieved in the past in transforming the tribal population for sustainable development is far from any satisfactory level. Time has now come to make a realistic assessment so that the welfare and development activities targeted for this vulnerable sections of the society may ensure satisfaction of minimum needs, control and management of productive resources, productive employment generation, maximum participation of the people in development process and the required national integration of tribals with other sections of the society. The welfare measures, hitherto initiated to meet the minimum needs in the tribal areas—food for work in the lean period, potable water, health and sanitation, housing, fodder, fuel, primary and non-formal education etc. tend to distort the self-reliance of the tribals.

A reversal of the approach is the need of the time. The minimum needs of the tribal population is to be met out by harnessing the forces of production and orienting the social relations of production in conformity with the tribal ethos of self management. The increased involvement of more and more elevated tribals for planning and implementing developmental programmes for the tribal area may be advocated as such attempts can be more realistic, productive and feasible.

The benefits targeted through the tribal area approach were disproportionately availed by the non-tribals and as such the plight of the tribals could not be improved in a desired manner. It is the need of the time to make a realistic assessment of the area development approach versus beneficiary oriented approach to ensure the tribal development a true reality.

ECONOMIC EMANCIPATION

India is the seventh largest industrialised country of the world, two-third of our population still depends on agriculture. The rural base of our economy is agriculture is yet to witness any significant erosion. Of course, the economy has moved on high growth path of over six percent, but the basic issues of population explosion, illiteracy, poor quality of life, poverty and regional economic disparities continue to haunt the planners and the policy makers.

The global perspective of the problem of sustainable development relates to the process of "development that meets the needs of the present without compromising the ability of the future to meet their own needs". This concept is dynamic since it encompasses the ever changing approaches to the exploitation of natural resources, the direction of investments, the orientation of technological development and institutional framework. The issue of sustainable development assumes alarming significance for the tribal areas because the human resource base of these regions is very weak to shoulder the development responsibilities.

Literacy level among the tribal social groups of Rajasthan is still around 20 per cent. The Tribal Sub-Plan Area concept has, of course, implanted some visible infrastructural masts over the whole of TSP Area during the last two decades. But the traditional socio-cultural fabric of tribal society perpetuates and still conditions the development parameters of the region spread over five southern districts of Rajasthan. Tribal economy continues to be governed by fragile agricultural and animal husbandry activities. The economy of this region is groaning under the increasing pressures of human and animal population. Land holding size and forest covered area is dwindling, droughts and famines continue to reoccur frequently and the land productivity is yet to surge up to a perceptible level.

Governmental initiatives in promoting the use of modern farm technology-improved HYV, use of chemical fertilisers, ground water exploitation for irrigation, distribution of farm implements, etc., do not seem to have established the roots in the tribal and landscape. Even the poverty eradication programmes executed under the IRDP (Integrated Rural Development Programme) scheme are yet to show their glow on the faces of poverty stricken tribal masses. This region has rich mineral resource base but the industrial activities have not developed on a large scale.

Mineral and industrial development responsibilities are primarily shouldered by the outside non-tribal entrepreneurial talents and the local masses are being engaged as wage labourers. Looking to the geophysical setup and the growing-population pressures, the secondary sector is expected to galvanise the tribal economy through the creation of larger and sustainable economic activities. As the situation exists today, no perceptible indicators are visible on the horizon of tribal region.

The basic traits of ignorance and inertia emanated out of the secluded settlement pattern of tribal social groups have made devastating contribution in withholding the speed of their socio-economic development processes. The panorama of unspent funds and under-exploited schemes persists because of the poor responses from the target groups. Geographical isolation has perpetuated tribal's fear psychosis and as such, this society has yet to become vocal for claiming its active participation in the development process.

The society at large has remained mute spectator to the manoeuvrability of outsider plunderers of the natural wealth of the region. This trend needs to be reversed in the TSP Area of Rajasthan to prevent any eventuality of the emergence of any organised and aggressive reactions from tribal masses.

The system of formal education has not yet succeeded in playing the dynamic role and hence the Tribal Area Development Department of the Government of Rajasthan has to make an effective intervention for mobilising the young and educated generation of tribals. Building up of effective awareness among the educated tribal youth to seek the development information as a right could be one such step in the right direction. Any systematic approach to empower the tribal youth through developing awareness about the available development opportunities and the process of availing of them will go a long way in mobilising the tribal youth in a big way.

The intervention has to be made both at the college level and at the school level through promoting the constitution of Career Counselling Clubs (CCCs) of tribal youth and ensuring the percolation of development messages to the tribal families at the grass-root level. The Tribal Area Development Department may effectively attempt to break the shackles of ignorance in the young generation. It will be the pragmatic approach to rope in the younger generation in launching on the information revolution because the future belongs to the youth. The youth has high stakes in protecting the eco-balance of tribal region and in preserving as well as conserving the natural resource base of the area. The mobilisation strategy shall help developing commonsense rather than erudition.

The tribal youth could be mobilised provided its livelihood interests are promoted through such Career Counselling Units (CCUs). In view of this, it may be necessary to provide avenues to the youth to upgrade their skills and aspirations and systematic assistance to move upon the ladder of job scale. Mutual cooperation constitutes an important trait of tribals' cultural menu. The time is ripe for organising the tribal youth through the CCUs down to the grass-root level. If the objective is achieved during the next one decade, the society shall be in a position to shoulder the development responsibilities of the region.

The transition from a protected economy to market economy would be smoother since the younger generation will be ready to withstand the challenges of 21st century. This strategy will constitute an important component of the human resource development strategy for the tribal society. Education is incomplete unless it helps in building up an award and alert society ever prepared to grab the development opportunities.

Community development is more than a programme of physical change. It is a form of guarantee that the economic gains brought through this approach will create deep impressions on the tribal mind. They may not be aware of its immediate impact but unconsciously they are being motivated towards a different socio-economic life. The development programmes are also trying to lead towards the promotion of democratic growth and social justice. But even after two decades, it has not succeeded to remove distrust, suspicion and fear of the government officials in the minds of tribal people and prepare the ground for the appreciation of the positive aspects of government activity. There has been least lessening of distance between the tribal people and the government functionaries. So far, the attempt of government officials forgetting the programmes accepted, adopted and propagated has been limited to a few families only. The general mass of the tribals are still to generate a habit of forward looking, flexibility in judging the new situation, spirit of innovation, respect for science and confidence in human ability to solve difficult problems.

COMMUNITY DEVELOPMENT PROGRAMME (CDP)

The Constitution makes the states responsible for the task of tribal development. Therefore, special efforts have been made for the development of the tribal areas and one of them is this CDP approach. The framers of the Constitution kept in view the special socio-economic situation of the tribal communities and made suitable provisions to ensure that no abstract principles come in the way of their development. Hence, they moved with the idea of community development as a consciously articulated method of accelerating the process of social, economic and political growth of the underdeveloped tribal areas.

Ideologically, the CDP is still to create a concern among the people about their local affairs and promote goodwill towards one another through collective activity and thus strengthen the foundations of community life. It is still trying to promote a sense of responsibility and dignity among the tribals, by weaning the people away from depending upon the government programmes. CDP failed to exert the desired impact on the tribal population in ameliorating their poverty which remained static for the most part as they were before the introduction of the development programme, which has still a long way to go, and for the present the tribals are in the grip of a various circle of poverty as the CDP propounded little for an all-round social progress.

Careful planning of development programmes is necessary to concentrate efforts on achieving the objectives; to keep the development worker and the people on the track without involving them in trivialities; to make the most effective use of the available resources of land, labour, capital, human, material and time; to provide for continuity of efforts towards the accomplishment of the objectives in case the personnel changes; and to time the utilisation of resources in a way that both short and long term objectives arc achieved. All the schemes of community development, viz., agriculture, irrigation, animal husbandry, communication, health education, social education, housing, and rural arts and crafts are planned at the centre and are implemented at the block level throughout the country.

The planning should have been made from below keeping in mind the local culture, religious customs, political system and economy of the tribals. It is now felt by scholars in the various fields that real development can only start from below, from the people at the bottom. Grassroots and barefoot words are now becoming the fashion. Now it is desirable that the ordinary man at the grass-roots should be the point of reference and the yardstick for judging the success or failure of the schemes.

Tribals in India face the problems of the basic requirements of human beings. The tribals have been shamelessly exploited by other people socially, economically, sexually and in other respects throughout the country. In such circumstances the central planning was thought to be best suited. Only planning by the central government could bring the tribal society into the mainstream of Indian life. Truely, it cannot be denied that in 30 years of continuous efforts of the central government the vulnerable tribal society has developed considerably. Now they know the world other than their own, they are trying to adapt fast to the changing world.

The tribal development schemes planned centrally are executed at the block level. The failure or success of any development scheme depends much upon its execution by the CDP workers. The tribal development programmes are chalked out at higher levels without discussion with the people and are ordered to be executed in a particular way. Orders are issued from the highest to the next subordinate authority, from the latter to its next and so on till they are received by the workers at the lowest level in the hierarchy. The latter are thus the persons who have to execute the orders. They have, in most cases, no say except to obey and execute orders, even though they feel that these orders do not suit their areas. There has thus developed a one-way channel of working between the higher officers and the people. Orders flow from the top to bottom without regard for the experiences of the people or the workers at the spot.

In the Five Year Plans of the country, all the schemes are chalked out by the government, and these schemes are finally sent to the blocks for execution year by year. So the schemes are chalked out by the block staff and it depends upon them to allot a development scheme to individuals. The village level workers bring the development schemes to the notice of only such persons who are dominant, rich, influential and easily approachable; and the rest primitive tribal communities and far off villages are always neglected. The people who are really primitive, poor, and in need of help, are usually sidetracked. The people, who come to know about the schemes, give application in the block office. The block staff take decision in regard to the distribution of the schemes.

Every year, a large number of development schemes are sanctioned by the government which are to be implemented in the block. The block officials do not find themselves able to spend all the heavy funds as it requires much paper work as well as field work. But to save one's own labour and to please the superior officers, there is a tendency among the block officials to fulfil all the paper requirements and to neglect the field work. Therefore, it results into lapse of funds and bad quality of work. As the weaker sections are usually unable to avail themselves of the facilities for economic betterment, it tends to strengthen the economic power structure sustained by those, who are already economically better off.

The tribal people want some of the benefits of modernisation but, inevitably, they also want some of the benefits in social framework and within a traditional culture and rhythm of their life. Cultural background must be taken into account while planning for the tribal development. An empirical field study on the different tribal groups must be done, and a well-thought special scheme should be prepared by the anthropologist in collaboration with other experts, who should be also associated with the various phases of implementation of the schemes.

Generalisation of tribes is one of the major difficulties of the development block schemes. Some tribes have highly developed judicial and administrative councils, through which they manage their own affairs and settle their disputes. Some tribes have communal dormitories which serve as centres of community service and give a kind of basic education. There is an endless variety in economic status and degree of cultural development. Different tribal communities have different needs, and the same tribal community has different needs at different times. The policy of the government is to encourage and develop everything that is good in tribal culture. But although this has been accepted enthusiastically by the higher officials and politicians, it must be admitted that at the block level only sporadic attempts have been made to carry out the policy. Tribal culture can be encouraged and developed by not doing anything that will discourage or destroy it. We have to adopt policy of non-interference on the one hand and helping them with technical improvements, wise and tactful guidance on the other.

The success or failure of any development scheme depends upon government personnel to a great extent. They find their job very difficult as they do not know the people of the tribal area and their culture among whom they work. Most of the non-tribals, while working in the tribal areas, take the attitude of benevolent paternalism, while others take their jobs lightly and think that it is impossible to make the tribals change. With benevolence on the one hand and apathy on the other, no attempt is made to involve the people with the programme.

In the tribal area, there are also influential non-tribals whose help and cooperation is easily available to the block staff. The non-tribals are delighted at the opportunity of gaining favour of the officials and then strengthening their hold on the tribal population. Their history as exploiters of the tribals cannot be forgotten by the latter, and, therefore, the Block officials became suspect in the eyes of the tribals. The Block people could also not be blamed as funds were meant not for tribals alone but for the development of all people living in the area. If they received ready cooperation from the non-tribals, it seems, there is no reason why they should not accept it. Moreover, cooperation from any quarter was welcomed as they had to accomplish certain physical targets in a short time. If they depended upon the tribals alone, this could not be done, as among them persuasion took a lot of time and the response was very poor. Thus most of the non-tribals became executing agents for the different constructional activities on which money had to be spent. There was a rise in the number of petty contractors, who invariably sprang up from the ranks of the recently expropriated petty landlords.

Under the CDP, the officers at state level have a feeling that they are the agency for executing programmes, and that their duty is only to issue orders and expect compliance from the block development officers, through district level officers. Instructions issued from the headquarters are thus mechanically passed on to the regional officers, and from them to the district officers, and to the block development officers and village level workers. This machinery, coupled with the existing administrative machinery, started ordering things to be done by the project workers without taking into consideration whether the programmes suited their areas or not. As a result of all this, the original concept of the community development programme has been lost sight of.

In CDP, the village level worker is regarded as the kingpin, round whom the development programmes in the villages revolve. His role is designed as a multi-purpose functionary, to serve as the common agency of all the development departments, and educate the people to adopt the programmes of technical and financial assistance. It is supposed that the passes over to his departmental superiors the sense of local needs and urgencies in order to obtain their recommendations for solution, but in reality the superiors do not heed his advice.

The achievements of CDP can be evaluated under two sub-headings—physical and non-physical achievements. The programme has covered almost all the areas of tribal development and has been categorised into meaningful sections. One cannot doubt the good intention behind it. There has also been sufficient provision of manpower to manage the various programmes. Right from the central and state governments down to the Block Officers, there is a long chain of personnel engaged in tribal development works. This multiplicity of personnel has its merit of check and balance and also demerit as presence of too many cooks. Lately, terms like single-line administration have come up to ensure coordination between working of the departments and the personnel. Similarly, in the last two decades; fund allocations have also shown variations. When the general CD Blocks were converted and given the status of special multipurpose tribal blocks, sudden increase of personnel and finance had been witnessed. The tribals were unable to receive so many guests at a time and, therefore, could not be benefited properly. This has further restricted the tribals contribution in developing their own lot.

One of the main aims of the programmes was to generate and utilise local natural and human resources. In the case of tribal development, the contributions of both these sources seemed to be absent. There was no programme to utilise and develop the local resources, and on the other hand the tribals were too poor to even meet their share of financial contribution under the CDP. The only contribution they could make, was that of their hard physical labour, but that too became a form of exploitation. The requirement of people's financial contribution has helped the non-tribal group of the area to come forward and reap the harvest of development schemes.

The major part of agriculture development schemes is not useful for many of the tribal ethnic groups. As an example we can take the case of Bishunpur block. Here the major agriculture communities are Oraons, Mundas and Kherwars, etc. The artisan communities like Lohra, Asur, Chik-Baraik and Mahali farmer, shifting cultivator and present agricultural labour group like Birjias, and the nomadic Birhors, are not being benefited by agricultural programmes directly. Looking at these ethnic groups, one feels that small scale industries should have been developed and then only the artisans could have been benefited.

Even the schemes of agricultural production have been utilised by the rich tribals and non-tribals only. Improved seeds and chemical fertilisers in general had not reached the poor tribals. The demonstration farms in every case usually belonged to only a few rich families. The distribution of improved implements could not function properly in the difficult terrain of Bishunpur area. In some cases, the small bullocks could not pull the heavy iron plough, and in other the weeder or thrasher became out of order too soon, or the irrigation pumps could not be used even for a short period due to mechanical malfunctioning. The construction of many of the irrigation wells dug in the tribal area could not be finished due to lack of sufficient and timely grants.

In the past 22 years of the history of the block, there has been the least effort to reclaim the cultivable land. It has made the majority of the poor tribals poorer. It is said that the development programme in the field of animal husbandry has been limited to the field of agricultural use only. The cattle could have been used to supplement their income and change their food habits. Though pigs and dogs were distributed, cow, goat and sheep rearing also should have been introduced side by side.

The presence of so many artisan communities has not given any idea to the planners to develop small scale industries also. We can find some exceptions in the shape of centres for rope-making, basket-making and weaving which today are simply a development vestige as none of them are actually working. Thus all the programmes and financial allocations for industrial development have gone to drains, and not a single family has been benefited. The construction of various houses and resettlement colonies has helped the tribals to gain new ideas of living, but practically they find the living unbearable. There is no arrangement made for their repairs, which becomes a necessity just after a few months.

There has been dearth of suitable road communication. The communication facility has great bearing on the introduction and maintenance of development schemes in tribal areas. The sense of cooperation is not new for the tribal world, but their binding values are different from those of modern cooperative societies and grain goals, instead there had been court cases for recovery of loans. This they could not tolerate and have become indifferent towards development through cooperatives.

There are schemes of social services, apart from the gains through CDP. They are primarily meant to minimise the social distance between the tribal and non-tribals. Through these schemes, it has been planned to develop health and sanitation, education, leadership and the nutritional standard of food. The low financial sanction for medicines, the very limited facility of doctors and hospitals, and the complete lack of preventive measures speak for the health and sanitational standard of tribal people. Perhaps eighty per cent of the tribal folk had not experienced any change in their health and sanitational standard in the last two decades of the existence of the block.

The construction of a few reservoirs for drinking water and latrines and bathrooms for a population or thirty-three thousand seems a mockery of sanitational effort. Again, the number of high schools and middle school's is a proof of the sluggish effort at development of education there. So far as female education is concerned, there is only one middle school and that too is meant for Tana Bhapts only. Thus a population of sixteen thousand females is deprived of the basic facility of schooling. Construction of community centres and Gandhi Chabutras and organisation of Melas, outside tours, leaders camps, and youth leagues were necessary for enlightening the tribal mind, but the outcome was insignificant. The non-tribal population of the area participated in majority, while the tribals were spectator from the sidelines.

Very recently the tribal development has Applied Nutrition Programme (ANP) for raising the general health of the people. The children and pregnant women and lactating mothers are to receive the products of poultry and pisciculture. But the Sanchalak and Sanchalika or the programmers being mainly non-tribals, its benefit had been restricted to a few rich tribals and non-tribals.

The development proposals have favoured the non-tribals and some of the ethnic groups like Oraons and Kherwars. There is marked difference also between a handful of Oraons families and the general community. We can find such examples among other tribal communities too, i.e., a few families of Chik-Baraiks and Lohras have pined at the cost of other tribal brethren. It will not be out of place to mention these special facilities given to some families on the basis of their religious inclinations by the Christians and the Tana Bhagats. Inspite of all the development measures, majority of tribal population has not been able to reap any benefit from them and they continue to remain in the same state of poverty as they were before.

So far as the few developing tribal families are concerned, they are under the purview of difference between the material and non-material aspects of development (cultural lag) and trying to adjust between modernisation and traditional culture. But to explain and compare the stages of development between the tribal masses at one hand, a few tribal and non-tribal families on the other, one can use the term of development lag. This term could be used to make it clear that there is marked difference between the development of the non-tribal community and the tribal community.

Each per cent of non-tribal population of the area has captured 35 schemes of development, while one per cent of the tribal population has only 9.7 schemes to be satisfied with. There are many families among the tribals who have acquired cultural characteristics of non-tribal societies and have begun to contribute to national development. The process of integration for these families has covered a considerable distance. It has been repeated so many times that we should not judge the results of tribal development by statistics, rather an ideological change to some extent should satisfy us, as an anthropologist we must judge it from the point of view of the majority.

Sixty per cent of the tribal population do not show any marked material change in their life pattern even after 22 years of existence of the block. And eighty per cent of development schemes had gone to only ten per cent of the tribal families mainly belonging to the Oraon community, followed by the Lohras and the Kherwars. Thus, the problem of unequal distribution of wealth still looms large. Wealth is being concentrated in the hands of a small minority, while the masses of the people live in poverty and on the margin of society. The government efforts are still trying to integrate the marginal people into the existing social structure.

The purpose of development, that the benefits will trickle down from the top to the bottom, had yet to reach a satisfactory level. The material advancement through these developmental efforts among tribal people has not shown marked changes excepting some solitary cases. Even the rich among the tribals, have begun exploiting the "have-nots". As had been thought at an early stage of planning, the majority of the tribals did not accept the 'gifts' of development. It was a shock for the planners to find that even the poor tribals have refused the immediate material gains. This had led them to think about finding the flaws in the tribal society instead of in the development programmes.

However, new terms like grass-root planning are being used to give due emphasis to the poor man. Perhaps, making an ordinary man as the point of reference, would lead to an overall change of the tribal development planning. The mass welfare has aptly become the concept of programming a development effort. In other words the human factor should have precedence over the economic and technological factors. To achieve this, a dialogue between the planners and the tribals, should do the trick. The two groups—the donor and the receiver—should come round the table to talk on equal terms, a real dialogue on the basis of mutual respect for each other's dignity.

Till today the development programmes did not care for local natural resources and the tribal mind and requirements. The tribal people should be allowed to develop along the lines of their own genius and we should avoid imposing anything on them from outside. We should also try to build up a team of their own people for looking after the work of administration and development. But none of these approaches has been attempted in the past decades.

The policy of non-tribal administration for tribal development is still being pursued. On the contrary, we should have planned for gradual handing over the developmental efforts to the tribals, themselves. By now the tribal masses should have developed a feeling that the developmental efforts are for their own benefit, they own the particular measure, how best they can take advantage from it, and from where they can muster the resources for continuous running of the scheme. A lot has been written by various authorities on the anthropological approach to the problems of tribal development. It still continues to attract the attention of the social scientists. They have regularly emphasised on the systematic knowledge of social, economic, political and religious life of the tribals along with their beliefs and values as the prerequisite for a planned change. Any innovation should be judged from the view of the tribal response.

One must be aware of the developing cultural lag because of the ensuing economic and social change, and attempt to keep it at the minimum. Identification of hard and soft cores of tribal culture has a lot to do with the success and failure of development programmes. A development worker is further required to gain faith of the tribal masses. Above all, one must bear in mind that a social change is a slow process.

The process of development is distinct under different cultural patterns. The role of culture in development is determinantal. Development conceived and produced by men cannot be culture free. Man is a part of culture and the culture of one society cannot be substituted by another, it can only be changed and influenced.

Framers of the Constitution while taking note of the centuries old injustice perpetrated against the tribal community have adopted two pronged strategy of tribal development which seeks to provide them protection from exploitation and assist them in their economic development. Protection is prerequisite to development, particularly during the transition period until they came up to the general level and joined the mainstream of the nation.

Protective discrimination has been provided for in favour of Scheduled Tribes in the Constitution, particularly under Articles 15(4), 16(4), 19(5), 46, 330, 332, 335, and the

Fifth and the Sixth Schedules. Similarly, provisions have been made for the economic development of these communities, under Articles 275(1) first provision and 339(2). These provisions assign special responsibility to the Government not only for drawing up of special schemes of development but also for providing them financial assistance.

Numerous efforts have been made since Independence for economic development of the tribals. The first attempt was made in 1954 when 43 special multipurpose development projects each with an additional outlay of Rs. 27 lakhs for five years, were started to supplement the CDPs which aimed at comprehensive development of rural areas. Since these projects were in the areas which comprised sparsely populated hill and forest regions, with poor communication and limited institutional infrastructure, they called for greater investment and personal attention by extension workers.

Elwin Committee reviewed the situation in 1956 which recommended a cautious approach in the introduction of multiplicity of schemes in tribal areas. On review, the projects were substituted by a less intensive model of tribal development blocks in 1957. The norm for a tribal development block was confined to an areas of 150 to 200 sq. miles and a population of about 25000. The blocks were supposed to work for tribal population under Intensive Development Programme. They were to concentrate on the following four main activities, viz., economic development, education, health and communication and were to have specific targets.

Comprehensive review of tribal scenario was done by the Scheduled Areas and Scheduled Tribes Commission, generally called Dhebar Commission, in April 1960 and it submitted its report in October 1961. The Commission noted that the pace of development in the tribal areas was slow. Investment and other protective measures were also inadequate and needed urgent attention of the government. It called for comprehensive legislation to cover all tribals living within the Scheduled Areas and outside, and a simple administrative system for tribal areas.

It recommended a scheme of tribal development blocks for all areas with more than 50 per cent tribal population. The recommendations of the Commission were accepted and the block approach was continued. By the end of Third Five Year Plan the scheme was implemented in about 500 blocks covering about 40 per cent of the total tribal population. It precluded a large section of the tribal population from the development programmes. The tribal situation, so far as protective measures and developmental programmes are concerned, remained almost unchanged.

In 1969, a Committee under the Chairmanship of Shilu Ao was appointed to review the tribal development programmes. It observed that most of the recommendations of the Dhebar Commission had remained unimplemented and urged that they should be implemented without any further delay. It disapproved the block approach as inadequate. The block was too small to function effectively as a basic unit of planning and implementation. It pointed out that the main problems of the tribals related to indebtedness, land alienation, economic backwardness and inadequacy of communication and suggested that those should be tackled on priority basis by formulating a comprehensive programme of development.

Six tribal development agencies were started during the Fourth Plan, as pilot schemes in four states, viz., two in Madhya Pradesh, two in Orissa and one each in Bihar and Andhra Pradesh. Subsequently, two more agencies were started in Orissa by the end of the Fourth Plan. Each agency covered a group of blocks and was expected to take up various programmes and protective measures on integrated basis by pooling up the resources. In the Fourth plan, about Rs. 44 crores were allotted to these agencies. The allocations were in addition to the normal outlays. In actual practice, however, the agency approach practically remained an agricultural development programme and failed to achieve the desired results.

TRIBAL SUB-PLAN

One of the important factors for the failure of the development programmes is that the Scheduled Tribes and tribal areas have been looked upon as a welfare problem as distinguished from development problem. The welfare of Scheduled Tribes has continued to depend on small outlays under the Backward classes sector and not on general sector outlays. The administrative structure in tribal areas lacks simplicity. It is beyond the comprehension of the tribals, and therefore, it does not evoke any response from them. Such a structure of administration may not, therefore, be suitable for carrying out integrated development of tribal areas. The Task Force recommended that to ensure balanced socioeconomic development of the tribal areas, a policy of integrated development would be necessary for the Fifth and subsequent plans. Therefore, a Tribal Sub Plan (TSP) strategy was evolved in 1974-75. This strategy emphasised area development with a focus on improving the quality of life of the tribal communities. Its immediate objectives were elimination of exploitation in all forms, speeding up the processes of social and economic development, building up inner strength of people and improving their organisational capabilities.

Any development activity for benefiting the tribal population will not succeed unless exploitation in various forms is prevented. For protecting the tribals from exploitation, it recommended integrated credit-cum-marketing service, marketing of agricultural and minor forest produce, supply of inputs and essential consumer commodities, credit for production purposes, consumption of social needs, redemption of past debts through legislative and executive measures and adoption of suitable measures for dealing with resultant liability. It also emphasised that the programmes for prevention of land alienation, restoration of land already alienated, termination of practices like bonded labour, solution of the problems created in the zones of influence of modern industrialised areas and review of excise and forest policies, needed special attention.

The TSP strategy recommended giving high priority to agriculture, land reforms, irrigation, improved methods of cultivation and completion of land records; special attention to vulnerable groups like shifting cultivators and forest villagers; generation of employment opportunities for better utilisation of available manpower through programmes in the fields of horticulture, animal husbandry and allied occupations; development of cottage industries based on the local raw materials so that the proportion of semi-processed and processed goods is maximised in the export mix of the region and development of basic infrastructure including legal, institutional and physical aspects for speeding up the socioeconomic development.

The TSP approach has been applied to certain identified areas in different states and two Union Territories. These are Andhra Pradesh, Assam, Bihar, Gujarat, Himachal Pradesh; Karnataka, Kerala, Madhya Pradesh, Maharashtra, Manipur, Orissa, Rajasthan, Sikkim, Tamil Nadu, Tripura, Uttar Pradesh, West Bengal, Andaman and Nicobar Islands and Daman and Diu. This approach has not been applied to four tribal majority states of Arunachal Pradesh, Mizoram, Meghalaya and Nagaland and two Union Territories of Lakshadweep and Dadra and Nagar Haveli as their entire plans are directed towards the development and welfare of the tribal population.

The main components of the TSP strategy are Integrated Tribal Development Projects (ITDPs), Modified Area Development Approach (MADA) and Pockets and Primitive Tribal Group Projects. For implementation of TSP strategy, 191 ITDPs have been carved out in the aforesaid States and Union Territories. Each ITDP comprises blocks/Taluks/ Tehsils or even whole district with 50 per cent or more tribal population. In delineating the project areas, the main factors viz., predominance of tribal population, contiguity of area and administrative viability have been kept in view. In certain States like West Bengal, Karnataka, Kerala and Tamil Nadu, here, concentration of tribal population is not in contiguous belts, a flexible approach has been adopted in delineating ITDP areas.

The MADA pockets have also been carved out in states, covering about 30 lakh tribal population. These are as comprise smaller pockets of tribal concentration having minimum total population of 10000 with Scheduled Tribe population of 50 per cent or more. In these areas, the emphasis is on family development by taking up family oriented income generating programmes.

During the Sixth Plan about 39 lakh tribal families were economically assisted against the target of about 28 lakh families. During the Seventh Plan, the target of providing economic assistance has been fixed at 41.56 lakh families. During the first four years of the Seventh Plan, about 42.58 lakh families have already been assisted. The quantum of assistance varies from programme to programme and is not sufficient enough to raise the family above the poverty line.

The TSP is being financed through the resources drawn from flow of funds from state plan outlays, sectorial outlays in the central ministries for tribal areas, special central assistance allocation for tribal areas, and institutional finance mainly from banks. Flow of funds from the state plan to the sub-plan from the resource base for the tribal development programmes and the outlays from other sources are supplementary.

State plan outlays comprise a divisible and a non-divisible portion. Those investments whose benefit do not confine to any specific region constitute the non-divisible portion. Quantification and utilisation of resources should be reviewed to ensure accrual of due benefit to-the tribal region. For the disbursement of funds within the divisible portion a weightage should be given to the tribal areas on the basis of their level of social and economic development.

The institutional finance should take into consideration the total ceiling for the state and special problems, if any, in inducing its flow to the tribal region. The likely flow of benefits from each programme to the tribal areas should be quantified. The special central assistance for the TSP should attempt to supplement the total resources which can be mobilised by the state plans, central ministries and the financing institutions.

After introduction of sub-plan strategy there has been substantial increase in flow of funds to TSP areas. But most of the funds have remained notional and as a result commensurate benefits could not accrue to tribal areas and tribal communities. For instance, investments made on major and medium irrigation, power, industrial and other projects merely on location basis accounted for about 50-60 per cent of the TSP. It has been shown as an investment under TSP but the proportionate benefits have not accrued to the tribals. In fact, such projects have benefited mainly the non-tribals.

In individual sectors the flow of funds from state plan to TSP has also been notional. Even in divisible sectors, allocation has been made on sectorial basis for the State as a whole and not for individual ITDP. It has rendered the monitoring of physical benefits to Scheduled Tribes virtually infructuous. Special central assistance funds have not been utilised as gap filler against specific schemes to-supplement the efforts of the state government. The disaggregation of these funds is made sector-wise and not ITDP-wise by the state departments of planning and finance. The project officer of the ITDP does not exercise any control over such funds.

The tribals have been treated as mere receivers of the benefits and they have not been involved either in the decision making process or in formulation or implementation of the plans and programmes. As the problems of the tribals are unique, it is essential that they are actively involved in planning as well as in the implementation of the programmes. Effective participation of the tribals in decision making would not only bring about successful implementation of the programmes but also create confidence among them in the policies of the government.

3

Tribal Education

The ultimate goal of education should be to meet the basic learning needs of all, children, youth and adults. These needs comprise both essential learning tools such as literacy, oral expression, numeracy and problem solving and the basic learning content such as knowledge, skills, values and attitudes required by human beings to be able to survive, to develop their full capacities, to live and work in dignity, to participate fully in development, to improve the quality of their lives, to make informed decisions and to continue learning. Education provides the necessary tools, skills, knowledge, values and attitudes required for the realisation of the four cardinal values applicable for all humans, viz., survival, security, prosperity and progress. The formal elementary education system in India is now a gigantic enterprise and is one of the largest in the world.

With the present trend towards globalisation, privatisation and liberalisation, the education system is getting more and more conditioned by the demands of the market economy as dictated by the ruling capitalist class. The school has become an extension of the market for moulding the child as per its specifications. Non-economic values such as equality, love, goodness and truth that bind the family, community and nation are being displaced by purely economic values of market relationships. Values like competition, individualism, hierarchy, money, hard work discipline, punctuality, etc., are being inculcated in the children. The emphasis is upon imitation, obedience, repetition, drill and control rather than upon initiative, creativity, choice, decision-making and freedom. The learning of humanities and the development of critical thinking are being discouraged. Instead an education subservient to the interests of the globalisation process, where competitive values are predominant, is being encouraged. Students are more preoccupied with learning how to compete with each other, and less concerned with enhancing personal growth and building up critical skills and the potential to transform society.

The tribals are the indigenous people of India. They are generally called *adivasis* which literally means original settlers. Under the Constitution of India certain tribes have been specified as Scheduled Tribes (ST). Only those tribes which have been included in the list of STs are given special treatment or facilities envisaged under the Constitution. According to the 1991 census 67.76 million persons belonged to ST constituting 8.08 per cent of the total population of India. There are 461 ST in India speaking more than 100 languages and dialects. Out of these about 30 tribes speak the Austro-Asiatic family of languages, none of which are recognised as a national language and included in the 5th Schedule of the Constitution.

The identity and culture of Indian tribals are closely linked to the natural resources and the environment amidst which they live. They have the total right on that part of the "Mother Earth", as they call her, bequeathed to them by their ancestors. They have developed various norms, values, beliefs and practices which regulate the use of the natural resources around them in such a way that nature always remained bountiful to them.

To tribals land is not simply a factor of production, but a source of spirituality as well. It is the land, that gives life and meaning to their whole being; for it is in their land that their history and identity are contained. Regarding the ownership of land the tribals have different concepts, often incomprehensible to outsiders. Ownership of land is vested in the community. No individual has the right to permanently alienate the land from the community. The community includes not only the living members but also the ancestors and future generations. That is why for the tribals land and blood are homologous. Their society, culture, religion, identity and their very existence are intimately linked to the land they hold.

The very existence of the tribals depends on their nature of the land they hold has enabled the tribals to develop an ethos which represents a quality of being and living which is far more integrated, more humane, and more egalitarian than the ethos of many modern civilisations. Their attitude is to enjoy the fruits of the present without risking the next generation, to ensure continual enjoyment of scarce resources in a situation of relative plenty. At the core of this ethos lies the concept of harmony—harmony with nature and harmony within the community. This harmony permeates the entire lives of the tribals and defines all aspects of their society.

Thus, the values of sustainable use of land and not of taking more than what is required have found expression in the various social institutions they have evolved. For example, it is an unwritten rule that everyone must take the necessary steps to ensure that his or her way of using the land will not be at the expense of future generations. Consumerism, the bane of modern society is rejected by the tribal society. There is a subsistent economy which is practically self-reliant. Economic activities are based on collectivism and cooperation; and individualism and competition are avoided. Dignity of both labour and leisure is acknowledged and down to earth living is very much appreciated.

The tribal society is basically an egalitarian society. They have a concept of men and women which places them in relations of equal respect and dignity, rather than the hierarchical conceptions existing in other societies that place women in a subservient position. In this connection it is interesting to note that the Austro-Asiatic languages make no distinction on the basis of gender, but only on the basis of having life. Tribal society is based on democratic political thinking. The democracy that is practised by them is participatory rather than representative.

The religious system of the tribals has originated out of their intimate relationship with nature and is a celebration of that relationship. They view the universe as a systematic, harmonic whole. Their world-view is cosmocentric rather than anthropocentric. The central concern of tribal religion is to preserve and maintain their intimate relationship with nature in such a way that nature would always remain bountiful to them. Thus, based on a world-view that is an antithesis of the dominant capitalist world-view, the tribals have been able to develop a highly efficient and viable social order that gives them a distinct identity and enables them to have genuine progress, a progress that is both sustainable and equitable in our search for solutions to our many global problems. Tribal cultures provide new opportunities by increasing the wealth of possible alternatives.

In the name of development for national interest the tribals are being robbed, oppressed and discriminated against by the rulers of the country. The basic phenomenon that characterises the situation of the tribals in India is that of dispossession. They are systematically and methodically being dispossessed of the ownership of their means of production, of the products of their labour and of the very means of human existence. They are dispossessed of their political autonomy and their communities are being broken up in the name of development. They are dispossessed of their cultures, their values, and their very identity through well planned policies, such as those of integration and assimilation, of bringing them to the national mainstream. As a result of all these the tribals are reduced to a situation of extreme poverty and powerlessness. The tribals are continuing their long-standing struggle to re-establish their traditional rights over their ancestral lands and resources, and for the right to develop and preserve their languages, culture, religion and social institutions.

Indian Constitution has specifically identified the tribals among the weaker sections of society and has made special provisions to check their exploitation and further their upliftment. Education has been accepted as one of the main means of achieving this objective. Special educational incentives such as opening of separate schools, reservation of seats in educational institutions, provision of students mid special scholarships, etc., have been introduced for the benefit of tribals. In spite of all these measures education has made little progress among the tribals.

According to 1991 Census the literacy rate among the ST was 29.6 per cent as against the national average of 52.21 per cent. The literacy rate for ST males was 40.65 per cent and for ST females 18.19 per cent. The corresponding national figures for male and female populations were 64.2 and 39.19 per cents respectively. In fact these figures for ST population was even lower than the corresponding figures for Scheduled Castes (SC) population. We exclude the North-eastern States which have very high literacy rates, the literacy rate of ST population in the rest of the country will be abysmally low.

In India tribal education is in a pitiable state beset with many problems. The educational system in India is structured on a world-view which is diametrically opposed to the tribal world-view and is conformed to the world-view of the dominant consumerist and materialist societies. Education no longer emphasises the need to maintain harmony, the central concern of tribal societies, but rather is now used to produce the necessary human resources for the continued pursuit of wealth. Values like competition, individualism and hierarchy as against the values of cooperation, collectivism and equality, held dear by the tribals, are being propagated through the present schools.

The present system does not impart tribal culture and does not develop in the students, both tribal and non-tribal, a love for the languages and culture of the tribals. Little or no education is imparted through tribal mother tongues. Hardly any attention is given to the development of tribal languages although some of the tribal languages like *Santali* have more speakers than some of the officially recognised national languages. Many of the tribal languages belong to the Austro-Asiatic language family. They are generally different from the dominant non-tribal languages which belong either to the Indo-European or Dravidian language family. Both in phonology and syntax tribal languages are different from non-tribal languages. Tribal children find it extremely difficult to learn in an alien language right from the beginning of their school days.

The present education systems have neglected the contributions of the tribals to the mainstream history and culture. Their rich oral traditions are branded as primitive and savage. The existing history books have been written from the dominant non-tribal high caste culture point of view. There are very few references to the tribals, mostly negative, in the epics and the *puranas* where they are considered as *rakshasas*, *nishadas*, *varanas*, etc., and treated as uncivilised and sub-humans. Although there were more than 100 tribal uprisings and revolts against British rule, the contribution of the tribals to the Indian War of Independence is not recognised yet.

There is hardly any concordance between the school and tribal culture. Schooling conflicts with the basic-education that tribal children gain from participation in their own culture. Tribal cultures generally require mastery of an elaborate and highly specialised knowledge of the natural environment, as well as special training in folklore, religion, technology arid other skills. The years that tribal children are required to spend studying the dominant culture's textbooks are in direct competition with the normal enculturation process.

Further, schooling deprives the tribal community of the important contribution that children often make to their subsistent economy. The great disparity between what the tribal children learn in schools and what they learn from other educative agents within their society leads to negative educational and societal consequences. The dominant culture based schools communicate negative attitudes to the tribal children about their culture. As a result, they become demonstrated and alienated from their own culture. In such a situation children become outcasts: not fully accepted by the dominant society and no longer fully able to play a part in their own deintegrated tribal culture.

Problems are associated also with literary field. Literacy carries with it the potential for much good. It contains also seeds of great destruction. In the hands of the dominant class literacy can become a powerful tool for exploitation. It can be used for opening up and increasing the reach of cosumerism. When not handled with sensitivity it leads to the destruction of local wisdom, traditions and practices. Eroding knowledge bases which have stood the test of time is extremely dangerous especially for the tribals with regards to their ability to cope with their immediate environment.

The transition from oral to written culture is very critical for the tribals. There is a false notion, propagated by the dominant society, that what is written is more authentic than what is orally transmitted. The history of the tribals is replete with cases where they were deceitfully deprived of their ancestral lands due to lack of written documents. These bitter experiences have gradually forced them to believe that what is written is more true than what is orally transmitted. They began to look down upon their rich oral traditions and started blindly accepting the dominant culture based written materials. Through a manipulative use of literacy the dominant classes have been able to create a superior/interior ranking between the written and oral knowledge systems. The present system of education has made the transition from pre-literate to literate stage a painful process for the tribals. Instead of being smooth it is sudden and abrupt as it does not build upon the traditions and practices of the tribals. Oral and written cultures differently condition the thought processes of their people.

Tribals, because of their oral culture, think, learn and remember differently. Due to the abrupt and painful transition to the literate stage and lack of scope to read and write in their mother tongues the tribals have negative attitude towards reading and writing. The present day text-books, teaching methods and teacher training programme do not take into account these difficulties and the entirely different learning style of tribal learner. For example, since oral cultures tend to use situational rather than abstract thinking, the tribals find it extremely difficult to grasp even simple abstract concepts. The word for 'to think' among the Munda speaking the tribals is *uru* which has also the meaning 'to worry' or 'to be in grief'. Thinking or abstraction is considered as an unpleasant activity by the tribals. Therefore, special textbooks and teaching methods are needed for tribal learners to make them joyful.

The overemphasis on centralisation and uniformity has made the present educational system rigid. The system is exclusively dependent on the bureaucracy and there is lack of healthy school-community relationship. As a result, the social institutions as well as the various teaching resources of the community are not properly utilised for educational purposes. In the government policy on tribal education the emphasis has been on concessional provisions. Little attempt has been made to equip the tribals with knowledge and skills through special educational programmes so that they can compete with their non-tribal counterparts on equal terms. Further, the education programme is not suitable to their lifestyle.

The present programme is institutional, full time and sequential with one-point entry. There is no flexibility in the choice, content and duration of the courses and it is difficult to adjust the curriculum and textual materials to the needs and interests of the tribals. The tribals who are poor do not have easy access to the educational institutions and cannot afford a full-time programme. They become drop-outs or push-outs from the system. The fixed school hours are not compatible with the needs of the tribal community.

The content of education also serves as a constraint. It alienates tribal children horn their society. It separates intellectual from manual work and does not invoke dignity of manual labour. It is not production-oriented and does not develop occupational skills. Often it is totally irrelevant to the needs of the community. The curriculum and instructional materials do not create awareness of the rich cultural identity of the tribal people as also of their enormous creative talent.

By imposing on the tribals the values and culture of the dominant society it perpetuates the existing unjust and inegalitarian social structure. The syllabuses and textbooks used in the schools are based on the life and culture of the dominant society. They are partial and prejudiced in favour of the dominant culture. They contain ideas, concepts and bellies alien to the tribals and create not only problems in learning but also a negative attitude among the tribals towards their own culture. The test procedures used in these schools are also biased in favour of the dominant class.

The use of non-tribal languages as medium of instruction and non-tribals, who consider the tribals as inferior to them, as teachers in the tribal schools also create serious problems for the tribal learners. Language is the main cementing factor that expresses the identity of a given community. There is a non-declared policy to suppress the language of the tribals and to impose on them the dominant language of the area. The tribal languages are merely corruptions of good speech and unworthy of survival. The suppression of the languages of the tribal people is one of the most effective ways of keeping them oppressed so that they can be easily exploited. Education in the present day schools has become a process of de-tribalisation for the tribals.

EDUCATIONAL TRANSFORMATION

Programmes of educational transformation must go hand with programmes of radical social transformation. The Jamtien Declaration had stated that the goal of tribal education should be to meet the basic learning needs of tribals. These comprise the essential learning tools and basic learning contents required by the tribals to be able to survive, to develop their full capacities, to live and work in dignity, to participate fully in development, to improve the quality of their lives, to make informed decisions and to continue learning and thus to preserve their very identity as a distinct people, enriching human society.

Tribal education, if it has to be relevant, must protect and promote what the tribals regard as valuable in their traditional culture. It must strengthen their spiritual and cultural values so that they may become involved in relationships based on their own identity and without jeopardising their symbiotic richness and community spirit. It must impart such values as cooperation, sharing, equality, dignity of manual labour etc., which are basis of their identity. Tribal culture is primarily oral and tribal knowledge and traditions are orally handed down from generation to generation. The transition from oral to written culture is a crucial period for the tribals. Literacy when not handled with sensitivity can cause serious harm to their rich cultural traditions. In order to make the transition smooth, right from the beginning, literacy programmes should primarily focus on the documentation and preservation of traditional wisdom so that generations yet to come will gain from it.

Tribal education must build upon the accumulated knowledge and wisdom of the tribal people and lend it the scientific and ecological credibility it so richly deserves. In order to foster a sense of love and pride for their culture tribal education must include celebrations of tribal festivals, tribal games, lessons on local traditions, folklore, music and biographies of important tribals. The rich history of the tribals and their contribution to mainstream history and culture must become an essential part of tribal education. Further, tribal children should be taught in their tribal mother tongues at the initial stages of their education, with arrangements to switch over to the regional languages later on. Once they learn to read and write in their mother tongues it is easier for them to transfer these skills to other languages learned subsequently.

A learner who already knows how to read and write does not have to struggle with the problems of reading and writing all over again. The essential process involved in decoding symbols and forming letters remain the same. Standardisation of tribal languages by developing scripts, writing grammars and dictionaries, and by making contrastive studies with other languages is also very essential for the progress of tribal education.

The present education system has failed to tap the rich educational resources in tribal culture. Several studies have shown how we can very effectively utilise some special aspects of tribal life and culture as positive resources for the education of tribal learners. Tribals possess many positive qualities such as cooperation, mutual aid, peer and group learning, egalitarianism, informality, sense of independence and responsibility, freedom from guilt consciousness and parental overprotection, warm humour, highly developed poetic sense, etc., which can be used as positive resources for teaching tribal learners.

In order to make an educational programme for the tribals very collective it should be based on such social and pleasurable activities. Tribals are often preoccupied with such pleasure-giving activities as singing, dancing, drinking, storytelling, hunting, fishing, etc. Their conversation is punctuated with riddles and word plays which they enjoy very much. Among the Munda speakers the word *rasa* (pleasure) is often on their lips and is very dear to their hearts. Their philosophy of life can be summarised in the word *rasa*. For the realisation of *rasa* they have a complete cycle of festivals. It is their main source of strength which keeps them going in the midst of all the sufferings and exploitations they undergo.

An important aspect of the tribal concept of pleasure is its social function. Real pleasure comes from group activities and community events such as festivals. In fact the tribals derive pleasure in giving pleasure to others. Tribal concept of pleasure has tremendous educational implications. For the tribals learning is an active and pleasurable event. The initiation of tribal children into new life experiences takes place through various pleasurable activities such as song, dances, folktales, riddles, etc., associated with different festivals.

Tribal history, the story of their origin, their customs, traditions, myths, legends, folktales, riddles, etc. are orally transmitted from generation to generation. Hardly any effort has been made to utilise this oral aspect of tribal culture to teach tribal learners. There are some basic differences between oral and written cultures. In written cultures one does not have to keep everything in mind because one can go back to the text when necessary. Oral utterances disappear in the air as soon as they are uttered.

Oral cultures use many techniques to preserve in memory the knowledge gained over the ages. Oral cultures are more redundant than written cultures. They use more words than is necessary and repeat key words and ideas in different ways so that the hearer can remember and assimilate what is said. For example, the Ho tribals in their songs and sacrificial prayers express almost every concept in doublets and many words have poetic parallel words, or words which are regularly used with them in parallel situation. Oral cultures are aggregative, whereas written cultures are analytic.

Oral cultures add lots of adjectives and epithets which the written cultures find cumbersome. Since tribal cultures are primarily oral, we must analyse their existing oral literatures like folktales, proverbs, riddles, etc., to find out their basic features and use these features in the textbooks for tribal learners. Some of the features found in these oral literatures, for example, are mnemonic patterns, use of doublets, word pairs, poetic parallels, and situational rather than abstract themes.

Features of oral culture could be very effectively utilised while preparing materials for tribal learners. There is need for research to find out also the various teaching/learning methods existing in tribal society. Learning for the tribals is a pleasurable activity and often it is done in groups, in the company of friends. Tribal children learn through songs, riddles, chain-tales, etc., which could be used to teach them reading, vocabulary, etc. Tribals stress teaming by memory. In order to memorise things easily they use repetitions, rhythm and music. All these features of tribal oral cultures can be profitably used for teaching tribal learners.

Some aspects of tribal culture are very harmful not only to the tribals but to human society at large. Some of them like witchcraft, superstitions, and excessive drinking of intoxicating drinks are taking the tribal society to the brink of ruin. Tribal education must create critical awareness among the tribals about these social evils, help them to find out their root causes and to organise themselves to remove these evils from their society. It must create a scientific temper among the tribals so that they are able to understand the real causes of various diseases, etc. Some of the evil practices like excessive drinking are due to the lack of alternative sources of pleasure in the present-day changed conditions.

Tribal education should provide access to new skills and technologies that could improve the quality of their lives and help to shape and adapt to the social and cultural changes that are taking place. It must enlarge their choices and opportunities and provide for their participation in decisions that affect their lives. Since India is a multi-cultural country it is necessary to develop positive attitudes towards other cultures. There is great need for developing mutual love, understanding and respect among the various cultures and religions in India.

An active involvement of the community in their children's education is absolutely essential. There must be constant interaction between the community and the school. A recent experiment conducted by an Non-Governmental Organisation (NGO) group shows how this interaction can take place fruitfully. The children were asked to collect informations from their parents on the different topics they were learning in the school. A rich variety of informations were thus collected. When the children presented them in the class, it was found that there were disagreements between the informations provided by some of the parents. The children told their parents about these disagreements. Then the parents themselves came to the school and after a long discussion together they came to an agreement on the various points. Here not only the children but also the village community was involved in the learning process.

Education must enable and motivate people to see that the way things are now, is not the only way they could be. Genuine education helps people to take responsibility for shaping their lives, their community and their environment so that the world provides a happier home for everyone. Tribal education, if it has to be meaningful, must, therefore, help to create critical awareness among the tribals about their own situation, empower them to transform that situation, enable them to build new society where they can realise their authentic humanity.

Process of liberative education can be aptly described as a person's search for his rightful place in society. This search has basically three forms: the process of self-discovery and image change, discovery of the societal reality, challenge to transform society.

The tribals have been undergoing various forms of exploitations for centuries. Continual exploitation necessitates the gradual degradation of the individual and his community. Through a well-planned process of domestication, stereotyping and categorisation, the tribals have been treated like sub-humans and made to believe that they are stupid, worthless and incapable of action by themselves. Over centuries they have not only patiently listened to these abuses, but have slowly begun to believe the same about themselves. Hence, if they have to think in terms of organising themselves, of wresting their rights, of struggling for a new future, a very significant and substantial change has to come about in their psyche. They have to begin thinking of themselves as capable, as intelligent, as useful, and as powerful. They have to conceive of their future as something that is of their own making, as something that they can achieve through their organisation and united action.

Educational programmes for the tribals should be designed in such a way that they help them to root out the false images, both conscious and unconscious, they have of themselves, the warped self-images that have been forced on them by their exploiters. These programmes must help the tribals to discover who they really are as persons and as a community and strengthen the positive attributes in themselves and in their community which make them proud of themselves. Creative cultural actions in different forms such as songs, slogans, symbols, stories, skits, dramas, rallies, etc., can be very effectively used in the educational programmes in order to enable the tribals to break force from the mental and emotional bondages that have enslaved them for generations.

Education should help the tribals to understand the present world and to identify the causes of their poverty and underdevelopment and the various forces that exploit and oppress them. They must come to realise that the root cause of their poverty is injustice and its end result is their dehumanisation. In order to surmount the situation of exploitation, oppression and dehumanisation education must help the tribals to critically recognise its reality, its causes, its structures and its systems. It must enable them to discover who they are and what they want to lie.

For the tribals, education is the pivot on which their success depends. Education disseminates knowledge. Knowledge gives inner strength which is very essential for the tribals for attaining freedom from exploitation and poverty. Due to ignorance arising out of illiteracy, the tribals have not been able to take advantage of economic opportunities. Opening of the tribals area in the wake of development process have brought in juxtaposition two distinct value system one based on tradition and ignorance and other on technology and innovations. Harmonious synchronisation of the two systems is essential for development of tribal people. The most important aspect of education in tribal areas is that of informing the community of the new innovations in science technology as well as the developments in the economic and political fields.

Due to lack of education and requisite skill, the tribals are not able to take advantage of the new economic opportunities which have been grabbed by the outsiders migrated to the tribals areas. Recognising the importance of the education, the framers of the Constitution have made specific provisions in Article 15(4) and 46 for promoting education among the Schedule Tribes. Article 15(4) is an exception to the fundamental right of the people of equal treatment irrespective of religion, caste, race or sex granted under Article 15(1). It empowers the state to make any special provision for advancement of any socially or educationally backward class of citizens or for the Schedule Castes or Schedule Tribes. Article 46 contains the directive to the state government to promote with a special care the educational and economic interests of the weaker sections of the people and in particular, of the Schedule Castes and Schedule tribes.

The basic responsibility of promoting education has been cast upon the state governments. The union government is responsible for co-ordination of facilities and determination of standards in respect of higher education, research, scientific and technical education. The main effort in the central sector to help the Schedule Tribes pertain to installation of post-metric scholarship, setting up boys and girls hostels and coaching centres for competitive examinations.

The Ministry of Education, which is responsible for the educational development in the country as a hole has, also been making special efforts for the educational development of Schedule Castes and Schedule Tribes. Some of the important facilities provided by the Ministry of Education include 7.5 per cent reservation of seats for Scheduled Tribes and another 15 per cent for Scheduled Castes in all Central Universities, Indian Institute of Technology, Regional Engineering Colleges, Medical Colleges, and Central Schools. In the newly started Navodaya School under the new education policy, due weightage is given to the students belonging to Scheduled Tribes. The educational institutions have been instructed to relax the norms for students seeking admission to the reserved seats for various courses.

Some of the activities taken up by the Ministry of Education for promoting education among the Scheduled Tribe are provision of scholarships, research fellowships, reservation of seats in hostels and research and training facilities for improving their educational levels. Priority is also given in the areas predominantly inhabited by Scheduled Castes and Scheduled Tribes for opening centres of non-formal education and adult education. Departments of Education, Tribal Welfare and Social Welfare implement the education programmes for Scheduled Tribes and operate the facilities of scholarships, hostels and *ashram*, schools, etc.

Literacy among the tribals has increased over the years. But it is still far below the general level. The position of female literacy is really a matter of concern. The rate of literacy varies from state to state. In some states like Mizoram and Nagaland, the literacy as per the 1981 Census, is as high as 59.62 and 40.31 per cent respectively which is mainly due to the efforts of the missionaries in inculcating interest for education among the tribals. In other states like Andhra Pradesh and Rajasthan, the literacy is as low as 7.62 per cent and 10.27 per cent respectively. Female literacy indicates an yawning gap in the states.

For poverty-ridden parents, education of their children is a luxury. The children assist their parents in earning their livelihood. Grown-up children also look after the younger ones when the parents go out for work either as cultivators or as labourers. Absence of child care centres, creches, *balwadis* etc., in the remote tribal areas, also has to share the blame for depriving the children of the poor parents of the facility of education.

Educational programmes for the tribals has to be carefully evolved. It has to take into consideration the sociocultural milieu of the Scheduled Tribes. Presently, the general contents of education have been extended to the tribal areas which in many cases are not relevant, particularly at the primary stage. The tribal areas suffer from inadequacy of educational institutions, boarding and lodging facilities. Even where centres have been opened, about 40 per cent of them are without buildings. The supporting services, such as the incentives in terms of scholarships, book banks, etc., are very insignificant and generally do not attract the children.

The problem of absenteeism of the teachers is one of the important factors affecting tribal education. They generally remain absent for days together due to absence of supervision over them and also due to lack of dedication to the cause of education of the tribals. The children and also the parents, cannot afford to waste their time and generally opt to drop out from the schools.

Even after 50 years of independence we have not been able to provide the tribals education in their mother tongue. The tribal children are not generally able to follow the lessons given to them in the school in the language which is totally strange to them. The tribals, undoubtedly, form linguistic minority groups and are entitled to facility of instruction in their mother tongue at the primary school stage. Article 350 (A) of the Constitution specifically provides for adequate facilities for instruction in mother tongue at the primary stage of education to children belonging to linguistic minority groups.

In spite of the recommendations and suggestions of various Committees and Commissions, no policy for the tribal areas has been evolved. In some states the school in tribal areas are under the control of Education Department and in some under the Social Welfare Department. Lack of administrative policy regarding the educational Institutions in tribal areas adversely affect the education of the tribals.

Contents of education should take into consideration the needs and aspirations of the tribal people. Education should be job-oriented. The curricula should keep in view the traditional local skills and crafts. The Tribals should also be taught elementary civics to familiarise them with their rights and duties. Due priority should be given for opening of educational institutions in the tribal areas and construction of school buildings should be undertaken under the normal funds of education as well as under the National Rural Employment Programme.

The medium of instruction should also be in the tribal languages at least up to the primary level. The teachers should be selected from the tribals themselves even by relaxing the educational qualifications, in case sufficient number of qualified teachers are not available. The non-tribal teachers who know the tribal language may be selected.

Steps should be taken for setting up of more and more Balwadis, creches and child care centres in the tribal areas. Suitable nutrition programmes should also be carried on in such centres which would not only provide nutritious food to the tribal children but also create among them an awareness about healthy and balanced diet. A system of effective supervision over the primary school teachers is essential. They should be placed under the control of the local panchayats wherever necessary. There should be effective participation of the tribals as also of voluntary agencies in the management of hostels. Non-formal and vocational education centres are very successful and should be able to provide academic education as well as vocational training to meet the needs of various industrial and other projects set up in the tribal areas.

NATIONAL POLICY ON EDUCATION (NPE)

In the case of scheduled tribes, their equalisation with non-scheduled tribes has not been explicitly so spelt out as a strategy. This is true of the other educationally backward sections also. In the case of minority groups, the policy does not speak of any strategy as such but generally of securing their constitutional guarantees and of their languages and culture.

The concern for removal of disparities in education by state intervention is manifested in the Constitution on considerations of: equality of opportunities (quantitative terms); and equity in terms of social justice. Article 46 of the Constitution, providing for social justice in promotion of education reads: "The state shall promote with special care the educational and economic interests of the weaker sections of the people, and, in particular, of the Scheduled Castes and the Scheduled Tribes and shall protect them from social injustice and all forms of exploitation". It is this package for promotion of educational and economic interests which form the basis of the Committee's perspective on education for the Scheduled Castes, Tribes and other backward sections.

Educational development should not be considered autonomously outside the other basic national policies concerning equity, social justice and economic development. This is particularly relevant in regard to programmes designed for this educational development of the Scheduled Castes, Scheduled Tribes and other backward sections. For these disadvantaged sections access to and retention in, educational system are functions of these policies. Unless they are put in possession of means of production and livelihood through measures such as land reforms; are meaningfully provided the essentials of life such as food, fuel and fodder; and are assured of fair wages for their labour, their participation in education will be a far cry whatever may be the nature of the educational programmes evolved and implemented for their benefit.

The Committee would also give a rather broad connotation for the concepts of equality of opportunities and equity in education. The concept of equality of opportunity in education started with provision for equal access. Later on equal input was considered necessary for equalising educational opportunities. Today, along with equal access and equal input, equal output is considered necessary criteria. The last one calls for measures of protective discrimination in favour of the disadvantaged sections of the society. The policy, then, should be one of providing equity package of educational and economic measures in terms of protective discrimination in favour of the disadvantaged sections of the society.

Most of the NPE/POA measures are those which have been under implementation even from before the formulation of NPE, in one form or the other. Moreover, many of them are being provided for delivery of education to other sections as well, though the policy apparently treats them as "attending to the specific needs of those who have been denied equality so far".

It is seen that the literacy percentage among the SCs is low in Andhra Pradesh, Bihar, Madhya Pradesh, Rajasthan, and Uttar Pradesh, when compared to the all-India Scheduled Castes literacy percentage. However, compared with all communities excluding SCs and STs, the literacy levels of SCs are fairly poor in most states and almost deplorable in the five states listed above. Even in Karnataka and Pondicherry, known as educationally advanced regions, SCs have only half the literacy rates compared to the rest. In terms of literacy levels of the STs, even the educationally advanced States/UTs present a fairly poor picture, with the literacy levels of the tribal people in Kerala, Karnataka and Maharashtra being less than half of that of the rest. The literacy levels among SC/ST women are dismal, with the all-India percentage being as low as 10.9 per cent for SCs and only 8.0 per cent for STs.

In some of the tribal communities the level of literacy amongst the males and females in the North-East is almost the same but in the case of Rajasthan the tribal women can be said to be still at a preliterate level with just 1.2 per cent amongst them being literate. Similarly the position of literacy amongst females belonging to Scheduled Castes in Bihar is abysmally low. The low literacy generally for SCs and STs in certain states and other Scheduled Castes and Scheduled Tribes women in particular, shows that the members of SCs and STs in these areas have not only received much benefit from educational inputs but also continue to face deprivation of the most serious king.

The global figures of literacy rates that are normally reported hide more than they reveal. The Office of the Registrar General of India has published individual caste-wise/ tribe-wise data for literacy rates for certain States/UTs on the basis of the 1981 census. The literacy rate for certain castes/tribes falls even below one per cent level. These data emphasise the need for adopting disaggregated strategies based upon micro-economic and cultural information, with both planning and implementation being decentralised to the level of Educational Complexes and individual schools and Village Education Committees.

The enrolment figures, at the primary stage, particularly in rural and tribal areas, do not necessarily reflect the reality and are often inflated, these can be taken as some kind of rough indicators. The enrolment ratios for SC and ST children in the primary schools are reported to have reached the level of 95.5 per cent and 91.6 per cent respectively in 1985-86, compared to 93.4 per cent for general population. In spite of the tendency to inflate enrolment figures, it is noteworthy that there are wide gaps in enrolment ratios in different States/UTs, with the levels falling down to 55-65 per cent in some States.

REGIME OF INCENTIVES

The concept of providing incentives to bring children into schools is based on the premise that children cannot come to school as they are engaged in economic activities both in and outside the home. Scholarships would hopefully offset the opportunity cost while free uniforms, textbooks etc. would relieve the parents from this additional burden.

Often, incentives do not have the envisaged impact. The working group on early childhood education and elementary education for the Eighth Five Year Plan opines that, "It is difficult to establish any clear correlation between the present distribution of these incentives and the relative position of different states in regard to progress towards UEE." The report of the Backward Classes Commission observes, "Whereas several states are extending a number of *ad hoc* concessions to backward class students, few serious attempts have been made to integrate these facilities into a comprehensive scheme for a qualitative upgradation of educational environment."

A series of studies should be instituted to investigate into the impact that the various incentive schemes implemented in different states have had on enrolment and retention of SC/ST children in the schools. Community profiles of educationally backward communities should also be prepared based on study of their current educational status. With reference to these profiles and the findings of the impact studies, on a disaggregated basis, appropriate and logical strategies should be established for the educational development of the backward communities.

EDUCATION ENVIRONMENT

Remedial coaching is proposed by NPE/POA as a special measure to improve the prospects of SC/ST students for further education and employment. While the basic idea behind this proposal is welcome and needs full support, there are aspects which demand attention. In spite of a long experience in organising remedial courses at +2 and even higher stages, the policy formulation does not seem to be based upon any evaluation of the outcome. There are limits to what remedial coaching can achieve.

The impoverished learning environment in the educationally backward regions and the economic deprivation in the homes of SC/ST children, can irreparably limit the learning skills of these students. Such barriers to growth in the capabilities for acquiring knowledge, are inherent in the iniquitous social system in which SC/ST children live. The impact of these limitations, set in early childhood and later in the primary stage can become the chief determinants of what is accepted as notion of merit and talent as brought out elsewhere.

Remedial coaching is now offered to the SCs/STs in the states from class IX onwards. The objective is to equip the SC/ST students to fare comparatively better in the public examinations. Even this scheme is implemented in a rather disorganised and ad hoc manner. Coaching is given only for about two to three months prior to the examinations in most cases. Not all the schools undertake this programme either. The government of India implements a scheme for remedial scheme, assistance is given to the states to meet the cost of remedial coaching but the coverage of SC/ST students in just fifty schools does not touch even a fringe of the problem. This scheme of remedial coaching should be re-organised such that on a phased basis, majority of the schools introduce the same. Instead of coaching being confined to two or three months of pre-examination periods, the same should be offered in a sustained way throughout the academic session in the concerned classes.

A strategy to enrich learning environment and the socioeconomic conditions in the tribal regions as distinct from mere remedial coaching should be evolved and brought under implementation. In the backward area including SC, ST habitats, a network of school-linked libraries should be established. For reaching out to smaller habitations without schools, a dynamic programme of bicycle-borne mobile libraries for para-school-based libraries should be brought under implementation. These libraries need to be enriched with creative children's literature. While the children's literature would be primarily in the regional languages, efforts should be made to increase the availability of children's books in the local dialects or languages spoken in educationally backward areas.

In order to nurture all kinds of talents and aptitudes in children, ranging from academic subjects to co-curricular and socio-cultural spheres as may be identifiable. Educational Complexes should organise a wide-ranging programme of specific theme-based workshops/work camps, using the best available resource persons in the area. This programme should encourage school drop-outs as well, to join and contribute in this collective endeavour towards excellence.

In the curriculum of the educationally backward, the following should be emphasised at all stages of education:

— Science and Mathematics;
— Expression, both oral and written, and creative writing;
— History and sociology of the Scheduled Castes, the Scheduled Tribes and other backward sections of society;
— Contribution of these communities to national life and development, including the freedom struggle; and
— Role played by women belonging to these communities in national life and development.

In order to bring about universalisation of elementary education among girls in backward areas, including those belonging to SC/ST communities, a network of ECCE centres should be established on a priority basis, with linkage to primary schools.

According to NPE, educational programmes for the ST children should be so designed as to preserve their rich cultural identity and make them aware of the same. Tribal cultural identities are relevant not only to the tribals but all the school going children. The rich diversity of the tribal cultural identities should be included in the common cultural heritage which is one of the elements of the Core Curriculum envisaged in NPE/POA.

SPECIAL COMPONENT PLAN AND TRIBAL SUB-PLAN

Every year, along with Annual Plan, the Department of Education submits to the Planning Commission Special Component Plan (SCP) for Scheduled Castes and Tribal Sub-Plan (TSP) for the Scheduled Tribes in respect of education programmes coming under the Central sector. The preparation of SCP and TSP, in practical terms, has been a paper exercise for the following reasons:

— They are not included in the budget document. Consequently, the discipline which goes with the implementation of budget provisions, does not exist i.e. the expenditure of allocations for the specific purposes for which they are given is not ensured.

— The Bureau Heads of the Department of Education to whom the copies of SCP and TSP are provided every year for follow up in implementation, are unable to ensure their implementation on ground though they issue general instructions/guidelines under the respective schemes.

— The present system of monitoring of implementation of SCP and TSP by the Ministry of Welfare is also not effective. Most of the inter-ministerial meetings organised by the Ministry of Welfare end up with reasons given by the officers incharge of implementation of schemes as to why they are not in a position to implement the SCP and TSP.

Recommendations

— Special Component Plan and Tribal Sub-Plan should be specifically exhibited in the budget document, schemewise.

— To the extent feasible, schemes meant exclusively for the Scheduled Castes and Scheduled Tribes should be prepared and included under SCP/TSP.

— Wherever exclusive schemes cannot be formulated, specific physical targets for coverage of Scheduled Castes/Scheduled Tribes under the schemes generally applicable to all, should be indicated.

— A more effective monitoring mechanism should be established in the Department of Education itself for the purpose of periodically following up the progress of implementation of SCP/TSP.

Implementation of educational programmes for Scheduled Castes and Scheduled Tribes should appropriately be based on a careful identification of their habitats and convergence therein or concurrent, collateral and complementary activities. At present this is not happening. The Department of Education does not also have feedback regarding the actual number of blocks with concentrations of Scheduled Castes and Tribes covered under important programmes like operation blackboard, non-formal education and adult education.

The Ministry of Welfare, according to the Business Rules is expected to do coordination in the implementation of programmes relating to SCs/STs. This Ministry should provide lists of blocks with SC concentrations. All the educational programmes should be implemented to the extent feasible conveniently in the same blocks of SC concentrations/tribal blocks so that impact of educational development is felt in a demonstrable and balanced way in the respective areas.

After the formulation of NPE/POA, communications were addressed to all the States to report on the overall status of implementation of NPE/POA so far as they would relate to SC/ST and minorities. For coordinated monitoring of all the educational programmes meant for the benefit of the Scheduled Castes, Scheduled Tribes and minorities, through inter-departmental exercises done by the Department of Education, Ministry of Welfare and the Planning Commission, detailed Performance Plans have been got prepared but receipt of information from the various Ministries of the Government of India as well as the State Governments has been quite uneven and erratic, apart from being out-dated and incomplete most often. This situation, *inter alia*, is due to the fact that educational programmes relating to SCs/STs and minorities are implemented in a fragmented way by different agencies and departments at the Central and State levels. A single focal agency in each State should be identified for the purpose of reporting to the Government of India comprehensively on all the educational programmes.

NPE calls for attention being paid to the minority groups which are educationally deprived or backward. It also mentions about attention being paid to the constitutional guarantees given to minorities to establish and administer educational institutions. The implications of constitutional guarantees for the minorities to establish and administer educational institutions have been elaborately gone into and brought out in rulings of several courts of law over the years. These rulings clearly establish that it would be within the powers of the respective States to bring into force regulations that would ensure the quality of education through measures such as prescription of proper qualifications, for the teaching staff, fair and reasonable remuneration for them, conditions of service based on principles of natural justice etc.

The Government of India formulated policy norms and principles for recognition of minority managed educational institutions in the light of these rulings and circulated them to the various State Governments, finding that not all of them had issued necessary guidelines and that the guidelines that had been issued by some States were varying in nature. Based on the policy norms circulated by the Government of India, the State Governments have been requested to issue detailed guidelines, so that side by side with protection of constitutional guarantees to the minorities, the standard in their educational institutions would also be uniformly maintained.

Government of India should establish a standing machinery to closely monitor issue of detailed guidelines by the States for the purpose of granting recognition to minority-managed educational institutions; to review the pace of disposal of applications for recognition of these institutions; and thereby to secure quality of education in institutions so recognised. The POA (Programme of Action) has identified forty-one districts as being as minority concentration. This should be a sound base or implementing education programmes on compact area approach.

All the educational programmes that are now under implementation should be concurrently implemented, to the extent feasible, in these districts on a priority basis after conduct of benchmark surveys as envisaged in POA. Community Polytechnics, as brought out elsewhere, is an innovative programme which helps in the use of the existing infrastructure of polytechnics for the purpose of imparting technical skills amongst the rural people.

The NCERT has been organising orientation and training programmes for Principals/Managers and teachers of minority-managed educational institutions. The objective of these programmes is to provide appropriate career for guidance for these professionals. They are also meant for training of teachers in teaching of English, science, mathematics etc. The orientation programmes for the Principals/ Managers and teachers of minority-managed educational institutions should be organised on a decentralised basis through SCERTs at the State level and DIETs, CTEs & LASEs at the sub-state levels.

The UGC has been organising special coaching courses for minorities in order to enhance their capabilities for successfully competing in recruitment for public services. In this programme, twenty universities and twenty-eight colleges participate. The progress achieved under this scheme having been found to be inadequate, the UGC itself reviewed the scheme and came out with recommendations for modifications, in implementation. These modifications included opening of more resource centres and additional coaching centres, regular interaction between Advisory Committees of coaching centres with UGC, improved monitoring system etc. Nonetheless, not much progress is in evidence in terms of number of those given special coaching.

Special coaching should be organised through reputed and progressive voluntary organisations, particularly those operating for the benefit and welfare of the minority communities. Open universities including the IGNOU should establish distance eduction programmes for imparting special coaching.

Education must impel the tribals to engage themselves in the construction of a new society, realising that it is only in a totally transformed society that they will be able to realise their authentic humanity. This new society will be based on the values of quality, justice and righteousness, supported by self-dignity, self reliance and freedom. A simultaneous and radical social and educational transformation is not possible unless there is a backdrop of a mass movement which is organised in fighting for the basic rights of the people. People can wrest their rights only if they have power. People's power can become a force only through their organisation and people's organisation is based on their unity and cooperation. Tribal education, if it has to be effective, must help the tribals to realise their power by bringing about unity and cooperation among them, and enable them to organise themselves into a mass movement for transforming society.

4

Religious Movements

In Gujarat the tribal population consists of 15 per cent of the total population, concentrated mostly in the highlands which cover the eastern parts of seven districts. There are twenty tribal groups of which the main are: Bhils, Vasavas, Dhodias, Gamits, Chaudhuries, Koknas, Rathwas, Warlies and Garasias.

Many tribes resented being called Bhils. Bhils of Panchmahals and Dang district are the most poor. In the popular imagination of Hindus of Gujarat the Bhil is projected as a dark man, robber and a murderer. The Bhils had some chieftains who ruled some areas. These chieftains also gave their daughters in marriage to the low-ranking Rajputs. The term Bhil stood for bowmen as they were generally seen with bows and arrows.

Tribals of Gujarat could be divided into three zones:

i) Tribals of the plains,

ii) Tribals of the hills, and

iii) Tribals of remote interior jungles.

Tribals of first zone have advanced technology and it monetised economy. Until about a century ago the tribals of the second zone were slash and burn cultivators. In the third zone one can still observe shifting cultivation. Capitalist penetration, enactment of forest and excise laws and land alienation have caused socioeconomic disruption in the tribal belt of Gujarat.

In a recent study by the Institute of Economic and Social Research the tribal belt has 31 out of every hundred poor in Gujarat. Huge dams such as Ukai, Madhuban, Sardar Sarovar and Karzan have displaced a large number of tribals. With little or no compensation they were flushed out into the plains as agricultural labourers or casual in labour markets mostly in the construction sector. Having pauperised the tribals by systematically robbing their resources such as forests, water and land the state throws some crumbs at them through poverty alleviation programmes such as Integrated Tribal Development. But schemes such as loans and subsidies are pocketed by corrupt officials, a large number of them being non-tribals.

Development in the tribal areas has multiplied opportunities for further exploitation of tribals. Political disintegration of tribal society is last taking place. Politics of crime and goondaism are spreading in tribal areas. Traditional social institutions of the tribals are sidetracked by modern institutions such as courts, constables, police and panchayats. Their customary laws, medical system and above all the religious system is under threat. The disappearance of the forests have destroyed the sacred geography of the tribals. The tribal population has been at the cross roads with their indigenous cultural, social, economic, political, legal and religious space being violated by so many agencies some of which claim to be working for furthering tile interests of the tribals.

There have been a number of socio-religious movements among the tribals. Social protest in India has been largely made visible through the religious idiom. One cannot but observe the social content in some of the religious movements. According to their origin tribals of South Gujarat may classify movements like Devi and Sati Pati as indigenous and the rest of the Bhakti variety movements as non-indigenous. In general, social movements among tribals have been seeking:

i) Political autonomy and formation of a state,
ii) Agrarian and forest based movements,
iii) Socio-religious movements, and
iv) Movements based on script and language and religion/ cultural movements seeking to assert and define tribal identity.

Common features found in most movements are as follows:

i) Society intensely dissatisfied with the social and economic conditions which it is forced to accept,
ii) Existence of emotional unrest with certain hysterical symptoms,
iii) Appearance of a charismatic leader,
iv) Demand from this leader for implicit faith and obedience from his followers,
v) Unquestioned faith and obedience consisting a radical change of life, and
vi) Threat of severe punishment of opponents and traitors to the movements.

DEVI MOVEMENT

The Devi Movement was a response to the impact of colonial rule on tribal society. The *adivasis* were peasants, practising shifting cultivation. Their world was filled with divine and semi-divine beings who had great power over nature. Though they lived isolated lives yet merchant capital in the form of non-tribal money lenders and *saukars* had some impact on their lives.

British rule started in this region around 1800. They introduced *Abkari* Act as a result of which liquor became a highly taxed commodity and land became a marketable commodity. The cost of liquor soared and liquor being indispensable to adivasis social and ritual life, drinking debts increased, forcing many adivasis to sell their lands. The adivasis were slowly exploited and pauperised.

At that point the Devi Salabai arrived in Kanpur village on 8th November 1922. She gave commandments to people through spirit mediums or oracles to abstain from liquor, toddy and meat, to bathe regularly and to boycott the Parsis who were running the liquor trade. Different groups responded differently to the Devi. However, a large majority perceived the commands to be a call to change their way of life and assert themselves against tile exploiting Parsis. The Devi reigned supreme for atleast a couple of years. In the meantime liquor dealers had little business. Though the adivasis resorted again to drinks, the consciousness created in them was later carried forward by Gandhians, Kisan Sabhas and so on. The Devi movement thus forged a remarkable change in consciousness for large numbers of adivasis who realised that change was possible, and that it could be brought about by their own actions, even as their understanding was coloured by gods and goddesses.

SATI PATI MOVEMENT

The Sati Pati movement came to Gujarat in the late fifties and became an autonomous movement under Kesri Singh. He was a rich farmer, gifted speaker and good organiser. Initially, he condemned drinking liquor, eating meat, wearing costly ornaments but eventually turned his attention to the sad economic plight of the tribals and began pinning its responsibility on non-tribals. He asked his followers not to pay land revenue, boycott schools, elections, government offices and courts and currency.

According to Kesri Singh the tribals were owners of land and the government had no right to collect revenue. He encouraged tribal tenants to grab land under Land Tenancy Act. Many tribals claimed land. This led to serious conflict between non-tribals who were owners of land and tribals. As a result in 1953 at Valod the police opened fire. Kesri Singh told his followers to face bullets as they will turn into flowers. But this did not happen and his followers got disheartened. Kesri Singh himself who advocated anti-government doctrine was imprisoned five times.

Both the movements began on a religious note but they were largely propelled by the protest against exploitation of tribals by non-tribals. The non-tribals with the connivance of the state managed to siphon-off the social protest component from these movements and what remained was religious rituals or spiritualism.

NEO-BHAKTI MOVEMENTS

Bhakti Movement with its stress on devotion, surrender to a personal God with monotheistic leanings appealed to the masses since 13th century. However, it may not be correct to say that it was a monolithic movement. It was an amalgam of movements.

There were at different times and different places in India different leaders who spearheaded specific movements within the wider called Bhakti movement. So in North India there were Kabir, Nanak, Dadu, Raidas etc., and in South India, Ramanuja, Madhva, Nimbarka and Vallabhbhai. Sufi movement was akin to Bhakti Movement among Muslims. Lower castes were left out of the mainstream Hinduism or Brahminism but had access to Bhakti movement. In the 19th century because of the onslaught of Christianity Brahmo Samaj, Prarthana Samaj and Arya Samaj reacted sharply to retain Hindus within the fold of Hinduism, especially lower castes.

The Neo-Bhakti movements began in the 19th Century. And (Neo-Bhakti movements) have been popular with tribals who interacted rather freely with Hindus especially in the plains. Bhagat Movement was one such movement. Bhagat movement subsumes a host of sects begun by leaders such as Mavji and Govindgiri. The various aspects of life prescribed for Bhagats are as follows:

i) They will refrain from eating meat and drinking liquor.
ii) They will give up bride-price, and leviratic as well as re-marriages.
iii) They will greet each other by saying *Jai Maharaj*, a symbol of this sect.
iv) They will wear a *tulsi mala* around the neck as well as a Vaishnavite sectarian mark on the forehead and a cotton thread around the neck.
v) They will wear white robes to signify simplicity and truthfulness.
vi) They will obey the will of the community which is supreme.
vii) They will give up a life of crime and lawlessness.
viii) They will embrace the philosophy of nonviolence and virtuousness.
ix) Their women will observe seclusion during menstrual period.
x) They will take bath early morning prior to any activity.
xi) They will abjure superstitions.

It was the *Ujte* Bhils (pure) and not the *Mele* Bhils (impure) who took to Bhagatism. The *Ujle* spoke contemptibly of the *Mete.* The Bhagat has consciously renounced faith in the primitive cult, labelled animistic, and developed faith in Hindu Gods and the associated religious principles. Further, he is one who has given up many old practices and taken to new ones which are considered essential requirements of the new faith.

The Bhagat movement was an attempt to Hinduise the tribals, reform them and give religious legitimacy to the upwardly mobile strata. The tribals had their indigenous belief system which the *Ujle* Bhils increasingly gave up to attain respectability before the non-tribals, viz., Hindus. The *Mete* tribals hung on to their indigenous belief system.

The *baniyas* (traders, shop keepers) were the first to interact with tribals and live in tribal areas. But they never sought any kind of integration with the tribals. They bought tribal forest products and agricultural produce through barter system in exchange for essentials of life. They looked down on tribal culture, society and their way of life. The *baniyas* were vegetarians, vaishnavites and puritanical in their way of life. They had nothing but contempt and ridicule for the tribals.

Even today it is noticeable in good measure in the *bazars,* shops and public transport. Continuous ridicule and contempt crushed the identity of individuals as well as groups. They were forced to look down on their own culture, way of life and social practices and developed inferiority complexes. The only role model offered to them was that of their exploiter, in this case the *baniyas.* Ironically the *baniyas* did not accept the tribals on the same religious platform. They did not concede equal religious status to them. They did not allow the tribals to visit their temples nor sit with them for singing religious *bhajans* (songs). Hence tribals did not have access to the Brahminic or Sanskritic variety of Hinduism.

It was in this context that the Bhakti movement came as a boon to the upwardly mobile tribals. Bhakti movement was an antidote for Brahminic or Sanskritic Hinduism and it appealed to the lower castes and tribals. The propagators of Bhagat movements asked the followers to do away with the indigenous belief system. What happened to the tribals when they desired to put on a new identity through the so-called religious movements? At one level there were *Ujle* and *Mele* or *Sarjela* and *Varjela* categories. Only the pure and well-to-do tribals got integrated into the mainstream Hinduism through Bhakti movements. But even those *Ujle* and *Vajrela* who opted for Bhakti movements and sought legitimacy and respectability did not totally throw overboard the indigenous belief system. Depending on the context and situations, they practised indigenous beliefs. If they lived in urban centres and amidst Hindus they shunned them to a large extent. But when they visited their natal villages they participated in them.

Those who indulged in Bhakti movements amidst tribals also showed differential behaviour. In public they subscribed to the proprieties of the sect but not so in private, especially when it came to drinking alcohol and eating meat.

Fragmentations at different levels are common among tribals. Half a tribe accepted a sect and the other did not. Those who accepted tended to sustain structural tensions especially in kinship and marriage sectors until it (sect) attained the endogamous status. Culturally the sectarians underwent changes in food, prayers, language and rites. Here again there was complete partial or incomplete cultural adoption. At the household, family, lineage and clan level too fragmentation took place. The most acute was at the household level. Some members or one person became a member of Bhagat movement and his or her puritanical behaviour separation and exclusivism had to be endured by other members of the household. So separate kitchens or cooking, separate vessels, separate diet for the member by himself within the same household had to be arranged. This gave rise to tensions. The fragmentation in households, families, lineage, clans and tribes gave rise to a kind of schizophrenia between the converts and non-converts, until changes at structural and cultural level were stabilized. The proprieties and expectations stood disturbed. If prior to the sectarian movement it was non-tribals who ridiculed the tribals, after the movement the convert tribals further ridiculed the non-convert tribals and looked down on them.

Generally, the better off sections of tribals sought membership into a sect first. The process of exclusion was at work viz., the better off converts sought to exclude themselves from the non-convert tribals. At the same time the non-converts attempted to include themselves with the converts. Thus there was plenty of anger, anguish and anxiety in sociocultural relations, until a complete identity was formed.

Formation of identity on sectarian grounds have two major components, such as philosophical, (the way in which life is viewed) and environmental (structural and cultural). A sect generated a new/alternate identity when it programmed the life of its members at birth, marriage, death; rites, rituals, economy, education, health; time (day, week, month and annual calendar) and space (sacred space, profane space, pilgrimages). Until a member was socialised in both the components of identity formation he/she remained torn and in conflict internally. It was only when one's socialisation was complete that one could speak of formalisation of ones identity on religious grounds.

Bhakti movements found resonance among tribals largely because they accommodated them, confirmed them and accepted them into the mainstream Hindu ideology. The mainstream ideology ridiculed tribals, looked contemptibly on them and at the other end sections among tribals looked for respectability before non-tribals through the only way open to them, viz., by accepting the Bhakti movements. Bhakti movements offered them new identities. But the million dollar question to be asked was did these Bhakti movements answer the vital questions and concerns of tribals, such as poverty, marginalisation, exploitation, deprivation, and pauperisation? The answer was no. On the contrary, these movements tended to blunt these vital issues and diverted the militancy and protest of tribals by giving them heady wine of spiritualism. They only drugged the tribals into saying, justice is not denied to you but it is merely delayed, it will come to you soon. What the tribals got was spiritual justice.

Even the exploiting *baniya* occasionally came and sat with the tribals for spiritual sessions and the tribals psychologically felt gratified of having secured equality with the baniya on spiritual grounds. It appears that Bhakti movements co-opted the tribals and diverted their anger, anguish, frustration and energies into another direction. The real issues got suppressed while acquiring a sectarian identity.

In the larger perspective tribals sensed that their real issues remained unanswered. Just when they came to this awareness another sect swept through the tribal areas. This was perhaps the answer to the question why so many sects swept the tribal areas like waves of the sea. They have come one after another. The tribal issues and concerns remained basically unanswered and new sects came offering old wine in new bottles. They were short lived. Bhakti movements have offered the same alternative time and again under newer labels. The agenda, manifesto and prescriptions of these sects have largely remained the same.

The state also played its role in encouraging Bhakti movements as they diverted people's militancy and protest. In the case of two earlier sects, Devi movement and Sati Pati movement, the state came down heavily because they had strong components of political and social protest and militancy. As long as a sect engaged the tribals into singing *bhajans,* teetotalism and regular bathing the state had no problem but the moment vital issues of land, water and forests rights were raised the state came down on these movements with an iron hand.

In tribal areas, through their *ashrams* Gandhians played an important supportive role to Bhakti movements. In the name of social reform Gandhians have preached it Vaishnavite kind of spirituality which consisted of introducing purity-pollution, vegetarianism, teetotalism, singing bhajans and so on.

On the plus side Gandhians have imparted education to tribals and expedited the process of Hinduisation among them. Hinduisation of tribals has gone on from ages. Plains' tribals were more Hinduised than the hilly tribals for very well known reasons. Setting up of roads and communications have expedited the process of Hinduisation, largely because of traders, contractors, spread of modern institutions like, law, literacy, medicine which have brought tribals and non-tribals into greater interaction.

The tribals have been asking for it separate state in Gujarat consisting of the eastern parts of Sabarkantlia, Panchmahals, Baroda, Bharuch, Surat, Valsad and the whole of Dang districts. The Adivasi Vikas Parishad of Gujarat issued handbill which invited the *adivasis* to awake and free themselves from the clutches of non-tribals, viz., Hindus. It claimed that *adivasis* were the original inhabitants of the land but were driven to the hills by the conquering Aryans. Those *adivasis* who remained in the plains were reduced to the status of bonded labourers.

In the last few decades the Hindus have come to the hills and systematically dispossessed the adivasis of their life support systems and driven them to the plains as cheap labour for the Hindu landlords. Besides, the *savarna* Hindus have blocked every avenue of upliftment by fighting against reservations. The handbill called for a separate state for the adivasis named Bhilistan. Most of Eastern Gujarat from Southern Rajasthan to Northern Maharashtra is the hilly habitat of tribals. The sentiments expressed in the handbill were not totally baseless.

During the nineteenth century a variety of communities of tribals had remained free, or at least relatively free, from the controls of state. But the colonial period was accompanied by an influx of traders, moneylenders and landlords who established themselves under the protection of the colonial authorities and took advantage of the new legal machinery to deprive the adivasis of large tracts of their land. This experience generated the spirit of resistance which incorporated a consciousness of the *adivasi* against the outsider. In the decades after independence the *adivasi* society has come in for greater disintegration.

5

Dalit Empowerment

Dalit empowerment movements emerged in Indian society during early decades of the 19th century. Such emergence was extremely fragmented, too far between and certainly not strong enough to have influenced the course of socio-political development of the colonial Indian society; and through the movements gathered some momentum during the mid-century, it was only during the closing decades that this emergence became collective, articulate and politically determinative.

With the stage now laid out for the political drama of confrontation between imperialism and nationalism, the lower rungs of the society were acquiring not insignificant leverage to advance their own cause, emancipation and empowerment. The game of one-up-manship between the two dominant actors required that each claim and project oneself as the sole saviour of the masses—the generalised lower classes, *shudras*, *ati-shudra* and other.

Ameliorative efforts, largely cosmetic in nature sprang up sporadically in the sphere of policy-making by the then rules and in the realm of the society by the rules-in-waiting; concern for the backward classes and later the depressed classes became the standard stock-in-trade for both the parties. But these classes themselves were beginning to show definite signs of growth along independent and autonomous lines, maintaining themselves equidistant from both and struggling to make the best out of a bad situation. With the process of devolution of power set in motion at the beginning of the present century the political significance of these hitherto submerged masses became crucial and the need for the nationalists to dominate, control and hegemonise them took on a serious note of urgency.

The terrain of struggle as well as the main contenders began to shift and change as the imperialists now increasingly were taking on the position of a referee. The confrontation between Gandhi and Ambedkar was only a personal metaphor of what was going on between two contending forces within society and in the realm of ideology. While the outcome of this historic struggle is the subject of many a writing and by now has become part of the popular lore, what has eluded most observers is the existence of and struggle between two ideologies and strategies for emancipation and empowerment of the masses within the specific context of the Brahmanised and peasantised colonial India.

The colonial mass movements were generally towards education, occupational diversification, migration and conversion. They were all a move away from one set of socio-cultural conditioning and a move towards another set of socio-cultural imagined or ideal situation of a society in which degrading caste-identities would not exist. The scores of socio-religious and self-initiated movements of the lower-castes and tribals-Adi-Hindu, Adi-Dharm, Namashudra, Neo-Buddhist, Ayya Vazhi, Sri Narayana Guru, Satnami, Birsa Munda, Sidhu-Kanu, Tana Bhaghat etc., the numerous cases of mass conversions and the several instances of mass migrations both within and without the country were invariably religio-cultural, emphasising egalitarianism in social life as contrasted to the now colonially empowered Brahmanism embodying sociocultural hierarchicalism.

The ideologues and leaders of these movements elaborated cultural scenarios, invented traditions and constructed histories in direct opposition to those of the dominant stream—which was Vedic-Brahmanic with Varna Caste as the ideal. Their emancipatory and empowering economic efforts necessarily flowed out of this anti-Brahmanic cultural trajectory. The uppercaste nationalists, too, in their general and particular concern for the lower-depressed classes did project a certain ideology and strategy of what they thought these classes deserve under the emerging dispensation. The totality of their different concerns could be summed up in the concept of 'amelioration' within a general patronising altitude of nobless oblige.

Beginning with the removal of untouchability in the most literal sense, the activities included a whole range of poverty-eradication programmes, however, in half-heartedly conceived and nominally implemented. With the transfer of power, largely into the hands of the nationalists, these concerns were recast into provisions of the welfare state within the overall attempt towards societal-national development.

The worldview or the *weltenchauung* that the shudras and ati-shudras in their own self-initiated movements had projected as the *conditio sine qua non* for their own empowerment which was religio-ideological in the sense of anti-Brahmanical and egalitarian, was slowly but successfully replaced by an another, alternative worldview or *weltenchauung* that of the dominant classes, which was amelioration, progress and economic welfarism sans religio-cultural or ideological orientation. This process of substitution of the ideology and strategy of the subordinated communities by that of the dominant communities has been slow and gradual, spread over several decades, often indirect and genuinely articulated and co-optative of selective sectional interests of the hegemonised and often not without some justification and truth.

At the risk of naive simplification and of being extremely crude in theorising, it is being suggested that these two ideologies are: abolition of Brahmanism on the one hand and economism and welfarism on the other; in other words what are being contrasted here are, culture, in its specificity as historically determined within modern India, on the one hand and economy and economic development understood in its generality of cross-cultural situation across the globe. While empowerment itself is a concept that is wholistic and straddles both the realms of culture and economy what is being distinguished and contrasted here, are the two ideological routes to the ideal and their repercussions on the struggling communities.

It is possible to construct two ideal-types in the Weberian sense, of the two contending ideological routes—culture and economy. Culture addresses itself to the historic specificity of the subcontinental society, while economy, to the generality of human condition as obtaining in several parts of the world. While culture seeks to reach out the totality of the collective concerned, economy tends to fragment the same into individuals and groups. Cultural address goes to the heart of the matter and affects the vested interests of the dominant groups, while economy neutralises the thrust into a generalised rhetoric of poverty-eradication.

Cultural struggle as abolition of Brahmanism and Brahmanical social order retains and reinforces the autonomy and self-determinative nature of the movement, while economic efforts as abolition of poverty has this tendency of shifting the focus to the dominant groups and particularly the State. Cultural thrust is the route to the politics of command while economic thrust leads to the politics of' demand only.

Onslaught on Brahmanism by the lower classes and particularly the Dalits indicts the entire society and delegitimises the existing order while economic mobilisation tends to grant legitimacy to the whole and narrows the problem of the lower castes/Dalit to the margins of society. Coalition on the cultural front is more easily lead by those at the very bottom of the social order i.e., the Dalits, while the same on the economic front, would relegate them. Cultural accusations implicate the entire social order and is more likely to bring about the larger social transformation than economic allegations.

Dalit empowerment through abolition of Brahmanical social order will encompass the entire Dalit community and scores of other non-Dalit communities, while the same through the route of poverty-eradication would leave behind the lowest rungs of Dalit communities themselves. It is certainly possible to discover many more facets to the problem.

In the order of temporal sequence in history, if culture-ideology of liberation dominated the lower caste/Dalit struggles during the colonial period as manifested in the scores of scattered socio-religious movements of both de-construction and reconstruction, in migrations—spatial, cultural, occupational and religious, politico-economic ideology of upliftment appears to have the upperhand now during the post-independent period. The broad alliance and non-differentiation between the untouchables and the touchable lower castes that was visible earlier has broken down through the anti-untouchability campaign of the freedom movement and the subsequent compartmentalisations by the state for the purpose of distribution of economic favours.

DALIT'S RIGHTS

Indian Constitution considers the right to equality as the very first fundamental right. The right assures equality before law or equal protection of law to all citizens. If any unequal society desires to move towards equality, the unequals of that society should be provided with special rights. That is the very basic principle of social justice. A just society can be constructed by treating those who have been treated unjustly with special opportunities so that the oppressed and the exploited move into the path of equality. It is essential that such opportunities are created not as favour or concessions but as acts of justice.

The state is not to discriminate against citizens on grounds of religion, race, caste, sex and place of birth. Dalits are provided access to shops, public restaurants, hotels, places of public entertainment, wells, tanks, bathing ghats, roads and places of public resort maintained wholly or partly out of state funds or dedicated to the use of general public.

Untouchability remains abolished. The offences against untouchability are punished under the Protection of Civil Rights Act, 1995 and the Atrocities of SCs/STs prevention Act 1955. In spite of the right to equality, social equality is still a distant dream for Dalits. In a system based on caste, equality is an impossible dream. Dr. B.R. Ambedkar had said, only when Hindu society becomes a casteless society, will it acquire the power and potency to defend itself. Even if the Hindus happen to get independence, with no inherent strength, it may result in taking one step back to slavery.

With increasing atrocities on them, the right to equality is something that is limited to the book of the Constitution. In reality Dalits enjoy no equality at the social and political level.

Right to freedom

When the whole community is not able to express itself the freedom of speech and expression granted to all citizens has no relevance to Dalits. Being the poorest among the poor and victims of oppression still, they are not in a position to form associations or unions. Their professions are still determined by their caste masters. Right to freedom is an elite right that makes no sense to Dalits. Only 37.41 per cent of the Dalits are educated. Hardly 5 per cent of them are in higher education.

Right against exploitation

The rights against exploitation prohibits traffic in human beings beggar and other similar forms of forced labour. There are Acts of Minimum Wage, Bonded Labour Abolition (1976) and Immoral Traffic Prevention (1986). Children below the age of 14 cannot be employed to work in any factory or mine or engaged in any other hazardous employment. Once again all these laws are more violated than followed as far as Dalits are concerned. The country has a big chunk of bonded labourers practically all of them from the Dalit community. As coolies and landless labourers Dalits till the lands and harvest crops for zamindars; at a salary decided according to the whim and fancies of landlords.

Freedom of religion

The caste system has looked down on the rich culture of Dalits and has termed it as inferior and polluted. They have no entry to Hindu temples. As untouchables, the caste priests do not preside over the religious ceremonies of birth, death and marriage. Though the progressive and radical among the Dalits claim themselves as non-Hindus and indigenous people, the caste system has kept them under the Brahmanic fold to be used for vested and selfish interests.

Their religion centred on nature, ancestors and community has not been recognised and esteemed. While the *Hindutva* forces want them to remain as untouchables to be made use of as instruments of exploitation for economic profit, the other religions too have not made attempts to learn from their egalitarian ways and communitarian ethos.

Right to Constitutional remedies

Right to Constitutional remedies assumes that the community is educated and wealthy. One cannot move the Supreme Court or any other court for the enforcement of rights without proper knowledge of rights. With the poverty and ignorance prevalent in the community, it is quite reasonable to assume that the Dalits cannot have access to courts. Besides, approaching the courts for justice in an expensive proposition. A poverty stricken community cannot approach the expensive judicial system for justice.

Therefore, the present kind of rights guaranteed in the Indian Constitution are meaningless to Dalits. They need new kind of rights, meant to provide empowerment and equality. If the state is serious about Dalit progress and development, the following rights should be provided.

Right to culture

Dr. Ambedkar provided an independent Dalit identity which challenged the age old caste system. Dalits may not need patronisers anymore. A section among them today are able to assert for their rights and define their identity. Whether their formation of identity will spread to all Dalits and whether Dalits as a class will embrace the identity as defined by themselves only time can tell. There have been two dimensions-denunciation and announciation in the formation of Dalit identity and establishment of their culture. Caste, priesthood and Hindu gods and goddesses are considered three chains of bondage and relentlessly to be denounced in the process of announcing self-respect movement for Dalits.

Periyar, Ambedkar, Bhakti movements, Buddhism, and Dalit Panthers have been sources of strength and support to Dalits in denouncing Brahmanic caste culture and various other superstitions surrounding the dominant culture. Periyar declared that the Brahmans were propagating caste culture for their own livelihood. While fire, water, air and earth were elements of nature, how can these be touchable for some and untouchables for others? He resolved to eradicate the evils of casteism, and to crusade against god and superstitions. Dr. Ambedkar wrote a number of critical articles on *varna*, caste, Rama and Krishna, symbols of Hindu culture, *Manu Smriti*, the *Dharma Shastra* of the Hindus was burnt by Periyar.

Dalits today are becoming aware that the survival of the caste system is due to the scriptures that attributed the caste system to God's creation. The internalised belief that guide behaviour have had so much influence on Dalits that they had come to hold that any breaking of caste system individually or collectively is tantamount to breaking of divine laws which would land the violators into hell.

The Bhakti saints who upheld the values of humanism were critical of caste. It is one thing to denounce *Hindutva* culture with its theories of gods, caste, varna and hierarchy while it is equally important to announce and affirm a culture of their own for Dalits. In this the Dalit panthers have been the most helpful. The Dalit panthers movement was a follow up of the movement initiated by Dr. Ambedkar that originated from the literature produced by Dalit scholars and intellectuals around 1970s. While denouncing caste culture, the Dalits need to affirm their age old culture. To the extent the state does not provide the necessary space for Dalits to create, live and proclaim their culture, Dalit empowerment will not take place. Special provisions under the Constitution should be enacted to provide cultural rights to Dalits as a first step.

Right to land

If 22 per cent of India's population are SCs and STs, they

must be provided with 22 per cent of land. It is acknowledged today that as indigenous people they were 'sons/daughters of the soil' and all land belonged to them. If majority of them have no land today, it is due to the manipulative caste system that has worked against them. Dalits are agriculturalists by culture. Ownership of land would help them to live in accordance with their culture with intimate relationship with nature and enable them to live as communities.

Land for Dalits is not an economic commodity to be bought and sold. It is a cultural heritage to live communitarian lives. Without land Dalits cannot live as humans. In fact, the government's law on "Panchami land" is precisely to protect Dalit land to permit them to live meaningful lives.

Right to education

The Dalits need an educational system patterned on their culture of equality agriculture, community and other values. In it, popular art forms different from the one representing their culture must find a pride of place. Popular literature, arts, sculpture and painting should form a part. The Dalit literature is a living literature closely linked to the life and culture of labouring masses.

In the Dalit educational system, it is necessary to create literary art forms that promote equality, work culture and a spirit of protest. The need is to creatively shape all the art forms like stories, anecdotes and songs to meet the needs of Dalit struggle. There is a wealth of literary heritage in the songs of the fisherfolk, the rhymes of the shepherds, the proverbs of washermen, the dance of the *holeyas*, the oral traditions of *madigas*, the songs of the tappers and weavers. An educational system geared to their needs can provide the spirit required to live it life of sell-respect for them.

Right to employment

Right to employment should be made fundamental to Dalits. In fact, it is a corollary to the right to life. Without employment one cannot sustain one's life. Right to work would immediately change Dalit lives. Education is meant to train them in knowledge and skills, appropriate to their cultural ways of life. Any community can fall back on the natural resources and exploit them properly if the system of education provides them with the necessary skills and attitudes.

Right to social integration

Socially, Dalits are ostracised when demands are made for social equality. In majority of villages and urban slums Dalits live as outcastes. They cannot draw water from public wells, walk on public streets and possess no right to marry outside their community. Private educational institutions and economic centres do not admit them for education or jobs. Right to social integration should include right to live in any part of the village/town/city, right to drinking water from private or public wells, right to jobs in accordance with their percentage in public and private firms.

Right to political power

It is through political power social and economic power can be obtained. The whole freedom struggle of India's elders was to capture social and economic power. There is a need to bring together all Dalits irrespective of parties to fight for political power on a common banner. In the present party system Dalits are co-opted to serve the interests of dominant castes and classes. Once they enter the legislatures as Dalits they will be able to work out their equations with other social groups and be able to reap rich dividends in the social and economic front.

Today we have the scenario of rhetorical competition as to which group in society is most concerned with the welfare of the Dalits, or who represents their interest best. The Dalit empowerment problem in general and in the context of recent liberalisation and globalisation process in particular is discussed in mainly, though not only, upper caste academic and political circles as if, it were a mere problem of economic loss or gain. The much noise about Dalit resurgence or insurgence often takes place within the benevolent auspices, may even the abetment of the dominant communities themselves.

6

Tribal Self-Determination

Indian Tribals are fighting for their right of self-determination, not necessarily in the colonial situation of a foreign power, but against the internal colonial situation created by the dominant groups of our own country, which is even more exploitative, suppressive and oppressive than the foreign rulers. Though encouraging steps are being taken, not least of them by the Indian government in increasing allotment to tribals, greater efficiency and elimination of corruption will be required for effective implementation. This is not beyond the realm of possibility, but ultimately the tribal peoples will have to resolve their internal contradictions themselves if permanent solutions are to be found.

Acculturation is an inevitable process. However, the indigenous people themselves should have control over the pace and nature of the developmental process. The difficulty is that indigenous people the world over rarely have a significant degree of control over their destiny. Many societies have simply marginalised them and they have spent much time in futile attempts to prevent encroachment on their traditional lands, to which they rarely have legal title. Part of the solution lies in better law enforcement, but on account of police corruption and the nature of the lower-level bureaucracy, this has usually been more of a hindrance to justice for aboriginal peoples. Since development and acculturation are inevitable, the problem is one of retaining the most appropriate and valuable aspects of tribal culture while introducing, in as non-traumatic a form as possible, developmental changes that will enable tribal peoples to survive in the modern world.

The environment in which this development must take place in South Asia is particularly hostile to tribal empowerment. The dominant South Asian Muslim and Hindu cultures are antithetical to some of the more emancipatory tenets of modernity. Islam has in its practice been repressive towards women, while Hinduism has exploited the lower castes. Even religions such as Christianity, Islam, Sikhism and Buddhism have adopted some of the prejudices of Hinduism despite the more emancipatory aspects of their own original tenets. The impact of this Hindu influence has been devastating. It is generally believed that the untouchable castes were aboriginal peoples whose conquest resulted in their exploitation and acculturation within Hinduism, to the point where a separate cultural identity is problematic and their origins are lost to history. It is significant that the dominant Hindu society considers this process a positive development, and feels threatened by any of these groups converting to more emancipatory religions.

Still, the tribals retain much of their culture though even here there is great variation, with some groups having lost their languages to regionally dominant groups. The dominant groups in the plains of South Asia have been gradually imposing their cultural taboos on tribal peoples in a particularly negative way. For instance, the attempts by dominant Hindu groups to prevent the eating of beef by tribals, when successful, are likely to lead to an inferior diet. In fact, the more regressive aspects of Hindu culture are being imposed on tribal groups by the most culturally unenlightened elements in Hindu society at a time when these values are being abandoned by urban middle-class Hindus. At the village level this social differentiation is manifested in varying levels of segregation.

According to a World Bank study, the non-SC/ST people often do not want their children to eat food cooked by a lower caste helper. There appears to be slightly less proscription if the food is cooked by a Scheduled Tribe community worker. No conclusive evidence was found of antipathy between the Scheduled Castes and tribal people either, although a Scheduled Caste community worker and some officials reported that tribal people will not partake of food cooked by Scheduled Caste workers/helpers. Both in Bihar and M.P., workshop participants confirmed that the situation of Scheduled Caste people is often worse than that of Scheduled Tribes. They are often poorer, and are exposed to caste biases even at the *anganwadis*.

When tribals come in contact with upper-caste cultural values, the attempts to assert superiority over other groups can have deleterious cultural and political effects. It is paradoxical that in many areas where tribes are exposed to the influence of caste Hindus just those features of Hindu society which modern India strives to discard are newly introduced among populations to which they had hitherto been foreign. Thus, not only the prejudice against certain occupations such as leather working and butchering, but also dietary taboos, child marriage, and restrictions on the remarriage of widows and divorcees are gaining a foothold among the hill- and jungle-folk at a time when they are losing ground in the larger urban centres.

This development is almost inevitable as long as throughout rural India compliance with puritanical precepts of Hindu morality remains the principal criterion of social respectability. The result of this process is likely to be the creation of new groups of untouchables rather than the elevation of the tribal peoples to a higher level in the modernisation process. In South India many primitive jungle tribes became low caste and untouchable when assimilated within the caste system. The traditional tribal practices are in fact superior to the local Hindu folk traditions in many cases and the adoption of Hindu values is a regressive process that will be psychologically traumatic.

The adoption of Christianity, which is more emancipatory than Hinduism, posed a threat to the Hindu-dominated nation-state. The struggle for the religious allegiance of tribals has been corrosive for tribal cultures, a fact which is now recognised by the major European Christian denominations, though this is not an issue in Hindu and Muslim theology. In countries where

Christianity is a minority religion, church members are often seen by tribal peoples as among the few allies they possess and the official state religions are seen as oppressive because they represent the dominant culture. In India, for example, Hindu organisations are now promoting policies of Sanskritisation in order to assimilate animist scheduled tribes. Retaining the many positive aspects of indigenous culture, while assimilating the skills and education required by industrialised society, is difficult, and few if any indigenous peoples have accomplished it.

In South Asia the Indian tribal-dominated border states have come closest to the ideal. Arunachal Pradesh is being seen as a model in this regard. However, the British colonial 'inner line' policy of excluding immigration and its pursuance for security reasons by the independent Indian government deserves the primary credit. As a general tribal policy it has not been well implemented elsewhere.

While the alienation of tribal land is beyond dispute, there is division on whether this represents simply the dominance of local landed interests or is part of a hidden agenda of the dominant society as a whole. The argument that it is merely the local interests that are responsible can be advanced by the state and national governments which have a considerable bureaucracy and legally binding statutes to prevent exploitation. That these laws are routinely violated and ineffectually enforced is pointed out by critics as proof of the lack of serious intent of the state. These tribal areas represent internal colonies being exploited by the dominant powers in Indian society.

This reflects the concept of tribal areas as a fourth world within the Third World which utilises their natural resources. Third World colonialism has replaced European colonialism as the principal global force that tries to subjugate indigenous peoples and their ancient nations. Invasion and occupation of indigenous nations once done by foreign white expansionist powers are now done by foreign brown expansionist powers. The majority of these artificial Third World states can only be maintained by the invasion and physical incorporation of lands and resources of hundreds of indigenous nations.

Movements which question this presumed identity between the people-nation and the state-representing-the-nation is denied the status of legitimate politics. Seen from this perspective, Third World governments are not legitimate representatives of indigenous minorities, making resistance and rebellion by indigenous nations legitimate forms of expression. This is essentially subversive of the political ethos fostered by Third World governments and the non-aligned movement, which seek to project themselves as representative of poor people in their countries. Once the nation-state is no longer considered legitimate, acts of subversion and rebellion are justified. From this perspective indigenous peoples become nations in their own right. However, this does not determine who will represent these nations, because indigenous groups are usually as divided among themselves as is the outside dominant society.

The standard criticism of indigenous movements is that they represent indigenous middle-class elites who are no more representative of their own society than are outsiders. These ethnic elites utilise their claim to represent their people to garner the lion's share of the benefits that the state provides indigenous groups. While this is a legitimate criticism, there are no other more authentic representatives of indigenous people than these ethnic elites. Traditional leaders may be more representative, where they still exist, but they are often uncomprehending of the wider world and lack the skills needed for negotiating with the state.

TRIBAL DIVERSITY

India has the largest tribal population in the world, representing 67.75 million people, or 8.08 per cent of the Indian population. Though it is too early to determine how their empowerment will work itself out in relations with the rest of society, tribal movements will undoubtedly have the opportunity of forming powerful combinations with other minority groups which could control state and central governments. These opportunities have yet to be realised, but the building blocks for such coalitions are being put in place. They represent perhaps the best possibility for the reconciliation of tribals with the dominant society. These new social forces for the most part have been a long time in formation, though they have only recently come to state power.

The tribal movements have the longest antecedents, having resisted Aryan invaders in prerecorded history, and in various phases opposed subsequent waves of invaders to the present day. It is generally considered that untouchables were tribal peoples who were enslaved and assimilated into the Hindu caste system, while those original inhabitants who escaped or successfully resisted domination by the invaders are the ancestors of the tribal peoples of today.

The tribal population is often depicted as unassimilated, but tribals in fact represent a continuum from peoples who have retained their own culture to those who have essentially lost their own languages and culture but retain a nominally separate ethnic identity. While both tribals and untouchables can be considered indigenous, those who came to be assimilated into the caste hierarchy are designated as untouchable. This has led to political divisions over who is indigenous. Untouchables and tribals both consider themselves indigenous, but the upper-caste-dominated Indian government accurately claims that documentary proof of the identity of the original inhabitants of India is impossible to obtain.

Some untouchable 'organic intellectuals' have claimed that they too are indigenous and would like in principle to be accepted immediately. Such an approach can result in further splits because there can be competition among the various groups for power and leadership. The tribals being a small minority may be outnumbered. Moreover, in many areas the Dikus (outsider exploiters) have used the dalits as their agents in exploiting the tribals. 'Organic intellectuals' may think in terms of a regional, national and even a global approach and may not always take the field reality into consideration. That may be one reason why there is less enthusiasm among the tribal leaders on this question than among the dalits. This difference may also be two different sides of a search for an identity viz., the tribals trying to re-assert theirs when it is under attack and the dalits attempting to attain a new one. All these aspects have to be taken into account and non-tribals should only support this search without pushing the issue beyond a point.

The tribals have populations concentrated in a few areas. This gives them opportunities for regional autonomy and secessionist movements which the scattered minority Scheduled Caste population lacks. The differences between Scheduled Castes and Scheduled Tribes in culture and living standards are not as distinguishable as is commonly thought. For instance, most plains tribals have abandoned shifting cultivation for the sedentary agriculture of their Hindu neighbours, and many tribals speak only the regional languages rather than their indigenous one.

Nevertheless, all tribals have an ethnic identity separate from their untouchable neighbours. Most of them have languages of their own and customs and traditions that separate them from other peoples. They are generally divided between those in the plains of peninsular India and the hill tribes of the Himalayas and northeast India. While the latter have for the most part achieved statehood, those in the plains do not control their state governments and partly as a result of that are considered more economically backward. This division of the tribal community between plains and hills has presented an insurmountable obstacle to joint tribal political action, which could have brought considerable pressure to bear on the Indian political system. A national-level attempt to politically combine all tribals with untouchables and other minorities has never been made.

The Indian Council of Indigenous and Tribal Peoples (ICITP) states: 'Dalits are our co-sufferers. Dalit organisations and individuals are invited as observers which will be enlisted under a separate Dalit Register. Such observers can also speak if permitted by the Chair but they cannot vote'.

Though the tribal leaders are often accused of being unrepresentative of their own grassroots communities, they are adamant about excluding Dalits from equal participation because of their tribes' perceived cultural differences.

However, the reality on the ground is that some tribes and lower castes are little different from each other in culture, having the same language and similar histories. The political distinction is made less on the basis of cultural difference than from fear of domination by the more numerous Dalits. However, the leadership of both groups often have more in common with each other than with their own grassroots supporters. The differences may represent the protection of turf rather than culture, and certainly these divisions have prevented any political unity in practice.

While Dalits have tended to include the tribals and untouchables as part of the 200 million indigenous peoples, the tribals have tended to see themselves alone as indigenous, with Dalits having lost that claim through cultural assimilation. The ideology of tribalism is a mechanism through which the indigenous elite is precisely the most vocal *adivasi* sector in proclaiming its tribal identity. The tribalist ideology permitted the *adivasi* elite to enter the political arena and dominate certain fields like that of education, for instance, through the channels provided by the missions, also promoting the tribal construct. The *adivasi* elite's self-definition as tribal helps push underground the class affiliations, privileges and ambitions of its members.

The tribal elites tended to take away all the benefits of development programmes, leaving the vast majority of backward tribals untouched. This view is common among administrators concerned with tribal affairs. A representative of the National Commission for Scheduled Castes and Scheduled Tribes felt that reservation should be discontinued after a couple of generations to encourage equality of tribal access, though this is not official policy. However, given the underfulfilment of the existing quota, such a policy would only reduce total representation, since there is as yet no intra-tribal competition for places. Not a few tribals, are also dissatisfied with the conduct of their educated tribal elite, though this does not usually enter the published record. In this respect they are no different from other elites who have the opportunity of preferential access to resources and patronage. The current situation of North-east as well as middle Indian the tribal people presents a striking contrast which is largely relatable to the place of education in the scheme of development in the two regions. In the North-East education preceded development of their economy which continues even to this day at the pre-agricultural stage. But in middle India economic development took precedence over education which has remained neglected. Whereas tribal people in the North-east are now ready for a leap forward in development based on the resources which have remained under their command, those in middle India have fallen prey to the adverse processes of development and are facing disorganisation, many of them having been rendered resourceless. The gains in tribal-controlled states have presented new problems which are no closer to being resolved than those of the plains tribals. Whereas plains tribals have been exploited for their cheap labour or through confiscation of their land and natural resources, the achievement of state power for most of the hill tribes has prevented the more egregious forms of exploitation by outsiders.

Statehood has presented its own problems, however. One of the main demands for state support and avenues for individual advancement is education. With the rapid spread of education in tribal states, the educated youth have only the state sector for employment, given the low level of private sector development activity that has been attracted to these isolated areas. The government, however, though expanding during the period when the tribal states were being created, is now facing budget cutbacks from accumulated deficits. As a result, the state will no longer absorb the educated tribal unemployment, which can create social problems of its own. Since most tribal states have armed insurgencies under way these problems cannot be ignored by the tribal state leadership and the central government.

The state had offered equal opportunity to all educated youth with regard to employment, the opportunities for the SC and ST youth cannot be said to be really the same at least for some more time unless there are specific reservations in their favour. There is a big differential in their preparedness for open competition not only in terms of quality of education but also the social background and other support which matter in getting employment.

Members of SCs and STs can look forward to only employment in the public sector which is now saturated and whose pace of growth is also slow. In fact, this provides one of the biggest motive forces for demands for establishment of smaller politico-administrative units. It is obvious that this cannot be continued indefinitely and contradictions are bound to arise sooner than later.

LAND REHABILITATION

Despite legislation to prevent loss of land to moneylenders and landowners, the alienation of tribal lands has been continuing. While much of the land alienation is at the instigation of local moneylenders and landlords in violation of statutes, the state has on occasion been involved in this process as well. The leasing of forest land to private logging companies and construction of hydroelectric dams have been the major causes of state-sponsored land confiscation. In effect, land can be taken by the state whenever it is deemed by the government to be in the national interest.

While this is a universal practice, in South Asia the compensation system is inadequate at best and often non-existent. The Narmada Dam project has been particularly controversial from both an environmental and ethical standpoint. This in itself represents an important break with the past when such practices were taken for granted. That the World Bank was eventually pressured to withdraw funding is indicative that the era of uncritical development implementation by governments is now over. This will not prevent the continued erosion of tribal lands which continues in both government and private sector projects, but it does indicate to government that the environmental and indigenous movement can no longer be ignored. Even if governments choose to ignore the protests, international lending agencies will be pressured to withhold funds by indigenous and international NGOs.

Laws have been passed prohibiting alienation of tribal lands to non-tribals almost in all states. In Bihar, 52,127 cases involving an area of 76,411 acres have been registered and in 27,454 cases the decision is in favour of restoration of land to the tribals. The area in question is 32,636 acres. Getting this type of decision from the government is one thing, but actual restoration of land is quite another. As a matter of fact, only 1774 acres have been actually physically restored to the tribals. In West Bengal, the land restored is a mere 1681 acres, in Madhya Pradesh 1500 acres and in Orissa 889 acres. In the face of a situation where very large areas have passed hands from the tribals to the non-tribals, the progress of work is rather dismal. Though the government has become active in restoring land to tribals, we do not know to what extent it will succeed, because most non-tribals are economically well off and are employing lawyers to defend their cases, while the tribals have no documents in their possession to prove their claim to the land and do not have the economic resources to employ lawyers to defend their cases.

Despite the laws, however, the tribals' land continues to pass out of their hands. This alienation was done, according to a study by the Department of Rural Development, through land sale in almost 40 per cent of cases, 25 per cent for public purposes, 25 per cent by mortgage or lease and the remaining 10 per cent through other modes. Eighty per cent of the acquisition in private cases went to non-tribal people. The study found that the tribals were generally unaware of the laws protecting them. Even in states where awareness is more, the tribals' poverty and the cumbersome process of law prevented recourse to the legal process. The laws contain certain inherent deficiencies such as the absence of a machinery to initiate suo-moto action, the general period of limitation of 12 years for adverse possession, lack of a provision against relinquishment, lack of a provision against trespass and lack of a provision against collusive or fraudulent transfers. The legal process suffers from delays, several stages of appeals and revisions and administrative delays in disposal of cases. Absence of free legal aid to the contesting tribals is often a constraint.

Much of the tribal areas continue to be unsurveyed or partly surveyed and lack of updated land records prevents quick action. In certain states, even after orders are passed in the tribals' favour, the law requires them to approach the competent authority again with an execution petition, setting in motion another round of litigation. The law does not prescribe a time limit for physical restoration of the land to the tribals from the issue of orders.

To make way foe development projects, tribal land's private encroachments are accompanied by government expropriations. This is particularly adverse in the case of dam construction which frequently results in the flooding of the forested areas tribals inhabit. According to the Report of the Working Group on Development and Welfare of Scheduled Tribes, during the Eighth Five-Year Plan (1990-1995), Out of the 16.94 lakhs (1,694,000) persons displaced by 110 projects studied, about 8.14 lakhs (814,000) persons displaced are tribals. The number of displaced tribals is, however, likely to be much more than this, if we take into account the total number of development projects executed so far.

The rehabilitation of the displaced tribals is a serious problem which has not received due attention. In States like Madhya Pradesh and Maharashtra which have made acts/ regulations for rehabilitation of displaced persons, including tribals, provisions have remained on paper only. The absence of a national policy for rehabilitation of displaced tribals has been the chief reason for the present state of affairs. Various guidelines have, no doubt, been issued from time to time regarding rehabilitation of the displaced persons including tribals.

Traditional economy of shifting cultivation is now undertaken by only 12 per cent of tribals. The erosion of the traditional economy has produced a marked decline in nutritional standards. The nutritional literature on tribal people holds that the most primitive tribes who subsist on natural resources which have not been interfered with by the 'outside world' are better fed and have better nutritional status than other tribal or non-tribal people.

Where natural resources have been exploited and are declining, groups which were dependent on them demonstrate worsening nutritional status. The small tribal communities, which were entirely dependent on forests, have not been able to face the challenge of the changing situation. Many of them have almost disappeared. Moreover, a few communities, which are still surviving in the forests, are being forced to move out. Their rights are not recorded. Therefore, they cannot hope, let alone claim, a sympathetic hearing. On the other hand the resources from which they have been making a living are dwindling in the face of growing pressure from more stronger communities or the government itself. In this way tribal communities got dispersed and they have ceased to exist as communities. Similarly, in many areas the economy of the shifting cultivators has collapsed. Only those shifting cultivators have survived, who did not come under pressure of the outside system. The need and usefulness of involving tribals in forest development has now been recognised.

There are confrontations between the forest department and the tribals. The tribals perceive the forest department as merely a controlling and a punishing authority. There is a potential of rejuvenating, and conserving the vanishing forests by winning the confidence of the tribals. This would also motivate them for participation in the programme and would also generate a source of employment for the tribals. There is a need to systematically tap the potential of minor forest produce and it would certainly contribute as a source of income for the tribals.

In a country where a third of the population suffers from malnutrition and grows by 12 million a year the pressure on land and resources is difficult to accommodate. Settled cultivation, which most plains tribals have adopted, however, represents a change of lifestyle to some extent. The introduction of settled agriculture implies greater entry into the cash economy and the intrusion of state institutions. Only the northeast tribal majority states have managed this transition under their own auspices. They can take their own decisions. Moreover, the system of self-governance at the village level is still continuing in these areas. The people still enjoy full rights over all the resources and the land within their respective territories. Therefore, they are in a position to prevail upon others to agree to their proposition.

This incorporation of development has uneven effects. The emerging tribal elites are generally educated and acculturated; and, in most cases, are estranged from their 'backward' brethren in different proportion. They move in the direction of emulation of the pattern of culture of the people of the higher state of the wider society, although it leads to the impairment of their ethnic solidarity. The need for community control of the development process to moderate the inevitable class and cultural differentiation that results from it places the tribal movement in a conflictual position.

In the northeastern states, tribals control their own destiny to a large extent, but the need for employment and education, and the lack of rapid enough development create social pressures. In the plains the total lack of control has meant land alienation, increased poverty and exploitation. With marginalisation and reduction to a minority status, the creation of a tribal state is no longer likely, but greater influence at the state level, and district council control by tribals. This compromise, while less than what has already been achieved in the northeast, would provide a large measure of protection to tribal interests without driving out the non-tribal population who have the skills and investment needed for development activities.

The tribal movement is so divided between hill and plains tribes and along many smaller ethnic, religious and political lines. As the tribal hill states have access to greater government resources than the plains tribals, the failure of the state governments in northeast India to take national leadership of the tribal movement must be seen as primarily their own responsibility, and a reflection on the internal divisions of the Indian tribal movement between autonomist plains tribals and oft-times secessionist hill tribals. While the plains tribals advocate more autonomy within the Indian Union, with which they are integrated to a large degree, the hill tribes of the northeast tend towards secession and independence. Traditional elites are finding access to universities increasingly difficult as reservations make them accessible to lower castes and tribals. The assertion of minorities and the lower classes in the electoral system is proving to be an important and growing counterweight to the influence and financial power of large corporations that bankroll the major political parties.

State commitment to tribal development has significantly increased since independence. From the First to Fourth Plans, the investment in tribal areas was meagre. Since the launching of the Tribal Sub-Plan (TSP) in the Fifth Plan period there has been a significant increase in funding. With the Seventh Plan, the percentage of proposed outlay (7.22) was almost as much as the percentage of tribals (7.76 per cent) in the 1981 Census which the Commission for Scheduled Castes and Scheduled Tribes found very heartening. The actual expenditures were even higher, at 8.39 per cent in 1985-86 and 8.68 per cent in 1986-87, anticipated expenditures at 9.52 per cent in 1987-88 and 9.67 per cent in 1988-89.

The per capita investment in respect of Scheduled Tribes is not a very clear indicator of the fact that the money invested has actually benefited the tribals. There is strong indication that due to poor infrastructure, comparatively heavy investment on development of administrative structure, leakages and other related factors, the real benefit of the investments made in the tribal areas has not been of the desired level. The Commission would recommend that keeping in view the poor economic status of the tribals, the per capita investment for them should be of a much higher order than that of the general population. Further, increased funding, given the admitted leakages and inappropriate development, will not necessarily improve the tribals' lot.

An analysis of investments during the first four years of the Seventh Five Year Plan has revealed that beneficiary oriented schemes may not have received more than 20 per cent of the total outlay under TSP during Seventh Five Year Plan. It is a matter of concern that this has been the state of affairs despite an increasing emphasis in every successive plan period on states to quantify more and more for the beneficiary oriented schemes. TSP is a plan within the State plan and therefore draws outlays from different sectors. The present bias in favour of infrastructure development schemes is resulting in an exaggerated and notional flow to TSP. Quantifications under TSP are presently made under the general plan schemes of different Departments as percentages of the outlay without any careful look at the relevance of the schemes to tribal areas and without any assessment of the likely flow of physical benefits to tribals. The investments in tribal areas, how so ever well planned and how so ever massive these may be, will only add to the miseries of tribal people if they are not provided proper protection umbrella. There is a strong concomitant need for stringent implementation of protective laws to ensure that the benefits of economic development are not taken away from the tribals. The loopholes in the existing laws should be plugged forthwith and, if possible, a central model law on prevention of alienation of tribal land, should be framed.

The quantification of funds under the TSP continues to be notional in quite a few cases and schemes that cannot be legitimately shown as flow to the TSP are actually shown as such. The detailed planning and exercise that are necessary on the part of each developmental Department to quantify the flow to the TSP realistically are seldom undertaken. The overall outlays for the TSP do not indicate the nature of investments in the area which are beneficial to the tribal people. It appears that all the states are not using a common frame notwithstanding the fact that the Sub-Plan exercises are now more than a decade old.

Major and medium irrigation projects, power and large industries are the most obvious examples in which more often than not, investment results in a severe backlash for tribal people and benefits may accrue partly to the area but not to the people. Power projects may be located in tribal areas but benefits go to the state as a whole. In some states, therefore, major and medium irrigation projects and power are not included in the TSP outlays. In some cases a *pro rata* share of these projects is credited to the Sub-Plan based on the quantum of benefits likely to accrue to the

Sub-Plan areas. But in some states no such consideration appears to weigh with them and the entire outlay on such projects is reflected in the Sub-Plan which highly inflates the figure of investments for tribal development without meaning much in real sense or even having adverse effects. In such a mixed affair the performance based on overall outlays and expenditure is misleading. Moreover, the heavy investment infrastructural programmes involving big contracts prove to be large sponges which absorb whatever comes in their way. The inevitable draw is on vital programmes like education, health and agriculture which are even otherwise difficult to operate and the strain on resources caused by such capital intensive projects becomes a convenient *alibi* for non-action.

The traditional exploitation of tribals by outsiders has left a legacy of tribal mistrust that makes well-intentioned programmes more difficult to implement. During the Sixth Plan all the TSP documents did not contain references to the part to be played by the financial institutions. However, it was assumed that around Rs. 800 crores would be the contribution of financial institutions in tribal programmes. Thus, on the whole, institutional finance has not so far emerged as a strong financial support to tribal development programmes. The reservation in the matter on the part of the tribal is understandable as he has had the bad experience of moneylenders who charged him exorbitant rates of interest and made him indebted.

In many cases alienation of lands and even bondage can be traced back to taking loans from moneylenders. Thus, there is a general reluctance to get entangled in schemes involving a loan element. Till the requisite degree of enlightenment and awareness among tribals is reached we will have to go carefully for those schemes linked with loan element. It will have to be ensured that schemes involving loan component do not deteriorate the economic condition of the tribals.

Besides all these protective laws to provide protection to tribals from exploitation by non-tribals, this has not received priority. There are still instances reported by states of tribal lands passing into the hands of non-tribals despite the existence of these laws. The moneylenders in tribal areas have been charging higher rates of interest and the tribal indebtedness to them continues, although the extent of indebtedness varies from state to state. Large Size Multi-purpose Cooperative Societies (LAMPS) have not been able to substitute the money lenders as viable credit agencies. In the area of marketing of tribal produce the price realised by tribals has improved to an extent in respect of certain items with the intervention of the State Tribal Cooperative Marketing Corporations/Federations, but it is still less than the market price.

The inefficiency of the Indian bureaucracy presents a dilemma for development agencies involved in tribal development. An established reputation among donor agencies and effective networking for foreign funding can contribute to a lack of independent evaluation of what is going on in tribal development projects. The existing networks often reflect old programmes, which may have lost their dynamism, and neglect new organisations with greater grassroots capability but fewer contacts in the capital. Development staff are too few to adequately evaluate large funding projects at the village level. Yet the trend is to decentralise aid operations to the local area. In the Indian context, this often puts more power and resources in the hands of those most directly involved in exploiting the poor. To avoid this problem, development agencies need to have grassroots intelligence about programme recipients which, on account of the prejudices and cultural barriers, can be difficult to determine, particularly when programmes reach a scale that precludes micro-level monitoring.

With corrupt low-level government officials and exploitative moneylenders and landlords, the tribal population is vulnerable to exploitation from both the state and the private sector. The laws in place for their protection often tend to be observed in the breach. On account of their, minority status, the tribals are unlikely to overcome these problems, but without active pressure on the political system their participation will be minimal.

JHARKHAND MOVEMENT

The Jharkhand movement is the most persistent attempt by plains tribals to create their own state. Though the hill tribes have been granted several states, no tribal state exists in the plains despite most of the tribal population residing there. The failure of the Jharkhand movement to achieve statehood is a reflection of the opposition of the state governments who would have to abandon territory for its formation. It is also a reflection of divisions in the movement, and the immigration that has now left the tribals as a minority group within their own Jharkhand region.

Attempts to create common agendas with local non-tribals for the promotion of Jharkhand statehood have been only partly successful. No united movement has arisen, yet the popular demand for Jharkhand among the tribal people and the indigenous peoples shows no sign of decreasing. While touring the Jharkhand region in Bihar it was found that there was popular sentiment in favour of Jharkhand among the tribals but also a cultural gap between this sentiment and the leadership of the movement organised around its advocacy.

As one of the oldest movements in the country and by far the most important tribal movement, the progression and frustrations are indicative of the problems faced by both Indian tribal and foreign indigenous movements for emancipation. In the eighteenth and nineteenth centuries there was a series of revolts in 1780, 1831, 1855, and finally in 1899 of tribal peoples against the encroachment of British colonialism. These revivalist movements were replaced in the 1920s by modernist Christian-dominated movements, most prominently led by the Christian tribal leader, Jaipal Singh.

This movement parallels the experience of the Scheduled Caste movement in what one writer sees as a betrayal of mass interests in favour of the ethnic elite's class interests. When the colonial government began to patronise such movements, their leaders also started forgetting the masses and got involved in a politics of backwardness. They now merely used the depressed socio-economic condition of their communities for obtaining some concessions that could hardly benefit the entire community. The masses, still hoping for a better world and having much less faith in the high caste Hindu nationalists, continued to support their caste leaders, but certainly not with the same keen enthusiasm as before.

As a result, such lower caste movements could not ultimately crystallise into a distinct alternative political force and these parallel streams were eventually captured or appropriated by the dominant nationalist mainstream when an end to colonial rule seemed imminent and there was the need for new political alignments. This phase ended with the integration of tribal political leaders into the Congress party and the eventual erosion of their legitimacy within the tribal movement.

In recent years there has been a resurgence of ethnic tribal politics outside the patronage of the state, but within the democratic political system. Tribal politicisation had led to an understanding of the need for pan-tribal unity, as the British colonial census and the majority electoral system pointed to the importance of numbers and the existence of ethnic identity. This was accompanied by the reservation or affirmative action policy which offered immediate individual benefits for tribal identification.

The colonial state has often been blamed for manufacturing ethnicity, but the identity was already there; the colonial system merely opened up the possibility for organisation on a previously unknown scale. While the late-colonial system did promote this as an attempt at 'divide and rule', the independent government continued the system, and in recent years has greatly expanded it under pressure from new ethnic elites. That this is more than a British legacy and is part of a global phenomenon is indicated by the spread of affirmative action programmes for minorities throughout the western world.

The tribal peoples had a majority population in the Jharkhand area which gave them in the late-colonial period a reasonable expectation of eventual statehood, given a colonial regime that was generally sympathetic to tribal emancipation. Gradually, immigration resulted in the relegation of tribals to a minority status in their own areas. The movement's orientation has also undergone a transformation. From being a struggle of tribal masses to preserve, strengthen and assert their distinct ethnic culture, identity, values, history and independence, the Jharkhand movement in the course of its long existence has slowly but steadily been transformed into a movement for the development of the tribals much along the same path as that of their non-tribal neighbours.

The tribals have been relegated to a minority position, which has made political alliances with local non-tribals essential for electoral success. As a result the distinctive cultures of the tribals have been downplayed in favour of class alliances and regionalist movements against exploitation by outsiders. At the level of political practice it is advised that unity of the people of the entire backward area would strengthen the movement or more directly that the movement would not succeed unless it wins over the support of the non-tribals.

Ethnicity is the idiom of the tribals while regionalism is that of the dominant communities and the movement is definitely moving in the direction of regionalism. The difficulty for a tribal movement which hopes to achieve some measure of local autonomy, if not statehood, is profound. The need to obtain allies compels the tribal movement to limit the divisive issue of ethnicity in favour of the common cause regionalism offers. How a tribal ethnic identity can be retained in this coalition is by no means clear. The argument that the indigenous leadership by adopting the developmental mode transfers the grounds of discourse to the outsiders' paradigm, begs the question of how a genuine tribal development can be achieved, given the low level of development that has hitherto existed in tribal communities. The obvious option of abandoning development altogether is no longer realistic since the people themselves want modern goods and services. Without development the tribals are doomed to what has come to be considered poverty, while the promotion of ethnicity relegates them to political oblivion.

The tribal leadership has attempted to overcome these barriers by promoting development under its own control and political power through strategic alliances with non-tribals. The extent to which the ethnic cultural revival has suffered as a result is open to debate. Certainly, there is a large gap between the tribal leadership and the masses, with no widely recognised leader or party to give the movement a clear direction. This is in part because indigenous peoples are divided culturally and politically along a number of tribal ethnic lines, and further divided between Christians and non-Christians both among the tribal leadership, and to perhaps a lesser extent among followers. Religion is an area of contest in India, with the Hindus attempting to convert tribals or at least undermine the efforts of Christians to do so.

There was a deep vacuum in ideology within the leadership in the Jharkhand movement. Ethnic rivalry, religious conflicts and inter-party competition absolutely disrupted the mobilisation of the people inviting pessimism and degradation for them.

The movement was repeatedly undermined by defections of leaders and followers to the ruling party. On a more subtle level, tribals with education could secure government jobs which, however, precluded political activity. A new phase of the movement began in 1973 with the Jharkhand Mukti Morcha (JMM) in which common cause was made with radical Marxist parties that had bases among the working class and non-tribal agriculturists, but these were alliances of convenience rather than a heartfelt political conversion. Internally divided and spread over four states, all of whose governments are opposed to separation, the movement faces seemingly insurmountable obstacles. The concession of district councils in tribal areas is possible, but with tribals now in a minority position in the Jharkhand region it is difficult to see what additional benefits this will bring.

While the assertion of a tribal identity is present, it is far from clear what this means in terms of empowerment, particularly in a poor country where the state largesse for ethnic development promotion is limited, and may decrease with structural adjustment. At a time when job reservations are being extended to most of the population, even while the public sector is not expanding, the relative position of tribals as beneficiaries of these affirmative action programmes could be diminished in favour of larger and more politically influential groups. In conjunction with a limited capability of the state to achieve social engineering comes a new concept of community empowerment in both India and the West. In the case of tribal populations this is seen as a return to traditional tribal authority and learning to achieve empowerment.

A major contributing factor for lack of peace and tranquillity in tribal areas is the waning authority of the community, interference by exotic agencies even in matters concerning their day-to-day life and their growing dependence on others in matters such as right over land and access to other resources. Since the community life in tribal areas is still vibrant and capable of managing its internal affairs it will be in the general interest of the people and their well-being if their authority is not allowed to get eroded. It will also help in engendering a sense of self-confidence amongst the people to face the new challenges from all sides and maintenance of their proverbial idyllic milieu.

As large an area as possible should be brought within the purview of specially constituted local institutions. These institutions should be responsible to the people of the village and not to ally higher authority either in the administration or even formal representative institutions. This approach of reconstructing traditional community authority, however is not without its problems. Non-tribal observers to the Indian Council of Indigenous and Tribal Peoples 1993 General Assembly noted that many tribal movements too are male dominated, with women's participation being minimal. The participation of women may be in contradiction of certain local customs, but most governments and activists would insist upon their involvement. Such reconstitution of traditional institutions is today usually a government-sponsored imposition, and how this is to achieve local legitimacy while maintaining a social reform orientation local participants may reject is by no means clear.

In the traditional social system of the tribals there are some inherent qualities which can be constructively used for building a just society. Some of these qualities are the spirit of cooperation and mutual obligation, community solidarity, sense of general equality and partnership among all, sense of equal partnership between men and women, honesty, sincerity, doing one's duty silently, democratic procedures for dealing with common affairs with emphasis on consensus, dignity of physical labour, etc.

Innovative programmes could be based on these elements of tribal culture and values to the extent they prove to be compatible with development. There are certain tribal values and attitudes which impede development, but there also are definitely some other types of values and attitudes which can contribute to developing a just society. Some so-called negative values and attitudes can be used for constructive work, if appropriate strategies are adopted. They can cope with the changing society or on giving them new meaning and make them function for the greater good of the society.

Despite over a century of missionary education in the Jharkhand region, tribal peoples have not developed an entrepreneurial base, and have remained at most salaried government employees. The development which occurred was undertaken by outsiders. Exposure to western education alone was not enough to launch the developmental process. The development that has occurred has been skewed towards tribal elites. By giving privileges to the tribal leaders, the British administrators not only introduced a degree of stratification in tribal society which did not exist before, but also created tribal elites who themselves exploited the tribal people and were later to do so to a much greater degree when in free India massive investment was made in tribal development. Ironically, affirmative action may have increased tribal differentiation. Notwithstanding a lack of funding for such policies, positive discrimination has secured many benefits for the tribal populations of independent India. Ironically, too, it has served to fortify an emerging tribal middle class, for it is this group which monopolises most of the benefits on offer. Again, this tends to undermine the ideology of undifferentiated tribal communities upon which tribal policy is based, and from which a traditional tribal politics derives.

The positive achievements of the movement in the sphere of language and identity have been hijacked by the activities of its leaders who carry on their squabbles and personal fortune making. The erosion in the movement caused by the performance of its leaders may be due to lack of ideological consistency and weak organisational network. Due to this, the movement could never reach a take off stage, not to speak of nationality formation. Though in recent years the religious divide in the movement between Christian and non-Christian has declined, the entrance of trade unions may have catered to the needs of mining and industrial labour in the area, and made a headway into non-tribal groups, but intrusion of diverging ideological trends only added further confusion to the movement. The import of class-caste-ethnicity issues, debate on nationality as a category, language and religion, etc., have all been mixed up. The movement and the groups were soon destined to be in disarray.

The culture of tribal peoples which has persisted despite the multiple defections and divisions in the organised movement. From this base new parties and tendencies will continue to arise, and some day may achieve a measure of local empowerment, and just possibly statehood. If this is to be achieved the leadership will have to resist accepting subordinate positions in ruling parties and be more effective in mobilising a mass base.

Each tribe has promoted its own interests, but failed to unite with others. The principal divide has been between the hill tribes in the frontier and those in the plains. As a result of factors such as missionary activity, limited outsider settlement, and government security imperatives, the hill tribes have been better placed to demand and receive government concessions, including statehood. This has not been obtained by plains tribals who are generally a minority even in their own areas. Only 13 districts have tribal majorities, and Madhya Pradesh and Orissa, with 22 per cent tribal population, have the largest minority tribal population.

The Jharkhand movement for a plains tribal state has not made significant headway to date, and even if achieved, would leave out many plains tribals and include many non-tribals within a newly created state. This is the dilemma of any ethnically based political entity. It only creates new minorities within its borders who in turn agitate against discrimination. The creation of ethnic boundaries may permit the rise to dominance of subordinate ethnic groups and the marginalisation of dominant ones, but this creates new injustices. While the inner-line policy certainly made possible the rise of a tribal middle class and political elite and general developmental improvements, the restrictions on the travel of 'outsider Indians' is at the very least incongruous in a democracy. However, when the alternative is the swamping of an indigenous culture, this is perhaps justifiable. If it can be justified for security reasons in the northeast then it should also apply for humanitarian reasons to the tribal people in the plains.

Hundreds of lives were lost in the West Bengal government's repression of the Gorkhaland movement in Darjeeling before a compromise involving local autonomy was reached. In the northeast the central government did impose tribal states through the partition of Assam, overruling the objections of the Assam government. Similar arrangements are legally possible in the plains. The creation of linguistic states during the 1950s is generally seen as resolving a number of destabilising issues that were endangering national unity at the time. Such protected enclaves, districts and states, however, will not be achieved without a movement that transcends tribal ethnic boundaries and will probably require support from other ethnic groups and interests as well.

The failure of existing hill states to press more effectively for protection of the plains tribals is a reflection of the ethnic atomisation of Indian politics. Their protection, however, cannot be entrusted to the locally dominant elites which control state governments. Only the centre can impose local autonomy for tribal peoples. At the very least the tribal peoples must control sufficient state power to prevent the locally dominant landed interests from alienating their land. While there are already laws to prevent this, local-level administration has proved unable and often unwilling to implement them. The administration is unlikely to change its attitude unless it is severed from locally dominant commercial interests and classes. Without local tribal empowerment and the prevention of encroachment, such a change is unlikely, since the administration itself is often involved in the exploitation through kickbacks from contractors or even outright extortion of tribals. Civil servants may on occasion provide some redress to tribals caught between dominant landed and moneylending village elites and corrupt bottom-rung officials, but without transfer of local powers to the tribals themselves, justice cannot be achieved. Such powers can only be provided by the state and national governments which have not been forthcoming in this regard. While the creation of hill states has precluded some of the worst effects of outsider exploitation, nothing of consequence has been done to arrest the erosion of tribal human rights in the plains.

Allegations of ethnic divisiveness, backwardness or separatism are often used by governments as cloaks for exploitation, authoritarianism and hegemonic privilege. Nowadays, in many parts of the world, people are resorting to their ethnicity as a sort of civil rights movement, to achieve the equality of treatment which had previously been denied them in the name of modernisation. Ethnicity has also been used to oppress others. While few would deny the right of tribals to assert their rights to cultural survival, the concept of ethnic identity is by its nature exclusive as well as inclusive, and this creates disunity among even like-minded tribal peoples which hinders their emancipation. It is therefore a mistake to place too high a premium on the retention of traditional practices which are counter-productive in modern society.

7

Development of Small Tribal Communities

In terms of their size, tribal groups less than 15,000 strong are considered as small tribal communities. Even in this group a subclass of 'dimunitive' communities has been identified whose strength is generally less than a thousand. All small groups are proposed to be classified according to their size, rate of growth, state of ecological equilibrium, isolation and confrontation with other groups.

No special theory of economic development appears to have been evolved for small communities. The general developmental programmes have been considered to be inadequate to meet their situation as well, particularly because their problems are of smaller dimension. The developmental processes, however, have either bypassed them or have had an indifferent impact. Other socioeconomic forces, operating in the larger areas, have been influencing these groups with different results.

The time perspective for the development of small tribal communities has to be longer. Initially first-aid operation with a pause to allow them to regain their confidence is necessary. In case of isolated communities, the target group has to be the next generation which can assimilate the benefit of new knowledge and yet is not alienated from its own society. In any attempt for the development of tribal communities special attention to the smaller groups becomes inevitable if the possibility of extinction of any small group by confrontation or maladjustment is to be avoided. In the first instance, it will be necessary to identify the differences in the social dynamics of a small group and of a larger group so that the processes are clearly understood and valid policy conclusions can be derived.

The very existence of a small group depends on its extreme cohesiveness. Consequently, dissidence is severely punished. Small groups are known to exist in extreme hostile circumstances in a state of continued confrontation. If they lose the nerve, they soon become extinct. But they continue tenaciously as a group by keeping the change to the minimum or accepting the change almost as a mutation when the whole community may accept a new behaviour pattern within a short period.

In India, the size of tribal communities varies from as small as a few dozens strong to as large as a few millions. It appears that a certain minimum size is necessary to keep a group going, or else its numerical strength, begins to decline for various reasons and, in due course, it may get extinct. The groups below this minimum size could be termed as 'diminutive' groups.

Similarly, above a certain size the groups become viable and can stand the socioeconomic pressures from other groups. However, even big groups may be helpless before a highly organised group or institution. These are exceptional circumstances where size is not decisive in the survival game. Between the 'diminutive groups' and the 'large groups' a distinct spectrum of 'intermediate groups' can be identified who can be said to be in a state of unstable equilibrium. They, may under favourable circumstances, cross the upper critical limit but under adverse circumstances may join the category of 'diminutive.' This category may be termed as a 'small' group.

Thus, the size-range of the small groups may vary from, say, one thousand to fifteen thousand. The upper limit of fifteen thousand is being suggested as groups upto that size are noted to have declined in number under adverse situation. Groups of a size smaller than a thousand are known to have perished in comparatively short spans of time.

A modern urban society draws its sustenance from a very large ecosystem which may be as extensive as the nation or the whole world. The small tribal communities, still depend on an ecosystem, which is not very extensive. The relationship of the community and the ecosystem in their case is direct in contrast to the indirect relationship of advanced urban communities. This distinction is not generally appreciated by planners who are themselves a part of the indirect relationship-matrix. Certain programmes, which, to a modern planner, may appear to be neutral or even beneficial to the local group, may tend to disturb its delicate balance with disastrous consequences.

At the beginning, tribal communities were in a state of ecological equilibrium with their environment. The numbers were small and natural resources abundant. The level of the technology was low. These communities initially sustained themselves as food gathers and hunters. As the numbers grow, some primitive form of cultivation like, cultivation by bum and slash, was adopted. In the normal course of development, with the growth of population, eventually the group had taken to settled cultivation and thus use natural resources more intensively.

During the early stage of development, ecological equilibrium may get disturbed due to natural or man-made causes.

The group may be outgrowing the natural resource potential without any change in technology. Alternatively, some change in the group's lifestyle may be leading to either destruction of over-exploitation of resources, thus resulting in disequilibrium. In some cases, the reasons for the disequilibrium may be external. There may be a secular change in the environment which may have adversely affected the fauna and flora or an epidemic may have dislocated the biological equilibrium.

There may be strong man-made forces to disturb the ecological equilibrium. A stronger group may have intruded in the region in search of better lands. With a higher-level of technology, it takes control of better resources and the original group may recede and may have to subsist on poorer and scanty natural resources. Some external pressures may be institutional in origin. A new organisation may be set-up in a backward region without honouring the unwritten rights of the local community. It may adversely affect the ecological equilibrium by over-exploitation of the resources.

There are considerable variations in the intensity of contact of smaller groups with others. Some groups retain their identity and way of life but they do not occupy a well defined area. They may be living on the margins of advanced groups. These groups generally subsist on forests which might have been over-exploited. Thus, the ecological equilibrium might have got disturbed and the group may be in a stage of confrontation with other groups or institutions. On the other hand, some other groups may still be in isolation for various reasons. These groups may not have been disturbed through force of circumstances as in some of the difficult hill regions, or as a result of an administrative decision. The undisturbed groups may be at different stages of ecological equilibrium.

However, when the ecological equilibrium has been disturbed, the first step has naturally to be to identify the precise nature of the ecological imbalance. This analysis should help in evolving a suitable strategy. If the contributing factors for ecological imbalance in relation to community are both external and internal, attention will have to be given first to the external factors. The external factors are superimpositions on the community and the community is legitimately entitled to get relief from those forces.

All external factors can be of two varieties, viz., institutional and individual. Those forces which are ascribable to an institutional source should be the easier one to influence since personnel interests are not involved. For example, if policy of the forest department or some other organisation is responsible for the mal-adjustment, that policy could be changed after due consideration in the first instance. Where the confrontation is amongst various groups, the problem is more difficult. In this situation, the interests of other groups, whether acquired legitimately or otherwise, become a relevant factor. It is well-known that compromises have to be found in these cases even when there are best intentions to help the affected groups. In these cases, one cannot depend on individual action alone; institutional methods will be necessary for dealing effectively with situation.

When efforts are made to neutralise the external forces, it will be necessary that first-aid operations are started to undo the damage which the group may have already sustained. A clear understanding of its health problems will be necessary. The diet pattern of the group will have to be carefully studied as the disturbance of the ecological balance may have deprived them of certain essential ingredients of their traditional diet.

The small groups are likely to have been affected on the psychological plane. The very confidence of the group may have been shattered. If there is no confidence, material assistance is not likely to be of much advantage. Small communities have a feeling of being friendless in the new context and, therefore, tend to become non-communicative and inward-looking.

Effective protective measures by a sympathetic band of workers may help in dispelling the group psychology of being all alone against tremendous adverse forces. External assistance, however, cannot create self-confidence. A social-therapy will need understanding of their perception of the socioeconomic processes, their world-view, the sources of their strength and their aspirations.

A small group, which is able to derive a reasonable sustenance from a limited ecological system, must be skilled. Lack of skill is comparatively a modern phenomenon and often a function of a specialised social and economic structure. Most of these groups, except those in complete isolation, have been in contact with advanced agricultural communities and have evolved their own adaptive strategies for facing the continued encounter. Their skills may not be of much relevance in the modern context.

In the absence of proper appreciation, even rare skills may not be duly remunerated by other groups, for example, the skill identification of herbs or taming of animals. In these cases, artificial equations could be corrected through state intervention. What is more important is that if their native skills are well recognised, the group will have a sense of pride and, thus, its confidence in itself can be restored. The future developmental programmes could be planned within the assimilative capacity of the community and on a well-understood skill-base.

Ecological disequilibrium arises generally because a community was not able to keep pace with the changing environment, both physical and human. An obvious answer would be to simulate faster pace of change in the community so that it can catch up with the rest of the society by freeing itself from the dependence on a narrow ecological frame and by sharing a higher specialisation and a bigger ecological field with the rest of the community. This has to be the ultimate goal. But while planning for initial phases of development, the fact of the 'loss of nerve' in many cases has to be fully taken into account. These communities are in the same position as an exhausted competitor in a race. They will require sometime for restoration of their balance and for acquiring inner strength which can enable them to go ahead with a renewed vigour.

The first stage of planned development has to be devoted to mend the shattered ecological equilibrium as best as possible. In this period, a benevolent outside contact may help them in getting over the 'confrontation complex' and establish new communication channels. The steps for removing the causes of ecological disequilibrium have to be as swift as possible. The pace of other steps, however, should be slow, preferably even imperceptible. A period of almost nonintervention, i.e., when no new changes are induced and the community is allowed to have a look around in a non-hostile atmosphere, would seem to be called for as an essential element of the strategy. It is at this stage that desirable agents of change may be introduced. But they should operate in such a fashion that the community should be able to view the new changes as their own innovations, which in fact may be induced, for meeting the changing situation. A better perception of the new processes and forces by suitable educational programmes will influence their world view.

A gradual process of change, which should always be within the commanding capacity of the group, will give them a sense of adventure and enable them in due course to quicken their pace to catch up with the rest of the community.

The comparative strength of the instrument of change itself is the most important feature which distinguishes the smaller tribal groups from larger communities in respect of planning development. In the development dynamic of smaller groups the very elements introduced for initiating developmental processes may themselves overwhelm the group and its socioeconomic structure.

This possibility is quite obvious in respect of diminutive groups where the population is a few hundreds but it is not clearly appreciated in respect of larger small groups which may be dispersed in thinly populated areas. One of the important constraints on the size of the developmental programme and administrative machinery in general developmental programmes of larger communities is financial. But in the case of diminutive groups, because of their extremely small size, financial resources cannot be a constraint for their development. Consequently, the size of the developmental effort can be decided independently of any financial constraint. In this situation, many hard policy questions may arise in relation to the strategy, for their development.

In the case of large small groups, also particularly in sparsely populated areas, although financial resources may have to be kept in view but they cannot be an important constraint simply because of the almost microscopic size of investment compared to the national or regional developmental outlays. Size of the development effort, thus becomes practically an independent variable. It also determines the size of the administrative apparatus.

Thus, the nature of a programme itself may become critical in the case of both the diminutive and the small groups because the very presence of instruments of development in these areas is likely to create a big impact.

DIMINUTIVE GROUPS

The crucial problem threatening the diminutive groups is of very survival. Most of the diminutive groups are not able to maintain themselves. Besides those cases, where assimilation in broader groups may be the main reason for the 'nil' growth rate, certain groups are known to be declining because of less of ecological equilibrium. The well known cases are Onges, Great Andamanese and Birhors.

In the case of Great Andamanese, their area of command got encroached by other groups, ecological equilibrium was lost and their numbers dwindled as they failed to meet the new challenge. Similarly, the Birhors are experiencing encroachment on their area of command. Onges are in a better position as they have remained comparatively isolated so far but some new developments have started encroaching on their command area.

Although these general formulations are well-known, deeper analysis of their situation is not available. It has, therefore, to be ascertained as to why a group is not able to maintain itself. Health and food supply are two relevant aspects. Health problems, if any, will have to be tackled to begin with. To the extent there is deficiency in their diet, it will have to be treated as a part of their health problem.

Another problem is their total economic situation. In view of their small size and no serious constraints of plan resources, a number of alternatives can be said to be available.

For example, in the case of Onges, the total population is 118, their habitant is one island of about 300 sq. miles. Natural resources are plentiful although external interference is now tending to disturb the equilibrium. One course could be that some *ad hoc* assistance, could be made available initially. Or the entire group could be employed on any modern activity which may be taken up in the island. In the meantime, perhaps the entire next generation could be put through a programme of residential school education. The basic question is that who is to decide about the course of development? What is the concept of the group identity? Has 'group identity' an independent value? Why should alienation which may arise from an educational programme, cause a concern for smaller groups only because similar alienation, is also arising in bigger tribal groups and other agriculture communities?

In the case of larger communities this alienation is accepted as a normal stage in the process of development. Conceptually, the group can be considered to be voluntarily taking a decision and accepting a new life style. A new leadership may be providing it the necessary sense of direction. However, there is an important difference. In the case of bigger groups, there is no possibility of a sudden structural change in the economic base. Therefore, group identity will remain unaffected for a sufficiently long time, say, at least a few generations, notwithstanding the process of alienation of their educated youth. The change, in their case, therefore, can be only gradual. In the case of very small groups, however, the change may have the character of a mutation for which the decision would have been taken by some one else.

No solution should be imposed which may threaten the group identity all of a sudden. The best way, perhaps, will be to try a gradual process of development and not overwhelm them with a programme which has the effect of sudden change and dissolution of the group itself. In the case of those groups as may have reached a state of confrontation, a phase of 'first-aid' type assistance will have to be envisaged during which the group regains its confidence. Thereafter, suitable programmes of development could be taken up.

Education will necessarily have to be an important element so that the communication barrier, if any, between this group and the rest of the community is broken. However, education must be adapted to their own environment with a view to avoid sudden appearance of the process of alienation and possibility of the very first generation educated group finding its traditional vocation uncongenial.

On the economic side, the group could be assisted either in its traditional occupations or some other activity akin to their traditional occupations. Thus, the group can be helped in overcoming initially the hardships arising from an adverse economic situation and lack of communication. Special attention to the problem of its health would help it physically. When the group reaches the stage of non-confrontation it will be in a position to share the fortunes of the rest of the community and partake in the normal developmental programme in the region.

Will it be possible to carry all the necessary programmes to each habitat of Onges? Of course, yes. But if approach is sectorial, the size of the administrative structure itself will be too big. In this case, whatever may be the formal programme content, the most important element will be the influence of the numerous functionaries who may be inducted in the area. While the programme content is planned, the human element will tend to become an autonomous force, unless effective planning is attempted even on that score.

Therefore, the general administrative and planning processes will have to be reversed in the case of such groups. More appropriate course of action would be that having got a clear idea about the objectives and the pace of change, a suitable team of two or three workers could be chosen. The criterion for the selection of such a team should be a clear understanding of, or capacity for understanding, the goals and a sympathy for the group. In such an assignment there is no place for considerations like the level of individuals in the hierarchy, etc. No person, who may wish to take up such a challenge is too high for the assignment.

The technical skill endowment of the team should depend on the programme design. Health, education and agriculture appear to be the three important components. But each member need not be a specialist except perhaps the medical man, who himself could be an educator and one who understands the ecosystem.

In brief, a motivated team, equipped with broad spectrum of advanced skills, has to be conceived as the primary agent of change in these communities, which will influence the process of change more by the very presence of its members rather than through formalised developmental programmes. In fact, this will very much resemble the process of acculturation initiated by torch bearers of new faiths all over the world throughout the human history.

LARGER SMALL GROUPS

Larger small groups, occupying sizeable geographical areas, give a first impression of being amenable to general developmental formulation like tribal development block programme or area development programme. Even when special character of the area may be recognised, planning concepts and techniques developed for advanced areas are sought to be applied which may not answer the need of the special area. These aspects can be better appreciated with reference to a specific area and its problems.

Consider the case of Abujhmar in Bastar. The total population is about 13,000. The total geographical area is 1500 sq miles. The topography is undulating, yet there are quite a few plain patches to support settle cultivation sufficient for the present population, even allowing for a substantial growth rate for the next few decades. The area can be considered to have good tourist potential. The main economic activity at present is good gathering, shifting cultivation and hunting with sprinkling of settled cultivation generally with hoe.

Even before 1930, inaccessibility had kept this area almost untouched. After independence sporadic efforts have been made for development of this area as and when attention of administrators was attracted to this region either as a result of personal fascination or because of special problems. The programme of tribal development block was started in this area in 1965. Except for a sizeable educational effort with ten *ashram* schools started in 1970, not much perceptible impact is visible. The benefit of medical facilities has generally not gone beyond the block head-quarter. Agricultural extension is confined to distribution of bullocks or giving vegetable seeds but no strategy as yet is available because the area is under shifting cultivation and there is little demand for settled cultivation. Drinking water wells have been constructed in some areas but their use is limited as yet. In a way, the area can be said to be virgin, both for exploitation of its natural resources and in respect of development effort by the state.

The Abujhmarias will become an insignificant minority; most of them will prefer to recede into the backwards and sustain in a comparatively poorer ecosystem; and such of them as do not escape to the more inaccessible and marginal lands, will occupy the substratum of the new socioeconomic structure.

In the national context, a tribal group becoming a minority in an area, which at one time happened to be predominantly inhabited by it, is not something unthinkable; but a decisively low position of the original inhabitants in the new socioeconomic structure should be a concern of every one. It appears that the level of technology and skill requirements for an industrial centre and its hinterland are so different from the existing skills and way of life of the shifting cultivators of Abujhmar that there cannot be an easy transition in a short span of time of a decade or so. As major decisions for industry or mining development are not normally taken with such a long-time perspective, the desirability of any heavy industry-based economy for this region has to be ruled out on sociological considerations unless these considerations are consciously over-ruled and social disruption of Abujhmarias is treated, in the national arithmetic, a necessary price which the group must pay for national development.

Necessary skills for some activities like construction are not available in Abujhmarias. Also, the local population may not like sustained work even in forestry and allied sectors and may come forward for limited work only. Thus, the total direct employment potential created as a result of new sector will far exceed the total usable labour in this area. This will require large scale immigration. The total immigration will, however, depend on the phasing of development programmes. It may be noted here that primary population immigration will soon be followed by a secondary migration of relatives of primary migrants, fortune seekers, traders and other groups. This may give rise to a state of confrontation in an area which so far has been kept immunised from all outside influence. Perhaps, the original inhabitants of this area will soon be reduced to a minority. This available land, which could not be put to use so far because of low technological base and lower pressure of population, may be occupied by the new groups.

As the capacity of the Abujhmaria to change in the short run is extremely limited and the technological skills of the two groups are widely different, the original group may tend to recede into the more inaccessible areas giving way to the new migrants in the regions which get opened up. With the new developmental inputs, agricultural production in the area will go up; out-turmain forests will increase; there will be considerable trade and transport activity and all indicators of development will show an upward trend. Yet the original group may be worse off.

The substantive developmental programmes in agricultural and allied sectors will strengthen the economy of Abujhmaria as well. But the gestation period of even such programmes, in terms of accrual of actual benefits to a primitive group, is rather long compared to the other influences which may arise because of the sudden high tempo of developmental activity directed from outside. Any model of development which presumes an unlimited supply of manpower will, in the first phase, displace the local population to their great disadvantage. The balance may never be regained since other interests would have appeared on the scene with an equally valid claim which would get strengthened with passage of time. These alternatives, therefore, must be rejected for an area like Abujhmar in the first phase of its development.

People's development

Area development is the main objective and development of the people has to be a corollary. Even a moderate road programme for Abujhmar may itself require deployment of the total available manpower in the area for construction in the earlier phases and for the maintenance of the network subsequently. Thus, the area could be visualised a public works department camp in which full time employment of the total population is maintaining the roads network, the level of road construction activity being limited by total available manpower. This is an extreme situation which is admittedly absurd. However, it brings into focus one important aspect of area development, viz., a single activity, in the area development frame, is sufficient to keep the entire population engaged.

Unless a comprehensive view is taken of the process of development, a single activity, howsoever important it may be, becomes meaningless from the angle of people's development. Often, road development is over-stressed in area development programmes and the manpower constraint is not kept in view. The result generally is large scale migration and the programme hardly touches the problems of the people.

Suppose exploitation of forest resources at optimal level is chosen to be the primary activity for this area. In this case, the entire population could be employed as wage-labour for exploitation of the forests and allied activities like maintenance of forest roads, etc. Thus, in this model Abujhmar will become a forest estate, the intensity of exploitation of forest resources being determined by the total available manpower.

In smaller and backward societies the association is more of a compulsive nature because of the unequal strength of the local community and the modern organised system which operates in these areas. The new activity is concerned about one aspect of the community life and is unconcerned with the rest. The imposition of change at one point, without attention to the rest, creates disruption in the social system with unpredictable results. The community may disintegrate. Even otherwise, a valid question may be asked whether we would be satisfied with subservient role of a whole community in an economic system where an abstract department or organisation is the overlord and the community provides casual wage labour according to its requirements. An individual enterprise, as a part of a larger system, cannot become an autonomous force and there are moderating influences. But when it is superimposed on a whole system, the matrix changes.

A programme of economic development even on forestry model is not likely to succeed in Abujhmar as the local population cannot be expected to change its traditional economic pursuits in a short period. Whatever may be the presumptions in the original schemes, unless the development of the local population is kept as the central theme, the programmes tend to acquire an independent identity and may be pursued for their own sake. Goal displacement phenomenon is well-known in social sciences. Thus, even forestry programmes may lead to large scale migration and its socioeconomic consequences in relations to the Abujhmaria may remain undefined if the question is not posed in the early stage and answered in categorical terms.

A very important policy question about the change in demographic structure arises which has to be answered in categorical terms. The demographic structure of a primitive region must be one of the most important points on which a conscious policy decision at a very high level must be taken. If in the interest of regional development or national development a decision, threatening the very identity of the group, is to be taken, it must be in full face of the facts as they are and the likely course of events in the next few years. What is not pardonable is to initiate a process of change without examining all aspects of critical importance to the local community and when the implicit inevitable begins to unfold self to say this is inevitable price for the development of the area.

Demographic structure must be taken as one of the most important constraints while planning development of the small primitive communities. The important aspects need to be noted and considered are: (i) the total available manpower in the region, (ii) the level of technology of the group and the possibility of its adaptation or upgradation in a given time period; and (iii) the permissible limit of introducing migration in the area so that a state of confrontation does not arise and the immigrant groups do not become dominant in the new socioeconomic structure.

People's development cannot be conceived in isolation—the ecosystem, including the environment in which they live, their effective command over resources and future potential, the resource endowment of the region, etc., have an interaction with their socioeconomic and cultural life and also provide a frame for their development. The new power of science and technology does make the choice of alternative courses of development available to planners very wide. However, the alternatives open to a primitive community, at least to its contemporary generation, are comparatively limited and are circumscribed by its assimilative power.

Among primitive groups, communication barriers are quite formidable; social systems differ; concept of a group life vary; the new is strange; preference is strong for being left alone. The Jarawas of Andamans or the Bondos of Orissa illustrate an extreme situation. Before planning for development, the nature of various influences on the primitive community will need to be clearly understood.

Changes associated with a variety of activities in different plans include the following:

i) *Manipulation of physical environment of group habitat*: mining, forest exploitation, large scale dairying, public health programmes.

ii) *Influence on the economic activity of the group*: agricultural extension, crafts and cottage industries.

iii) *Superimposition of new institutions*: a) political (panchayats, elections); b) administrative (revenue, forest and police administration); c) economic (co-operative societies, marketing); d) social (laws affecting social life and behaviour like marriage by capture) and e) pseudosocial (educational and health institutions)

v) *Interaction with other groups*: They include traditional neighbours, new migrants, extension agency, general administrative personnel, traders, contractors, casual visitors etc.

v) *Induced social customs and personnel behaviour*: Generally spread-effect of more and more of migrants, extension agency and educated tribal youth.

Formal enumeration of these elements for a region will not be sufficient to assess the extent of their influence on the role in the ongoing processes in the region. What is the degree of effective interaction in each case will be relevant for planning purposes. For example, forest regulations or land revenue system may have been formally extended to an area for a long period, yet its effective coverage will start only when an implementing agency is introduced in a local area.

Formally, Abujhmar is subject to the same land and forest laws as the rest of the state, though in practice they have not been extended. Thus, formal and actual situations differ widely. If the process of change, is not planned, the pace of effective coverage in the wake of new development effort in different sectors may vary considerably.

It is generally found that, unless consciously planned otherwise, regulatory activities of the state are first to appear on the scene and beneficial ones lag far behind. For example, as a result of conscious state policy, the police, revenue and forest administrations were withdrawn from Abujhmar. Extension and education activities were promoted subsequently. On the other hand, in the absence of a clear policy frame, the Bondo hills have a full-fledged police station for a long time now while educational and extension coverage remains weak. A differential and uncoordinated coverage by different elements unsettles the life of the local communities in an unpredictable fashion. In such a situation, vested interests of all varieties—institutional, group and individual—tend to take advantage of the new situation.

In Abujhmar, the community is still in a state of ecological equilibrium. Some areas where the cycle of shifting cultivation has been reduced and there is moderate pressure of population. As a result of conscious state policy, there is no confrontation in this area as yet. However, some pressure points are developing on the northeastern corner from cultivators from the plains as also along the only forest road cutting across Abujhmar in its northern fringes from communities raising cattle. The rate of growth of population is almost nil. Little is known about the precise reason for this. Generally, they enjoy good health but wild animals and diseases seem to take a heavy toll of life.

The whole territory is supposed to be owned by the community in which each village has a well-demarcated area. There are rich forests particularly on the periphery. Some areas have got denuded; yet each village has some forest under its command and also within its reach. There are vast stretches of plain land in the plateau with possible good irrigation potential. The total available manpower is about 3000; literacy is negligible; the people are used to an extensive form of agriculture.

There is contact with the neighbouring communities and induced change even in agricultural technology is evident in those areas which are experiencing moderate pressure of population. Extension agency and ashram schools have introduced government functionaries in this area, some of whom are becoming the new contact points between the Abujhmaria and the outside world. There is some reaction to the pressure from outside communities in the n orthern fringe. Forest on the outskirts of Abhujmar is providing the community in the border villages seasonal employment.

There is no conscious policy direction with reference to development of Abhujmar. The immunisation of the area through administrative tradition is fragile since it has no legal base. The fear of the unknown amongst the outsiders is gradually giving way with greater contact and the weakness of the local community will become a public knowledge with greater contact. The potentiality of the area will also be better known with the passage of time. Even government may be tempted to exploit its potential. Therefore, this area is fast reaching a stage where it may face large scale changes and considerable pressure from institutions, groups and individuals. To tame the change-process is the major problem.

Regulation of change in legal frame: A change in the legal frame becomes an important compulsive force, particularly when the two sides are not evenly balanced. Already the local practice and the formal legal frame in Abhujmar are at variance. The normal administrative structure, therefore, can be extended to this area at the mere wish of the local administration. Administrative practice is consciously formalised which could have elements for change as may be thought best for this area in the context of the developmental programme for future. The traditional panchayats at the village level may be brought into picture. There is no panchayat for the Abhujmar as a whole. One institution may be established drawing mainly on the traditional leadership.

Regulation of in-migration: The Abujhamarias trace their origin to a number of villages in their plains of Bastars and Naranpur. Although Abujhmarias are an endogamous group, but there is no bar to inter-marriage with the Gonds of Narainpur. There is also a local practice that in case a person from outside Abujhmar wishes to settle in Abujhmar, the village community as a whole can take a decision and assign land to him. It, therefore, appears that the manpower deficiency in this area, to some extent, can be made good through selective in-migration of persons from the neighbourhood which may be in conformity with their present practice. Migration, which may start as a trickle, may assume larger proportions upsetting the balance. After sometime local community may find itself helpless to stand the new pressures. Hence, it will be useful if an absolute limit to the number that can be allowed for in-migration under this provision may be fixed so that the balance does not become unfavourable to the local community.

Regulation in economic activity: In view of the sparseness of population, it will be necessary that extensive agricultural practices requiring comparatively smaller manpower are adopted in this area. Here we will have a clear departure from the strategy of intensive agriculture in the plains having higher density of population. This will mean that this area specialises in cattle rearing and horticulture. These are also nearest to their traditional economic activity and, therefore, can be said to be within the assimilative capacity of the local community. Shifting cultivation may co-exist for sometime but as greater income accrues from horticulture and cattle rearing, there will be lesser dependence on shifting cultivation as the primary economic activity. A greater contact with the extension agency in regard to these two areas can be used to slowly induce the community to meet its food requirements from settled cultivation and other needs from horticulture and cattle rearing.

There are some good plain stretches of land with potential for irrigation. These lands, even at the general peasant technology of Bastar region, will require considerable additional manpower. Here it can be considered whether a modern collective farm or co-operative farm with the use of machinery will be feasible. The pace of development of such a farm economy, however, should depend on the pace with which the concerned village communities can be prepared to participate in it at semi-skilled levels with induction of minimum number in key positions from outside. Such a farm may not be an immediate feasibility but if it is planned to be established, say after five years, it may be possible to train up local youth in the relevant activity who can take up the semi-skilled positions in this cooperative venture.

In the context of the present socioeconomic situation, any intensive economic activity appeals to be ruled out for a decade or so. Even for taking up any such activity after 10 years, adequate preparation will have to be initiated right now. Therefore, a comprehensive assessment of resources may be made early to explore the possibilities, if any, of taking up modern activity in this area.

If certain clear indications are available, an element of greater certainty in respect of such programmes may be ensured so that a longer term manpower planning can be taken up right from now. This brings us to the second aspect of change, viz, the preparation of the recipient group to the new change. The policy of non-extension of normal administration to Abujhmar and keeping it rather closed, has helped in maintaining the status quo. But, on the other hand, the preparedness of the local community to enter a new stage of socioeconomic development also remains, more or less, the same as, say, some two or three decades back. Thus, if a faster change is to come about through other compulsive forces, a good opportunity of making the transition even slower is low.

The developmental programmes taken up in the last ten years have not been tailored to its special needs. Therefore, they have had a very limited and partial impact. So far as the preparedness of the local community is concerned, there has been greater contact with an extension agency which did not carry with it the authority of regulatory administration and, therefore, was not oppressive or unconcerned with the wishes of the local community.

Communication and education are also the necessary infrastructure, to varying degrees, for taking up the economic development programmes. There is one more distinguishing feature of these two inputs. While it may be possible to plan the change-process, to some extent both these elements tend to acquire an autonomous character and behave as independent variables having a big impact on the local community, which may not be all in the desired direction.

As the communication network and the level of development in the advanced regions appear to be co-related, their cause and effect relationship is taken to be established. The usual arguments for the communication network are how else agricultural inputs, benefits of agricultural extension services, health and educational services, etc., can be reached to these areas. The relationship, on the fact of it appears to be so obvious that arguments become convincing. Having once conceded a high priority, a pre-condition for any developmental effort, financial resources are made available on a liberal scale resulting in large capital investments in roads development programmes.

If communication network is an essential infrastructure, it must support substantive economic activity and only then substantial outlay on it can be justified. The economic benefit from a road-network may be immediate and/or in the long-run and may be directly relatable to the local community and/or to the larger economy. Road construction, itself generates employment and a substantial part of investment on it is in the form of wages. Even, after the construction phase, a road-network requires sizeable manpower for its maintenance. In sparsely populated areas even when there is low coverage, road-length per unit of population is very high. But, accrual of benefit to the local community in this direct employment is not automatic and depends on a number of other factors in the local economy.

Road is essentially an infra-structure which must serve other needs and justify itself. Therefore, we may identify clearly the other socioeconomic benefits with the development of this infrastructure. The most immediate benefit in this category can be in the marketing of agricultural and minor forest produce. There is net addition to the production and there is a direct benefit to the community which gets fuller employment in a traditional activity without any structural change.

Education is the most important element in harnessing the process of change to the advantage of local community. Educational element will need to be viewed in two different contexts. Each development programme will define its own 'capsule' of educational effort. But all these capsules put together may not be able to give an unambiguous picture. Therefore, a broader frame will be necessary so that the picture which emerges is meaningful. The terms 'easy comprehension,' 'meaning,' etc., cannot be taken to have fixed connotation. The content of these terms will change with the passage of time. The change in the beginning in absolute terms, will be small, but, in relative terms, it will be very large because the base line, from which the process is being initiated, is very low. These small changes will have to be carefully taken note of, particularly because the extension agency, which is used to deal with matters of a different dimension, may not be able to appreciate the delicate balance in the primitive tribal situation.

Therefore, extension education inputs will need constant review and a well-designed feedback system. Interactions of a small group are not limited to certain well-defined programmed activities only. There is an important autonomous sector of interactions whose influence may be decisive in some cases. The outside contact itself means bringing to these communities new ideas, new knowledge and new situations. New situations are very important. The group does not have any past experience to go by; therefore, its context is entirely different. Its responses, therefore, are not rational. The extension agency by its very presence initiates spread-effect. It is well-known that some information is easily assimilated while aspects completely alien are hard to grasp. Therefore, the community is to be consciously prepared to stand the challenges of the new contact; it should be enabled to understand the nature and processes in the larger society and should be provided the necessary and useful information.

An educational scheme, framed in one specific context, may leave large gaps in a different context. This problem is being faced generally in the rural-urban context—an urban elite oriented education bring super-imposed on the multitude of rural masses. The disharmony becomes much larger in the case of backward tribal groups.

It will be necessary that special syllabus both for general education and for the adolescent and adult age groups is prepared. The education will have to be intensive so that in the next 5 years or so the level of literacy is at least 10 per cent and every adult has been brought within the net of citizen education. The local institution of youth dormitory, which is the meeting point of all the youngmen every evening and the entire village community occasionally, can be effectively used for this purpose.

It is not necessary that a school may be opened in very village but 'shala complexes' can be developed which have within their jurisdiction a specified number of villages and who may be given the responsibility of effectively implementing the citizen education and general education programme.

DEVELOPMENT OF DANDAKARANYA TRIBALS

Tribals are the indigenous population with special socio-cultural traditions. The current problems faced by the tribals are depletion of forest resources due to over exploitation and lack of repletion of minor forest produce. At this stage it is necessary to supplement their income from sources other than those forest produce, on which the tribals have been traditionally dependent.

Action for Welfare and Awakening of Rural Environment (AWARE) is an internationally reputed organisation working for the past 22 years for upliftment of rural population with special attention to tribals, scheduled castes and other weaker sections, with an integrated rural development approach based on Gandhian approach of self-sustainable rural communities. It is a development organisation engaged in the systematic formulation of annual and medium term programmes through a process of bottom-up participatory planning, coordinated and consolidated with the help of AWARE's field staff and higher levels of the apex organisations.

Its programme combines an "access strategy", empowering target groups for the access to development infrastructures created by Government etc. with a "parallel" channelling financial and technical support from AWARE itself to its beneficiaries; so far, of these two strategies, the former has the most important one as in AWARE's philosophy public funds are people's funds and they help, guarantee sustainability of development.

Dandakaranya Tribal Development Programme includes security and fulfilment of the basic needs of life like, safe drinking water, shelter, higher literacy rates for adults and children, expansion of tree plantation area. It also targeted at the provision of irrigation facilities, guaranteed employment and accomplishment of Rs. 27,000 income per household per annum in the year 2001 AD, so as to push them above the poverty line. These programmes have been implemented during 1992 to 1996, causing a great degree of quantitative and qualitative change in the village. In 1992 AWARE adopted many villages in the Dandakaranya region covering both Andhra Pradesh and Orissa states. A benchmark statistical data base has been established on the beneficiaries in that year. The data cover the socio-economic factors such as—land utilisation, rearing of animals, utilisation of schemes, health and food habits, literacy, and political leadership qualities.

There are a higher percentage of landless households (24.8%) in non-AWARE villages than in AWARE villages (13.2%). A small percentage of AWARE households (22.6%) possess less than one acre of land while in non-AWARE villages this is 33.5%. Even though the median size of the land holding is about the same (about 2 acres in AWARE versus 1.9 acres in non-AWARE) there is a significant skewness in the data. A similar comparison between 1992 and 1996 indicates that there is an upward mobility in the possession of land by AWARE households in this period. First more land was brought under cultivation even though it may be dry land in the beginning.

There is a decrease in the percentage of households holding wet land even though the size of land held by them is substantially more, many of them are holding more than 4 acres of land. Due to the efforts made by AWARE more land was brought into the hold of tribals. In the beginning this is dry due to lack of irrigation facilities, later it will be converted into wet land. It will be seen as a progressive step in bringing more land into the hands of tribals and also providing irrigation facilities gradually.

The total income of the household consists of the following sources of income—land, milch animals, small business enterprises, rents from financial assets, and other alternative forms of resources. A large percentage of AWARE village households are possessing milch animals, stock animals, sheep and goat besides poultry. In support of schemes introduced by AWARE towards, animal rearing and milk production type of schemes.

Interestingly the expenditure pattern of the targeted population is also on the rise in the time period under consideration. The median level of expenditure of AWARE village households was Rs. 4300 in 1992 has gone up to

Rs. 8300 by 1996, which is still less than the median level of income received per household. It can be expected that over time, savings will be built up and reinvested to boost the income even higher. Between 1992 and 1996, as per the data is available, AWARE village households are venturing into milch animals, sheep and goat, business, and improved wage position, and creating financial assets. Some of their features for the improvement of AWARE village household living standards were multiple cropping techniques, application of technology like tractors, fertilisers, pesticides, HYV seeds, marketing techniques like avoiding the middle man and selling on their own at a higher price.

From the education point of view, at primary level as well as at higher levels, AWARE villages are doing remarkably better than non-AWARE households. AWARE village households are more careful in food preparation not only in the context of nutrition but at also in the context of hygiene and preparation habits. The availability and utilisation of medical facilities have improved in AWARE village households. They are using all types of medical practitioners, away from the traditional faith healers. In case of safe drinking water AWARE households are drawing water from safe sources like well and bore well.

The non-AWARE village households are still using the non-hygienic sources of water forms like, *kundi* and *chervu* (open water pond) which are in open areas shared by animals as well as humans. AWARE has also provided these water sources nearer to the living areas in many villages.

As a part of human resource development effort in villages, AWARE aimed at establishing Village Associations, Mahila Mandali, Balasangam, and Youth Association. These associations helped to improve or solve problems related to agriculture crops, irrigation, health centres, schools and other infrastructural activities. Besides institution building, training constitutes the other important component of the human resources development through which AWARE wants to empower people. Training camps are organised and besides development problems issues relating to the economic and social aspects of the village life were discussed at these camps.

It is the philosophy of AWARE that to make development a people's movement, they must recognise their strength and establish their own leadership. Mahasabha—mass rallys, are considered as a symbol of demonstration of the strength of the poor. The study indicates that there was cent percent participation of the people in the Mahasabhas. They discuss, besides development schemes and programmes, a number of economic and social issues relating to education, untouchability, political association, awareness, equality, unity and reservation.

The awareness and other development programmes implemented by the Development Service Societies, with the support of AWARE aimed at improving the living conditions of people. Seventeen out of 21 Sarpanches indicated that there was significant difference in terms of better living conditions, better awareness of political and social issues, and their overall development. In non-AWARE villages 50-70 percent of the families continued to be below poverty line, as expressed by half of the Sarpanches. These villages are facing illiteracy, lower wages, bonded labour, lack of basic amenities including health services, harassment and atrocities on women.

The people in the villages generally come in contact with various individuals and institutions to deal with the problems, such as politicians, police, landlords, panchayat raj institutions and government departments. According to the opinion expressed by 69 per cent of the Village Association presidents in AWARE village households were able to deal with these problems effectively than non-AWARE village households. There is a significant improvement in health services in terms of accessibility to train mid-wife and village health workers.

Socio-economic profile of the respondents is a valuable key to understand the dynamics of the society. The social, political and educational attainments of a person shapes his/her personality. Moreover it also determines one's role as a political participant. In non-AWARE villages, wage rates, alcohol, illiteracy, bonded labour, untouchability, lack of basic village amenities, land conflicts, lack of funds for development seem to be some of the important problems that the villages are facing with. In AWARE villages these problems are of less importance due to the leadership and perception of problem. AWARE village households are more articulative and comprehend ground realities of a village life.

AWARE insists on access, control, and benefit to various resources to women. In this case the response was not too high but majority of women belonging to AWARE villages have access and control as well as benefits from the resources like—land, loan, health, education, and crops. This type of involvement for women in non-AWARE village households seem to be very negligible. In general, men belonging to AWARE villages are more helpful to their wives than their counterparts in non-AWARE villages.

The basic education for girl child is one of the important national level objectives as well as AWARE's target. Nearly 95 per cent of the women in AWARE villages want their girl child to be educated as compared to 286/6 in the non AWARE villages. AWARE efforts to bring a change in the attitude towards a girl child has given the desired results. These women of AWARE villages are ambitious and expect their daughters to be in a good position like teachers, government officials, doctors etc. The women belonging to non-AWARE villages could not express at all.

Participation in election is an important device in a democracy. The activity level of participation in the election by the people also shows their awareness about socio-economic and political factors. The survey identified that women in AWARE are having higher participation when compared with non-AWARE village women. This is an overall trend where women are exercising their voting rights more now than before. It also indicates that they are voting on their own decision. Savings schemes are the backbone of development of a society as well as the nation. AWARE is playing a significant role in this regard. Savings by women are of more importance. Over 60 per cent of AWARE families respond in savings schemes. There is no such saving scheme in non-AWARE villages.

In forming a concerted effort to mobilise women, Mahila Mandalis plays an important role. They meet more frequently based on the concerned issues, conduct training camps to discuss nutrition aspects, population, education, use of local resources. It is important to note that the mahila mandalis are taking an active role in awareness regarding their development in all aspects. It has been pointed out that the training camps have improved their development activities. There is a reduction in the gender disparities. Promoted child education, elimination of alcoholism, concern over unwed mothers is negligible.

In cases of trouble or conflict, they make them sit together and solve the problem. In some instances, they caution them and even impose fine on them. This is a healthy tradition to solve the issue amicably. The Mahila Mandali members also meet with other associations like Youth Associations, Village Association and offer some help. Mahila Mandalis take up the issue of voting at the time of political activities. Women contest for the position limited to village panchayats and the elected women mostly focus upon the important social issues such as drinking water, drainage facilities etc.

Women participation is an indispensable component in socioeconomic and political life. Particularly the women empowerment is the strategy of AWARE. The strength of women in AWARE villages is derived particularly from connecting with other women through their own medium of Mahila Mandali. Substantial impact of AWARE was felt in the life of women on the issues such as enhancement of leadership qualities, awareness about economic and financial developmental activities including changes in their life with the knowledge of education.

Through various programmes undertaken by AWARE—land utilisation, different income generating sources, social programmes, political activities for leadership, formation of Village Associations, Mahila Mandalis, Youth Associations—a sustainable socio-economic development is possible. The important contribution of this investigation is the role of women in the society by having access, control and benefits from the household resources.

DEVELOPMENT OF MARIA TRIBES

The Maria are first mentioned by Glasfurd in the western part of the Abujmar mountains and called the tribe who were settling there 'Marees'. Maria means merely man of the woods. With 70.82 per cent the Maria have together with their subgroups the Kammri and the Zarya the greatest share of the population. Kammri and Zarya are subgroups which came into being because of their professional specialisation that is of smiths and fisherfolk. The more significant separation of these two subgroups from the Maria took place only during the last decades and can be interpreted as a consequence of the increasing contact with outside cultures. From 18th century up to now, ethnical minorities immigrated into the territory settled by Marias. Within these minorities the Gond and the Pardhan were the first to become resident here. The Gowari and the Kummal followed. About 1900 the Teli entered this area. They were actually the first real alien element which effected a change of culture in the settling area of the Bhamragarh-Maria that had been up to this time an almost homogeneous territory.

This area in the beginning of the 15th century has seen the invasion of fleeing Chalukyas from Warangal. The fort on the Morameta mountain is a relic from this period, which proves that this breaking of the Chalukyas who were fleeing the Muslim invaders, produced a retreat of the resident owners of the territory. And it was these retreating owners of the territory, who settled then on the Morameta mountain. The second historical invasion took place as a consequence of the conquest of the Chanda-Gond Empire by the Marathas in 1751, which produced a retreat of the Gond into the Bhamragarh area.

A higher quality of life exists in the alluvial plains, as well as it may be interpreted as an economically conditioned east-west migratory tendency from the mountain area into the plains. The share of the small settlements is dominating. Most of these settlements are semipermanent ones. They are a proof of the highly dynamic element, which is one of the characteristics of the population of the

Bhamragarh-Patti. Religious ideas stamp the kind of organisation of the population, which can be called a clan-society. Clan is a social group which is unilateral and exogamous, whose members regard each other as relatives because of their common, mythically founded descent from a specific ancestor or another being. It consists of a number of families, and, therefore, every family that belongs to one of the different clans, shall be counted under the name clan-family.

We call a society a 'clan society' when it consists of different population-groupings, when it has unilateral clans and when its common characteristics are the veneration of a certain number of gods. The veneration of the clan gods is not always the same. There are two different forms of veneration: on one hand there exists the veneration of an individual god and on the other the veneration of a god-family. Both forms are inextricably interwoven, as the individual god always belongs to the god-family which is venerated by the clan. The individual god is only revalued in comparison to the other members of the god-family, because of the particular relation of this god to the village, that is mostly when his residence lies not far away from this certain village.

In the Bhamragarh area, the clan exists in two variations such as a clan with a clan-territory and a clan without such a territory.

If one regards at first the clans with clan-territories, one can find so many different clan-territories which have to be differentiated in real and unreal clan-territories and collecting and hunting areas. Real clan-territories are those territories where the head of the family which settled first in this place took, together with his relatives, possession of the land and established the stone of possession, as a sign of his new property. Because of the mobility, economically conditioned relatives of the same clan as well as people of another clan followed and settled on the new land. This happened especially then to the relatives of the same clan, when the population in the clan-territory increased so much that their land offered not enough space for them. But, nevertheless, they orient themselves according to the existing religious centre of the clan which was already settling there.

The second form of the clan area is the form of the unreal clan-territory. This is an area which is occupied by several clans, sometimes simultaneously, sometimes successively.

A third form of the clan-territory may be called a roving area, which corresponds to the way of living of the temporary settlers. This form is also a real clan-territory, but, nevertheless, there are changes in the clan-dominances which result from their specific economy in connection with the particularly high degree of mobility of the population of this area.

From the analysis of clan-territories it has become clear that the four-god-group which originally settled in the northern part of the Bhamragarh Patti, the five-god-group which lived in the central area, the six-god-group from the south and also the seven-god-group. In former times the territory of god-groups consisted of the settling area of a Patti. From this we can very well recognize that the god-group was the earliest form of organization of the Maria tribe.

Human beings are interested in the participation of the goods and values of a strange culture, as soon as there are communicative structures which are valid for all cultures. Traditional ways of thinking incorporating the spiritual values in a healthy tribal culture, are handed down by oral transmission in the form of myths. At the same time these myths point, in their content, to norms on which the social positions in the tribe are based. Cultural change means nothing else but the fact that strange mechanisms influence this circulation of reorientation in the transmitted ways of thinking by newly emerging cultural patterns.

The social anthropologists have to start a specialist examination of the spiritual values. They should be firm in their minds to preserve the old system of their common work. Otherwise the social unity of the community will be lost and the ensuing decay of the social structures would be accompanied by a loss of the transmitted ways of thinking. This process has already begun in the western area of the

Bhamragarh-Patti. The consequences are the following: spiritual impoverishment caused by a lack of reflection—a consequence of their doubts in their traditions which have set in and which are accompanied by the lack of self-examination by which a culture shock can arise. It may be a shock which might lead to a total dissolution of the existing structure and hence the destruction of this culture. We have to take measures in order to oppose such development and to aim at the preservation of the spiritual culture which is the very essence of their social values, and at the creation of a special mechanism of conduct: i) in a culture-transmitting institution ii) in a technical consulting institution.

Institutions which transmit culture must do so by word of mouth as well as through the written word and can thus create a base for a stable tribal identity. The signs are hopeful for, on the one hand, the age-grouping structure is wide at the base; on the other hand, there exists no better influential unit than the 60.2 per cent inhabitants of the large numbers of villages. The family structure with its enlarged nuclear families and an average size of 5.44 is a culture supporting element. The Maria element dominates even when the density of the population and the map of the tribes show that at those centralized points one can already find a diversity of tribes.

Social anthropologists have become familiar with the system of values of the Maria-culture. That includes also the learning of their language and very intensive studies of their culture. The spiritual leaders must be convinced that they are the very persons to disseminate the way of thinking of their tribe. One has to introduce a script for the tribal language which should emerge out of their own culture. From this a tribal literature should develop which will reflect their culture and traditions while at the same time it should help in communication with people outside.

The technical consulting institution should consist persons with a training in social anthropology. They should be able to attain a more intensified production in the economic field. An individual identity and a sound economy evokes a new religious awareness among the people.

8

Tribal Identity

There are distinct tribal differences to be met with among primitive peoples and that one element in tribal solidarity is the sense of strong physical similarity and resentment of, or hostility towards, those of different physique or appearance. This is even now the most powerful element in the racial strife from which the world still suffers. Yet it is also true that tribes are often simply local subdivision of a larger people, or folk-groups, also all physically alike, and that an infinite variety of relations may come into being among that group of people.

The social life of the whole people may be patterned, for instance, upon the most elaborate totemic system, deriving its authority from the same religious or priestly background, transcending the tribe, in which case intermarriage on a wide scale may not simply be tolerated but openly encouraged as necessary to the tribal health and to the economic well-being of a whole region. On the other hand peoples of the same breed or race, and, therefore, of the same physical appearance, divided into tribes which are mutually exclusive and even normally at war, and in which from time to time a pattern of relationships will arise in which the victorious tribe will dominate others in a fashion which we can describe as imperialist. When that imperialism involves intermarriage with the conquered, then obviously the tribal gene has been told to go and hang itself.

In human society it is the parts which bring the society into existence for their purposes. They maintain it, modify it, transform it, even abolish it if it fails to suit their needs.

Human history is full of examples of how men have survived the destruction of their most cherished institutions and political forms, and gone on biologically functioning nevertheless.

If man has a natural community in the animal sense, it is the family, or the loose horde or band into which a family might easily develop. There is perhaps every reason why that horde should remain together even after the infant members of the original family have attained maturity. The natural gregariousness of man would explain the desirability though not the economic practicability of this loose association. What is impossible to conceive in purely natural terms is why such a family, or group of families, or horde of like beings should ever develop the structured society which we recognise as a tribe, exercising a firm but invisible discipline over its members, even over those members who have passed puberty and are by nature, therefore, fully equipped to go off and found independent families of their own.

For Hobbes and Locke and Rousseau, man in a state of nature was free and sovereign. He was under no man's rule, and subject to no tribe's tyranny. And the atomisation of primitive mankind in this way was to them such an inescapable human birthright that the real difficulty was to show why man ever surrendered his animal freedom and gave to society that dangerous sovereignty over his life and liberty which had once been his private gift from God and which society anyway so often and so openly abused. These thinkers disagreed as to the nature of the inducements which caused man to surrender his liberty, but they were at one in describing society as an artificial contrivance of man, and not as the given basis of man's humanity.

No known tribe is satisfied simply with the distinction which its private pattern of genes awards it. The natural physique is not enough, and every human group seeks its own style to enhance or transform its original endowments. The artificial decorations may be wood or paint or clothes, headdresses, armbands, necklaces, girdles, weapons and the other endless contrivances of humanity for the better display of their own bodies; or they may be cosmetic activities.

The initiation rites of the northern tribes of Central Australia for boys are very strange. These are not the only initiation ceremonies of these tribes. Some of the coastal tribes practise the knocking out of one or more of the upper incisor teeth. The youths who had arrived at the age of puberty were taken away and isolated by the old men of the tribe, and subjected to rude buffets and tests. Blows were aimed at them, or food kept from them, or they were set to climb, or fell large trees, or to swim in crocodile-infested rivers, and to endure these humiliations and dangers without grumbling. Only at the end when this initiation was safely accomplished, were the youths shown the tribal bull-roarer, whose voice, women believed to be that of a spirit which came down from the sky and took the youths away into the bush from which they were to return initiated men.

Among Urunna tribe, when the time has come for the boy's initiation, his paternal grandfather seizes hold of him and after some ceremonies before the women which are meant to mark him as an initiate, he goes upon a journey with his mentor, rather like a *chela* with his *guru*, visiting different groups and inviting them to the ceremony. Upon this journey the persons of the boys and his guardian are sacred and may not be attacked by fellow tribesmen. Upon their return there follow several nights of ceremonies before the boy is finally circumcised by the elderly male relatives tradition assigns to the task. He is taken away into the bush and kept *incommunicado* until he has recovered, and then brought back and immediately, with as much ceremony, sub-incised. When this is over, he is shown, on the same night, more sacred totemic ceremonies, and the elderly male relatives who have supervised the initiation tell him that he is now a man and not a boy. He must not attempt intercourse with *lubras* other than his lawful wives, and he is not on any account to interfere with the *lubras* belonging to other men. If he breaks the taboos he will fall down dead like the stories.

Tribal ceremonies are of infinite complication, but in the main what is common in them all is that the boy is taken away from the women's camp in a ceremonial fashion which marks the end of his childhood, he is shown to those tribal groups which should attend the ceremony, he is brought back to sacred grounds normally taboo to women, and there ceremonies are endlessly performed within his hearing though not always within his sight. The dances and ceremonial plays and displays may go on for several days, before the dazed child is circumcised: the moment when this will occur is normally hidden from him, and he cannot know what to expect, save that he may be put to death and brought to life again by the tribal or totemic spirit, as the women will have warned him. The initiation may include mock attacks on him with spears, but as no initiate ever reveals to those younger what he passed through, he does not know that one of those spears will not presently pierce him. When the ceremony is over, and only then, his sacred totem or totem sign will be revealed to him, and it is made known that he is now a man and can sit with the men and take a wife.

Many primitive groups practise circumcision of males at or near puberty as a sign of virility, and of acceptance into the tribal maleness. It is the uncircumcised boy who is jeered at as a woman, and made the object of general mockery. In African tribes, it is the uncircumcised one who is the irresponsible one, free to break tribal taboos, defiance of which would strike his elders down dead.

Many of the tribal ceremonies of initiation encounter a psychological resistance: the more painful they are, the greater the reluctance of the initiates to face them, and the greater, the suffering of the parents and other adults at the pain they have to inflict. All such acts of mutilation have to take place against emotional shrinking: indeed much of their value arises out of the general resistance which has to be overcome. The ritual heightening of the ceremonies of initiation has precisely the intention of making the whole event tribally memorable and spiritually significant. Long preparatory rites and ceremonies and elaborate dances produce exaltation in initiates and participants alike. They launch the whole tribe or village or clan into a spiritual glissade which gathers momentum, and of which the climax is the painful mutilation of the young. And once launched upon the ceremonial cycle, it presently becomes inconceivable that the whole drama should not mount to its great climax.

One tribe may permit action forbidden in another, or eat foods taboo in another, or worship as friendly gods which others regard as hostile: there is no aggressive intent in these practices. They simply represent in their totality a different but equally valid pattern of life. The element of cultural aggression enters when one tribe or people discovers that another commits things on which it has set the seal of its disapproval. A conflict may result in which the ways and ideas of one tribe penetrate peacefully the life of another. On the other hand the penetration may be understood as a threat to tribal unity and resisted by war.

The elaborately structured tribal society gives birth to an immemorial pattern of settling these issues before they can destroy the people. Custom decides all, and the tribal leadership lies with those who have the right to decide wherein, in matters under dispute, the true path of custom lies—with those who have the greatest experience, in fact—the tribal elders.

9

Policies for Tribals

Tribals are among the weakest sections of the Indian society. The failure of the state apparatus to protect the livelihood and culture of the tribals led to the growth of voluntarism in many tribal areas. These voluntary and essentially non-governmental initiatives gradually started contributing to some of the important aspects of tribal life, for example tribal education, health, social development, nutrition, women and child-care etc.

In the past two decades, because of their participant observer position and having gained critical understanding of issues linked to tribal life, these voluntary groups and individuals received recognition from the state. Their tremendous impact can be judged from the fact that increasingly the state is looking, towards them and soliciting their help in policy formulations. The past two decades saw voluntary groups and individuals coming together and getting actively involved in policy formulations on forests, wildlife displacement, rehabilitation and resettlement and likes.

Their orientation has been to project a pro-people policy as an alternative to the state policies. Their concern for the holistic development of the tribes in India initiated them in recent years to work on a National Tribal Policy Project. It is problematic to identify the elements of an alternative paradigm for tribal development. Much of the understanding presented herein are based on a definite pro-people perspective and framework advocated in voluntarism.

The tribals remain marginalised in spite of the Constitution providing for a comprehensive framework for their socioeconomic development. Eight states have tribal areas which have been declared Scheduled Areas under the 5th Schedule of the Constitution, which imposes a special responsibility for peace and good government of these areas. It empowers the Governor of the state to formulate necessary regulations and the Central Government to direct the State Governments for proper administration of these areas.

Laws have been framed to prohibit or restrict transfer of land by or among members of Scheduled Tribes (STs), regulate allotment of land to members of such tribes and to regulate the business of money lending in the tribal areas. Looking beyond the problem of exploitation, Article 46 of the Constitution requires the State to promote with special care for their educational and economic interests. Articles 330, 332 and 334 provide for their representation in the legislative bodies, while Article 335 calls for reservation of seats for tribals in matters of recruitment.

The tribal development component has regularly been emphasised in the Five Year Plans besides the specific Tribal Sub-Plans. Both retributive and restitutive arrangements are made available to the tribals by the Constitution.

Most policies that are in force today focus on particular issues and were formulated according to needs that arose at different points of time. Comparative studies illustrate that many are incongruent and contradict each other on principles and content. Therefore, rather than aiding the process of amelioration of the tribals problems, they have created new problems for them. The State's contribution to their socioeconomic development is based on the understanding that the axis of tribal development is their ultimate integration in the mainstream of national life.

The frame of reference for the analysis of tribal life in India has, therefore, been integration: both social and cultural. Most are critical of this approach and see in it an attempt to integrate the tribals into the mainstream society as a low status group, even though traditionally they have lived in an egalitarian and unified society in which women have a fairly high status. This has tacitly legitimised vested mainstream interests to force the tribals into a relationship of the worst forms of exploitative dependence on the mainstream society.

The tribals resented the extension of British control and the intrusion of the colonial administration in their territory and many a time their resentment gave way to open rebellion. Most of them objected to the penetration of money-lenders, traders and revenue farmers who were the instruments of the British in bringing the tribals within the influence and control of colonial economy and exploitation. Today, the same process continues. It is therefore important to probe the question of the historical rights of the tribals in land and forests.

PANCHASHEEL POLICY

In 1958, when Prime Minister Jawaharlal Nehru announced the Panchasheel for tribal transformation, it was generally accepted to be the official viewpoint on the question of tribal development. The principles were understood as guidelines in the formulation of future policies. The Nehruvian Panchasheel was based on the hope that tribals should be allowed to develop along the lines of their own aspirations.

The Panchasheel policy includes:

i) People should develop along the lines of their own genius and we should avoid imposing anything on them. We should try to encourage in every way their own traditional arts and culture.

ii) Tribal rights on land and forests shall be respected.

iii) We should try to train and buildup a team of their own people to do the work of ministration and development. Some technical personnel from outside, will no doubt, be needed, specially in the beginning but we should avoid introducing too many outsiders into the tribal territory.

iv) We should not over administer these areas or overwhelm them with a multiplicity of schemes. We should rather work through their own social and cultural institutions.

v) We should judge results, not by statistics or the amount of money, spent, but by the quality of the human character that is evolved.

Finally, it pleaded that achievements should be judged not by statistics or the amount of money spent but by the quality of human character that has evolved.

It is estimated that the tribal communities comprise of over nine per cent of the total population of India. Tribals are minority communities in North Eastern parts of the country, About 80 per cent of the tribal population resides in these States. Several provisions for the protection of the interests of the tribal communities were made in the Constitution. While some of these provisions were for regions where tribal communities were the main group, many provisions were made for the tribal communities where they were in minority.

In their drive for the rapid economic development the Union and the State Governments initiated several mega-projects, many of which were located in tribal areas. Two of the big iron and steel plants at Bhilai and Rourkela are located in the tribal areas. This was also true of the hydroelectricity and the irrigation projects. This led to the massive displacement of the tribal population. So far, more than 10 million members of the Scheduled Tribes have been displaced by these projects. The displaced persons were never properly rehabilitated.

Development of transport and communications opened up avenues in the tribal areas to the outside non-tribal traders. Increasing the land hunger due to the high prices for agricultural products induced non-tribal farming communities to move into tribal areas. This led to an unprecedented alienation of the cultivable lands owned by the tribal households. Rapid deforestation also affected the tribal communities adversely by depriving them of their main sources of livelihood like food, fodder, small games, timber for the construction of the huts and for the manufacturing of the agricultural tools.

Thus, the Panchasheel Policy remained mainly on paper. Aware of the plight of the tribal communities, the Union and the State Governments made several plans for the tribal development.

On the contrary, the actual principles on which later tribal development policies were formulated and worked were just the opposite on all counts. Tribals were subjected to all forms of exploitation and the state, through its policies, rather than curbing this tendency implicitly abetted such exploitation. Instead of allowing them to develop on the lines of their own genius, the state continued and still continues with the process of opening schools and colleges in tribal areas which impart education in languages which are alien to them.

Rather than safeguarding their rights on land and forest, state legislations continue to project them as encroachers and potential destroyers of forests and thus demand their physical relocation. In the name of national development their territories are increasingly being opened to outsiders. Irrigation schemes, industrial mining and forest based industries etc., are allowed to prosper in large numbers, that too without the consent of the tribals. Today, the state boasts of having a special law on tribal self-rule.

THE FIVE-YEAR PLANS

The Planning Commission is entrusted with the task of laying down the objectives and strategy of tribal development from time to time. It evolved the concepts of sectoral, integrated and area development. Its most popular product the Tribal Sub-Plan (TSP) is rested on three parameters: i) recognition of the existence of great ideal of variation in the economic, social and cultural milieu among the different tribal communities; ii) demographic concentration in parts of some states and dispersal in others; iii) primitive tribal communities lived in secluded regions. The TSP took note of the level of development and pattern of distribution of the tribals. It envisaged Large-sized Multi-Purpose Cooperative Societies (LAMPS) to save the tribals from the clutches of moneylenders by buying back their farm and forest produce; by marketing the consumer goods available to them at reasonable or at controlled prices and, by offering them production and consumption credit at reasonable rates of interests.

The first three Five-Year Plans (FYPs) were based on the premise that socioeconomic development of the tribals was general goal and could be achieved through the implementation of sectoral programmes, implying no special concern for tribal development. The 5th FYP for the first time introduced definite programmes of action for tribal development, but then it did not look beyond economic development and thus made little social impact.

The 5th Plan introduced the Tribal Sub-Plan (TSP) strategy based on the twin objectives of socioeconomic development of the STs and to protect them against exploitation. The TSP continues to remain the cornerstone of tribal development even though it only partially fulfils the aspirations of the Panchasheel.

A wide variety of schemes under five heads, namely, education, economic development, health, housing and other allied schemes, relief and rehabilitation and development of communication evolved from the TSP. The financial allocations for tribal development in the FYPs is incongruent to their population and socioeconomic situation. The first FYP allocated 1 per cent of outlay (Rs. 19.93 crores out of 1960 crores) to tribal development programmes. In the 2nd FYP the allocation was 0.91 per cent. (Rs. 42.92 crores out of 4672 crores) of the total and it was further reduced to 0.6 per cent in the third FYP (Rs. 50.51 crores out of 8577 crores). The Annual plan of 1966-67 also provided 0.6 per cent of the total expenditure (Rs. 32.32 crores out of Rs. 6756 crores). The same was reduced to 0.5 per cent (Rs. 75 crores out of Rs. 15902 crores) during the fourth plan. But it increased to 3.01 per cent (Rs. 1182 crores out of Rs. 39,322 crores) in the fifth plan period. Manifold increase in the budget for tribal development was made in the seventh (1980-85), eighth and ninth Plan periods. However, the actual utilisation of Plan allocated funds has never been more than 80 per cent.

NEW ECONOMIC POLICY

The basic principles of the new economic policy of

liberalisation, globalisation and marketisation blurred the national boundaries. However, it is not noticed is that they seek to blur even the social and the community boundaries. In their zeal for industrialisation, modernisation and marketisation the governments world over are trying to relax the reservations and the protective provisions for indigenous communities.

Impacts of modernisation on the tribal communities is through the processes of land alienation, displacement and deprivation of the control and the use of natural resources.

Tribal land alienation started in India with the development of railways, the establishments of the land records and the growing market for the agricultural products. This began by about 1860 after the British rule was firmly established in India.

The dominant agricultural communities from Gujarat entered the tribal area of Dhule district and took possession of their agricultural lands mainly through force and fraud. By 1975, the State Government tried to prohibit further land alienation and even to restore the already alienated lands. Several states also passed similar laws.

With the adoption of the new Economic Policy, the governments are gradually removing the restrictions on the alienation of lands occupied by the *adivasis*. Till the advent of the new Economic Policy the lands were mainly taken away by the states for different projects. After 1990, it is the private industries and enterprises that are taking hold of the tribal lands by offering high prices. The governments lack the political will to check this and the process of tribal land alienation has accelerated.

Tribal communities have lost more than a million hectares of land for the construction of dams, hydroelectricity and other projects. A preliminary estimate states that from 1951 to 1985 about 14.5 million persons have been displaced due to the mines, dams, industries and wildlife sanctuaries. The estimate was revised upwards to 2.13 million persons from 1951 to 1990. The estimate is restricted to rural displacement.

The process of economic development is gradually usurping the natural resources of water, land and trees vital for the subsistence of the tribal communities.

The construction of large dams or the supply of water to the industries, urban centres and agriculture were started by British. A number of projects were started for the supply of water to the cities. Many of these are located in tribal areas. The schemes contain no provisions for the supply of water to the villagers. For example, all the projects to supply water to the city of Bombay are located in the tribal area of the Thane district. New techniques have encouraged the harvesting of the ground water. Shallow surface wells in the tribal areas are drying up due to tube wells by the non-tribal big farmers.

It was earlier due to the acquisition of lands for the public sector projects like irrigation dams, hydroelectricity projects and the iron and steel complexes. From the beginnings of 1990's the tribal land is being purchased by private enterprises. At present, national parks and wildlife sanctuaries have become a major cause for the deprivation of tribal lands and the displacement of the tribals.

Tribals depend upon forests for several basic needs like fuel, fodder, etc., for houses and agricultural implements. They also get a major part of their cash income from the collection and sale of non-wood forest produce like tender leaves, grass, seeds gums etc. It is estimated that the forests provide for about 30 million persons, year's employment for the collection of non-wood forest produce and there is further scope to increase this to 40 million per year. Rapid deforestation is depriving these communities of the means of livelyhood and also cash income. It is reported in the Forest Survey of India that the dense forests, the real forests with a crown density of over 40 per cent, have decreased by nearly 18,000 square kilometres since 1995. It is also stated that about 66 per cent of the total forest cover lies in tribal areas.

In the Melghat tehsil of Maharashtra 1000 deaths of children due to malnutrition have been reported during the last thee years. The Government of India has adopted a new forest policy resolution in 1988 stating that the principal aim of the forest policy must be to ensure environmental stability and maintenance of the ecological balance including atmospheric equilibrium which are vital for the sustenance of all life forms. It is also stated that the life of tribals and other poor people living within and near forests resolves around forests and the rights and concessions enjoyed by them should be fully protected. Six years after the adoption of the forest policy resolution, the Ministry of Environment and Forests prepared a draft bill to replace the old Indian Forest Act of 1927. Voluntary organisations all over the country have proposed several amendments to the draft and have proposed an alternative draft.

The need to have greater powers to Gram Panchayats in tribal areas was recognised in the 73rd Amendment of Indian Constitution and a special committee was appointed to suggest suitable provisions for the Panchayats in the Scheduled Areas. The Committee submitted its report on 17th January, 1995. Acting on the report the Parliament passed the Provisions of the Panchayats (Extension to the Scheduled Areas) Act, 1996. The Act made certain provisions to protect the rights of the panchayats in the Scheduled Areas for the development purposes. The Act empowered the Gram Sabhas to prevent alienation of land in the Scheduled Areas and to take appropriate action to restore any unlawfully alienated lands of the Scheduled Tribe. The Act also gave the Panchayats, rights over the forest produce and planning and management of minor water bodies. The Act laid down that every Gram Sabha shall be competent to safeguard and preserve the traditions and customs of the people, their cultural identity, community resources and the customary mode of dispute resolution.

It is to be seen how far the provisions help the tribal communities to retain these rights over the natural resources and prevent their ususrpation by vested interests. On the one hand, natural resources providing subsistence to tribal and other forest dwelling communities are being appropriated in the process of economic development; on the other hand the governments are making some provisions to retain the control of these communities over the natural resources in the areas under their jurisdiction.

The process of economic development did not benefit all the people but actually harmed some people particularly those at the lowest rung. The World Bank published a special manual titled "Tribal and Economic Development—Human Ecological Considerations". It was pointed out that approximately 200 million tribal people, roughly four per cent of the global population and who were among the poorest of the poor, were adversely affected by some development projects.

INTERNATIONAL TRENDS

Tribals deserve special consideration under World Bank Projects, both to ensure that they will benefit, though in the longer run from projects presently financed and that they will not be affected negatively by development projects. It is not the Bank's policy to prevent the development of the areas presently occupied by the tribal people. However, the bank will assist projects within areas used or occupied by such people only if it is satisfied the best efforts have been made to obtain voluntary, full and conscious agreement of the tribal people or that of their advocates and that the project design and implementation strategy are appropriate to meet the special needs and wishes of such people. It was further stated that certain basic needs must be acknowledged and accommodated if tribal groups are to benefit from development projects. These fundamental needs are equally important and each must be met for continued physical, socioeconomic and cultural survival in the face of development.

The 'Operational Directive' published in September 1991 categorically stated that the Bank's objective and policy was towards the indigenous people, as for all the people in its member countries, is to ensure that the development process fosters full respect for the dignity, human rights, and cultural uniqueness. More specifically, the objective at the centre of this directive is to ensure that the indigenous peoples do not suffer adverse effects during the development process, particularly from Bank-financed projects and that they receive culturally compatible social and economic benefits. Following these directives the World bank appointed a Special Commission to enquire into the effects of the construction of the Narmada Dam in the tribal communities in India and took the decision to stop the aid to the project. The guidelines issued from time to time on the development of the tribal communities and the need to take special care of their vulnerable position in the economy can be used to formulate a proper policy for tribal development.

The Commission on Human Rights appointed a special working group on the indigenous populations to lay out their rights. After a period of 10 years and after several meetings with the representatives of the indigenous people, the Working Group has formulated it draft declaration on the rights of the indigenous people. The Government of India took a position at these meetings that the tribal people in India cannot be termed as indigenous. Even if this controversy is put aside, the standards in the draft declaration can also serve as guide to formulate a policy for the tribal communities in India. One of the articles in the draft declaration states that the indigenous people have the right to adequate financial and technical assistance, from states through international cooperation to pursue freely their own political, economic, cultural and spiritual development and for the enjoyment of the rights contained in this declaration.

The International Labour Organisation (ILO) had adopted a convention on the indigenous and the tribal populations. This was later regarded as paternalistic and the representatives of the indigenous people demanded a revision. The ILO adopted a revised convention called "Convention Concerning Indigenous and Tribal Peoples in Independent Countries". The Convention applies to tribal peoples in independent countries whose social, cultural and economic conditions distinguish them from other sections of the national community, and whose status is regulated wholly or partially by their own customs or traditions or by special laws or regulations. And peoples in independent countries who are regarded as indigenous on account of their descent from the populations which inhabited the country, or a geographical region to which the country belongs, at the time of conquest or colonisation or the establishment of present state boundaries and who, irrespective of their legal status, retain some or all of their own social, economic, cultural and political institutions. The convention lays down the principles for a proper policy to protect and to further the interests of the tribal communities.

Any proper policy for tribal communities should ensure their survival, identity, and development.

Tribal communities are under threat mainly due to the erosion of subsistence base. These communities mostly practice subsistence cultivation and get a large part of their consumption basket without any cash payment. Due to deforestation and strict imposition of rules by the forest officials, it has become very difficult to collect these commodities. Many tribal households derive a major part of their cash income from the gathering and sale of non wood forest produce which includes tender leaves, gum, resins and a variety of grasses. With the development of transport and communications, tribal lands are no more inaccessible. These are being taken over by the governments, private enterprises and non-tribal households.

To ensure the survival of the tribal communities, it will be necessary to take massive programmes of afforestation, that would include trees like *mahua* and *sal* which give produce necessary for the survival of these households. It would be also necessary to see that alienation of lands occupied by tribal communities does not take place and adequate compensation is paid whenever such lands are taken over. In case of displacement on account of public sector projects, it is necessary to provide them alternate lands and sites for houses.

Indian Tribals have failed to evolve an All India General Tribal Identity as the tribes are divided into over 250 small and big tribes like Santals, Bhils and Gonds. Their members do emphasise the specific tribal identity. Assertion of self-identity depends mainly on the members of the tribes. What the government and others can do is not to destroy this identity. While reallocating the tribal hamlets, efforts must be made to give them a common place.

Development has affected tribal communities in two different and opposite ways. A number of projects like irrigation dams, hydroelectricity and roads have displaced tribal communities. Development of transport has also made it easier for the non-tribal communities to move to the tribal areas. Tribal communities have been adversely affected by displacement, alienation of lands and loss of control over natural resources providing subsistence base.

The development of infrastructure has also provided some opportunities to tribal communities. There is an improvement in the educational and health care facilities. To develop tribal communities they will have to give up subsistence cultivation and resort to improved agriculture practices. It will also be necessary to train tribal youths in different technical vocations. Efforts must be made to conserve and augment natural resources to eradicate the prevalent abject poverty. This has become possible due to the new legislation governing the Gram Panchayats in the tribal areas. The process of development is bound to go on and affect tribal communities. This will to some extent change the lifestyle of tribal households. However, culture extends beyond the dress and consumption basket of a community. The essence of tribal culture is the belief in the continuity of life, affection and regard for nature and the innate optimism.

Tribal areas have been experiencing massive natural resource exploitation and concomitant industrialisation and urbanisation since the past few decades. This dense concentration of population in a limited space qualitatively changes the nature of social interaction, outlook, world view, values, beliefs and cultural practices of the people. Scholars studying urbanism contend that, city life promotes plurality of lifestyles, a high degree of elitism in cultural life and dominance of the literal tradition of learning and skill in economic and cultural domains. Socially it is characterised by a predominance of conjugal families, faster pace of work pattern and time budgeting.

Urbanism promotes emergence of overlapping cultural and social enclaves based on region, religion, language etc., in which people interact at different levels of social and cultural contexts. Unlike in a village, a city does not show a congruence between physical and cultural levels of social intercourse. All these affect tribal social and economic systems. The contradiction between the tribal way of life and urbanism has implications for the tribals living in urban areas.

The Department of Culture prepared a draft paper on the National Cultural Policy in 1996. The draft recognises the need to develop strategies to sensitise people, especially the young, to creative expression in a framework of values accepted as those which enrich the quality of life. One of the important recommendations of the policy was preservation of folk and tribal cultural forms that are dying out or are being distorted.

The existing paradigm and its strategy needs rethinking. Many international conventions, covenants and policies, especially those that may have a bearing on the lives of the tribals, have changed radically in the past few decades. The international community has arrived at new understandings and have developed consensus on older contentious ones. Though the state had declared certain progressive policies and statistically proved that output and incomes have gone up nevertheless the level of living or the tribes has deteriorated. This is also substantiated by different government and non-government reports on the socioeconomic situation of the tribals in the last few decades.

This decline in the level of living is generally attributed to the incongruity between the different issue-based policies on one hand, and the policies and practices on the other. In the name of development and resource exploitation large tracts of tribal territory have been taken over for use by non-tribals. Their social and cultural institutions attacked in the name of reforms intended to initiate them into the mainstream. Rather than facilitate the enhancement of their skills to take up the task of administration and development. The legal system refuses to recognise their customary rights over land and forests.

There is always a danger of confusing development with economic growth and economic development. Gunnar Myrdal, Schumpter, Amartya Sen and Paul Streeten cautioned against treating economics as a complete universe. Schumpter even went to the extent of saying that, we can either begin or end our causal explanations with economic factors but we cannot do both. Data show that our policy makers took this narrow view of equating development with economic growth. Dams, industries, mines and other symbols of economic development were built in large numbers in the tribal areas so as to magnify the economy of the country in general and the region in particular. The argument was that, tribals will be absorbed into these economic activities and thus their socioeconomic situation will automatically improve.

India took a fragmented approach to tribal development rather than a holistic one, and we were slack on the action or policy implementation front. The policies we started with were not implemented in their totality. Adhocism, piecemeal efforts and regional variance marked our approach to tribal development which at this point of history, needs to be rethought and rectified. This can only be achieved by evolving a National Tribal Policy (NTP) which will be in essence an integration of all the existing policies that may have a bearing on the tribals. Integration of different aspects of tribal social life into a meaningful whole and linking this whole to the national democratic structure should, therefore, be its point of departure.

The International Covenant on Economic, Social and Cultural Rights of 1976 mentions that all people for their own ends can freely dispose of their natural wealth and resources. In no case may a people be deprived of its own means of subsistence. Our development paradigm with its stress on industrial growth and Gross National Product (GNP) impugns this clause. Land and forest which have been the mainstay of the tribal subsistence economy have been usurped in the name of national development and environment protection. They are forced to move out of their traditional habitat because the rational-legal system recognises only the legal *pattas* and government notifications. It is, therefore, important to mend our legal system so as to broadbase our understanding to include the notions of customary and community rights.

The World Intellectual Property Organisation (WIPO) of the UN, which administers most international treaties on patents and intellectual property rights and the newly formed World Trade Organisation (WTO) are pressurising the government to reformulate its patent laws in the light of recent international agreements. It will ultimately result in the tribals being robbed of their knowledge and natural resources. Its impact on the tribals can be understood from the fact that, more than 70 per cent of the health care needs of the tribals are met by the use of biodiversity materials.

The Programme for Tribal Studies of the Indian Social Institute, New Delhi, organised a series of meetings of tribals, scholars and social activists in different parts of the country during 1996-97, in an attempt to sketch the substance of a National Tribal Policy. The main purpose was to generate a wider debate on major issues concerning the tribals. Themes like, tribal learning and pedagogy, land alienation, forests, rehabilitation, tribal women, customary law, malnutrition, health, self-rule etc., were debated at each of these meetings. In this context two aspects were seen as important. Firstly, the policy should touch all the major issues concerning the tribals in India and secondly, the tribal leaders who have come with this proposal have to be given all the support they deserve to ensure that the policy that may be formulated will be the result of reflection at the grassroots level and a genuinely collaborative exercise. Tribal problems require tribal solutions and this requires a paradigm shift in the very perception the perception based on cooperation in lieu of competition; convergence in lieu of conflict and holism in lieu of hedonism. This was the perspective in which the process was envisaged.

During the meetings it was clear that respect for tribal culture whose basis is sustainable development, conservation of the environment, egalitarian distribution of resources, respect for women and protection of their social systems and their rights over community resources has to be integral to any comprehensive policy on the tribals. This was because all those who participated believed that sociocultural federalism has been India's *sui generis*. At the initial meetings the deliberations were structured to two prime objectives: i) understanding the basis of the tribal policy along with the issues that need reflection and ii) discuss the contributions of non-tribals to the policy and the support that they can provide to this essentially tribal initiative. Discussion papers were prepared on diverse issues like tribal learning styles, tribal resources, intellectual property rights, tribal culture, tribal women etc. In order to make the process of reflection diverse and meaningful all irrespective of their social and intellectual position were requested to participate.

Regional differences, intra and inter-community disparities; and historical, social and economic relationships have to be understood and translated into workable policy components. The tribals are already involved in issue-based policy initiatives like the policies on the forest, rehabilitation and resettlement and land alienation. Some policies like the one on the question of tribal self-rule have already been prepared by the tribals. All this needs to be integrated.

With the onward march of rationality, aided by science and technology, scientific temper will displace religious values. But there is no evidence of science displacing religion. What happens is that certain aspects wrongly attributed to religion—myths, magic and superstitions—disappear challenged by science and technology. Religion necessarily undergoes a new definition, takes on new forms and meanings but does not disappear. However, mainstream evaluations of tribal religions refuse to accept the existence of similar adaptation mechanisms in them. They are labelled as primitive, animistic or superstitious and, therefore, require cleansing.

Because tribal identity is derived from their culture which in turn is a subset of tribal religion, attempts to alter it will adversely affect their identity. A corollary to the above mentioned process is linguism, which manifests itself in forms such as dislike for other languages and linguistic groups; claims of superior status of one language compared to others and imposition of one language on other social groups. The new national policy has to address these problems and contain mechanisms to negate the process of evolving monocultures so that tribal identity, culture and knowledge can prosper.

10

Bhils in Rajasthan

In the process of the implementation of tribal development programmes, the members of high castes get an opportunity to establish the hegemony of caste society over the tribal society. The historical prejudices between the two societies instead of becoming weak have got strengthened, particularly in the context of reservations. The Constitution has provided certain safeguards and securities to the weaker sections of the society, namely, Scheduled Tribes, Scheduled Castes and Socially and Educationally Backward Classes popularly called as OBC. The wider society as a matter of fact is stratified into two segments: caste society and tribal society. The relations between these two societies are historically structured.

The tribal society structurally is egalitarian. It consists of the institutions of clan and kin. Anthropologists all over the world analyse the tribal society as a web of kin and clan. The relations in this society are informal and close. The caste society on the other hand, is hierarchical, the Brahmins being at the apex and Dalit at the bottom rung. Though there are *gotra* and kins in the caste society their ranking is determined by the criteria of pollution and purity.

The basic difference between tribal and caste society is that of egalitarianism and hierarchy. The caste society is based on the values held by Hinduism. Caste and Hinduism are coterminous or synonyms. The tribal society on the other hand, at least today is not defined in terms of values belonging to a particular religion. It is held together by professing different religions. The forces which make it cohesive are ecosystems including hills and forests and physical isolation. Another force which has kept them united is that of history. They were the original settlers to this land. They shared the common sufferings inflicted on them by the non-tribal rulers, caste traders and exploiters.

Quite unlike the caste society, the tribal society has been organised into local divisions which the anthropologists call clan. The tribal society is different from the caste society in terms of its clan structure. Actually, the origin of clan among the Bhils goes back to the period when they resided in western India before the ascendency of Rajput power. The Bhils lived in small bands. Each band had its own clan. The leader of the clan provided protection to the clan member.

The Bhils consisted of a large number of localities, i.e., villages, each of which was under a hereditary Chief, *naik*. In this band there was no system of taxation, which would have enabled them to accumulate a large surplus and thus, set themselves apart physically from other fellows. The naik, i.e., the hereditary chief received occasional offerings from their Bhil fellows.

Whatever we get about is through their enemies, i.e., the Rajput rulers and their chronicles. It is because of this that we only learn about the war-like chiefs and their bands and know nothing about the agricultural practices of the Bhil peasantry. It is probable however, that these peasants lived in small scattered clearings in the forests, practising slash and bum cultivation, without the use of a plough, supplementing their agriculture with gathering from the forests as well as the occasional raids.

Normally each village is a particular clan village. The Bhils observe clan exogamy, and, therefore, they invariably have village exogamy. The rules of marriage, therefore, help the Bhils to maintain village and clan solidarity. Such an organisation of clan, kin and marriage provides characteristics to the Bhil society which distinguishes itself from the caste society. The Bhil society and for that matter, the tribal society is found in certain pockets. This also differentiates itself from the caste society. In some cases the caste society has such a broad spectrum that it covers a very large area of the country. When the anthropologists label the tribal society as kin-clan society they mean a society which has physical proximity. None of such specificities is found in the caste society. Being a kin-clan close society, the show of strength can be displayed without any loss of time.

The Bhil society attained its first social formation since the time when it had its rule over the former states of former south Rajasthan.

Before the invasion of Rajputs in eleventh century, the whole of eastern Gujarat, western Madhya Pradesh and southern Rajasthan were dominated by the Bhil chiefs. The social formations of the Bhil society which we find in their clan, kin and wider ethnicity have come in interaction with the caste society. This process of interaction has been analysed by Jan Breman as a process of 'colonisation of the Tribal Hinterland'. Before the onset of the process of colonisation the tribal society not only in south Rajasthan but in the whole of north-western part of the country was clan based.

The implementation of tribal development programmes through the agencies of several government departments and non-government organisations has given a refreshing agenda for tribal development. Tons of money has been spent on a variety of programmes, Whatever, assessment that we get about the progress made by the tribals very precisely shows that little development is visible among the people. Our hypothesis is that those who implement the programmes, that is, the government personnel and the social workers of the non-government organisations invariably belong to one or the other caste. When these workers or officials go to the field they carry away with their caste culture, caste hegemony and consciousness. They forget it that the tribals have been looking at them, historically as their antagonists.

The relations between a Bhil and a caste member are not the relations between two citizens. These are the relations between two members of tribal and caste society. The Bhils fail to forget the distressing fact that although the various periods of earlier history they have been exploited and oppressed by the ruling groups and the members of the high caste society.

11

Primitive Tribes

Many tribal communities are labelled primitive irrespective of manifold varieties which they present in their social organisations and cultural patterns. When we think of the term 'primitive', it means that whatever has preceded us is less advanced. Of course, it is true in many respects. But in many other respects the cultures of those whom we call primitive is more highly developed than are the civilised or advanced cultures. With the concept of primitive, the idea of statics is largely associated. It is taken that the societies and the cultures called primitive are almost in a state of equilibrium.

Change is ubiquitous in all human societies. But subject to the environmental conditions and psychosocial orientations, the rate of change is bound to vary from one society to the other. The rate of change in some communities which are isolated from the main stream of cultural change is slower than that in those communities which exposed to the cultural interchange with other peoples. The habitat also sets certain limits beyond which, it is not possible for the culture to develop unless radical changes are introduced from outside. All societies and cultures do not have the same or similar opportunities for rapid development. It is for these reasons largely that human societies differ from one another.

According to sociologists one of the consequences of considering some communities primitive is failure to think that they are capable of achievements. The more we learn to understand the primitive man, the better we understand ourselves. In the rapidly developing world in which we live, the so-called underdeveloped regions of the world will witness their most spectacular advances in the areas of human development. It is of the first order of importance that we the so-called civilised peoples of the world understand the various processes involved in the evolution of various stages of development and act upon these facts. In the new strategy for tribal development, it is appropriate to look critically at the term 'primitive' to consider both its meaning and its implications. The relevance of critical examination of the term primitive in the changing context of tribal societies is twofold.

The present day primitive societies are thought to resemble the early man remote in time in a number of significant respects, such as use of crude tools, hunting and gathering and slash-and bum-agriculture. They present least change in major aspects of their cultures. As physical organisms, the primitive people are contemporary with ourselves. They are in our time, but not of it, because they belong to another world, the world of the past. The concept primitive may have neither empirical validity nor theoretical utility and our use of this term is through mere force of habit and has been intellectually unproductive.

It is a sheer mistake to think of 'primitive' as opposed to civilised or advanced. Some small societies which are called primitive are endowed with highly sophisticated urban qualities. The kinship system of a highly complex industrialised society may be extremely simple but kinship system of a tribal community labelled as 'primitive' may be the most complex in the world.

The term 'primitive' is connected also with various shades of inferiority. We can without difficulty determine that some usages or items of a culture are more inferior than other items of usages in the same culture or in the other cultures. When we developed into more abstract aspects of culture, such as, religious system it becomes difficult to settle which items of that system is inferior and which superior. The primitiveness or otherwise of cultural traits comprising monotheism as against those associated with polytheism, is by no means easy to settle.

The psychological and political climate of the country today is just unfavourable to the continued application of the term primitive to any people who have been very much politically conscious and are all out for emotional integration with the rest of the nation. Today many of these once voiceless people have been articulative and have been participating in the elective political system as full-fledged members of the independent nation. Many people of their communities have emerged as political elites and have been increasingly taking their places as equals with their most powerful brothers in the political structure of the nation. In such a situation no one of the so-called primitive communities will regard with delight, the designation of 'primitive' as applied either to any aspect of their society or to their society as a whole no matter how scientifically the concept 'primitive' is defined.

Increasing industrialisation, nationalism and development of road communication are other major forces which work in bringing about rapid change among different sections of the country. Industrialisation and nationalism have been the two major goals which the people of the country want to achieve irrespective of their caste and creed. In this respect the superior characteristics of the primitive, are incompatible with modem developmental processes. Therefore, the glorification or the continued use of the concept 'primitive' will be a formidable barrier to progress.

Designating a society or culture as primitive and assuming the inferiority of the primitive on the standards of our own cultures and societies, suggest a kind of ethnocentrism which is detrimental to the progress of the nation. The anthropologists seem to show considerable unwillingness to use the term 'primitive'. But finding no alternative they continue to use the term 'primitive' in so many differing, unprecise, conflicting and meaningless ways.

Primitive societies usually rest on communist economic bases. Those material means essential to the survival of the individual or the group, are generally held in common. True private property does not exist among the primitives in the form of ornaments, tools, house, etc. But such items do not constitute the essential things for the survival of the group. These items which constitute private property can be readily duplicated and, therefore, need not be owned communally. However, the private property does not constitute primitive capitalism. Individuals also own incorporeal property such as songs, magic, spells, curing rituals, etc. But they are almost irrelevant to the communal economic base of the primitive community.

Economic exploitation of man by man as we see it in civilised societies, is conspicuous by its absence in primitive society. No man need go hungry while another eats; production is for use rather than for individual profit. Correlatively, there are no economic classes in a primitive society. No permanent group owns the means of production. Primitive economies are natural economies; they lack true money. Exchange among the primitives is usually effected by barter system.

In primitive societies major functions and roles of leadership are communal and traditional; not political or secular. The leaders of the primitive community are respected as embodiments of their cultural heritage. Obedience towards the leaders is a sign of respect for the tradition of the primitive society. The society operates through custom and by well-understood informal sanctions not by means of a legal apparatus, administered from above. This means that there are no codified laws in the primitive society. The consequence of conservatism and slow change is the lack of internal turbulence endemic in contemporary civilisation in which the technological advancement is most rapid.

Lack of institutional conflicts is another reason which is favourable to the primitive society to function as a system without much disruption. The primitive society is taken to be part of the natural order and it is sanctified by myth, revealed in ritual and buttressed by tradition. The social network is perceived as a more or less permanent arrangement of human beings vis-a-vis each other. Since the basic need for food, clothing, shelter and personal participation in various socioeconomic activities are satisfied in a natural manner and also in a socially non-exploitative process, revolutionary activity is hardly known in the primitive society.

Primitive societies lack economic diversification and the ordinary members of the society participate in all segments of their socioeconomic life. For example, the average Bonda male is an expert hunter, a craftsman who can make excellent bows and arrows and a direct participant in a variety of rituals and ceremonies. He is likely to be well-versed in the legends and tales concerning the origin and migration of his tribe. The major reason for this functional integration is that they control the processes of production; that is, the primitives manufacture their tools from the very beginning to the end and use them with skill and also possess them and control them.

The customary law recognised the freedom and independence of every member of the primitive society. At the same time all are bound up together socially, politically, economically and religiously by a system of mutual help. The fundamental reason for the holistic basis of primitive life is that it is organised on a kin hot on a political basis. The personalism is the most significant feature of the primitive life and extends from the family outward to the society at large.

The primitive society is a community, springing from common origin, composed of reciprocating persons and growing from within. It is not a collective; collectives emerge in advanced societies; they are functional to specialised ends and they generate a sense of being imposed from outside.

There is a great need for classification of human societies on the basis of cultural and societal parameters. Different kinds of descent, inheritance and succession may provide one basis for classification of human societies. Different gradation of economic practices and organisations also provide another basis for classification. Some societies have well-knit political organisations and others do not have such elaborate political organisations. Different societies have different political structures based on different patterns of leadership selected either by majority vote or by general consensus.

We can classify these societies on the basis of their political structure and leadership pattern. Language may also serve as a basis for classifying human societies. Some societies appear to be acquisitive, forward looking and materialists while other societies seem to be traditionally directed and conservative. The lifestyle of some communities is based on mutuality of obligation and reciprocity whereas that of other tribal communities is characterised by individualism and self-reliance. Such qualities of personality may provide scientific guideline for classifying them into discrete categories.

In the light of the above considerations we can classify of the tribal communities into (i) backward tribes, (ii) peasant tribes and (ii) semi-urbanised and industrialised tribes.

Backward tribes generally speak their own dialect. They live in partially isolated-pockets. They depend largely on shifting cultivation and forestry. They have less monetised economy and have low literacy percentage. They have organised political organisation with leaders of their own.

Peasant tribes largely depend on settled cultivation influenced by monetised economy. They live mixed with other castes/tribes. Their percentage of literacy is neither high nor low

Semi-urbanised and industrialised tribes depend on settled cultivation and wage earning from agricultural, mining, industrial and urban activities having largely modernised.

Culture is dynamic—all cultures, primitive or modern, Eastern or Western, peasant or industrial. The only completely static cultures are the dead ones. The difference between one culture and another, under the aspect of change, is that some cultures may change faster than others. While there may be more resistance in some, others may be more receptive to innovations. The effect of some innovations may change the face of the receiving culture beyond recognition. Some of such cultures may lose their, moorings, and be swept off their feet by factors contributing to the change. Changes may occur in certain aspects of culture only, while the fundamentals may remain intact.

All these phenomena of culture dynamics give important leads to investigation and study both from the theoretical points of view and from the angle of applied anthropology. The canvas of tribal culture is fast changing because of contact with alien peoples, and alien ways of life. The process has been continuing for a very long time; and with increased facilities for communication, the isolation of the tribal villages has been broken. In place of the simple life that the tribals are used to, a pattern of costlier living is developing. To a certain extent this is unavoidable because one cannot hold up industrialisation.

Constant living with non-tribal castes in villages, the growth of townships in the interior of the tribal regions, the increasing industrialisation of the area due to the wealth of its mineral resources, the work of various Christian missionaries as well as the growth of political consciousness—all these factors have brought about a great deal of change in the life of the tribes. Administrative authorities, forest officials, businessmen, contractors, and moneylenders have given further fillip to culture change.

All aspects of the life is touched by change, but it is proposed to leave out certain fields, like changes in the linguistic structure or vocabulary in folk songs and folk literature, in plastic arts, and in the technique of dance and song. From an analysis of the changes that may have occurred in the aforesaid sectors, the rate as well as the direction of change will emerge.

Sometimes, the changes may be so pervasive that a change in the basic personality structure may take place after which there may be further fillip to culture change. In spite of widespread changes which they have undergone, the tribals have still maintained their distinct identity. They have not suffered from loss of nerve, and their population is steadily increasing.

12

Social Stratification of Tribals

By and large the tribal social order, which is obvious from the very definition of tribe, was taken as homogeneous in contrast to caste heterogeneity. Such an assumption was even supported by a predominantly reported homogeneous character of tribal communities, more so when such communities were marked by an acute form of isolationism. But the study of stratified social order, which could always be reported among some of the tribes and which has assumed more prominent form under added acculturative influence, remained largely unattended. The social analysts have recognised the universality of stratification in human societies. They attribute it to diversity of functions which are required to be performed by diverse individuals for a smooth running of society and the connected ways of life thereof. Since different kinds of persons and their expertise are required to perform corresponding roles, they are accorded differing values, rights and privileges differentiating them from others. When there is inequality of rights and perquisites, the society is bound to be stratified. In addition to roles, the stratification also reflects through prestige and esteem. Norms for each category are set involving ranking in terms of superiority and inferiority. Therefore, stratification may be taken as referring to ranking involving the elements of high and low among groups.

Stratification Theories

Social stratification refers to the differential ranking of the human individuals who compose a given social system and their treatment as superior and inferior to one another in certain socially important respects. For ranking statuses a large number of factors are responsible. These may at times be common, as also differing from society to society. Taking these into account, as also of the social stratification characteristics of its inevitability and perpetuation, the theorists have come out with various theoretic concerns in respect of stratification. While theorising on social stratification, three approaches have prominently been reported. First of these is popularly known as functional approach, or functional theory. Second one is the conflict theory, which is considered as an alternative approach with Karl Max as its propounder and the third one is coercion theory proposed by Dahrendorf.

The functional theory was advanced by Davis and Moore. In the background of this theory it was assumed that functional differentiation is inevitable. This has been true throughout the history irrespective of time and space. A major presupposition behind this thinking is that there are different functions to be performed in society. And one person cannot perform all these functions and rules. Such persons of different ability, intent, skill and understanding are required to perform different roles and duties. Some of these functions are rated higher than others, and so are the persons performing them.

According to this theory, the concept of stratification simply refers to the unequal rewards that are attached to positions. Davis and Moore argue that in all societies varying levels and kinds of rewards are in some, unspecified, way, built into positions. These rewards are the duties, rights, associated with a position and its privileges. They argue that if the rights and perquisites of different positions in a society must be unequal, then the society must be stratified, because that is precisely what stratification means. They seek to explain, in functional terms, the universal necessity which calls forth stratification in any social system. An empirical-universal inequality, must have some purpose, must fulfil some need of society.

Davis and Moore explains functional necessity of stratification in following way. First, all societies have a division of labour, a set of interdependent positions that have to be filled. These positions can be seen as clustered in four functionally necessary areas; religious, political, technological and economic. Second, people must be motivated to fill positions and enact roles. Social inequality is, thus, necessary in order to motivate people to fill functionally important positions and enact roles. Social inequality is, thus, unconsciously evolved device by which societies insure that the most important positions are conscientiously filled by the most qualified persons.

Davis-Moore thesis is similar to other functionalist analyses of stratification, especially Talcott Parson's. Parsons argues that the fundamental reference point in studying stratification must be the values dominant in a society. These values reflect functional importance in that one societal subsystem is seen as making the greatest contribution to valued ends in the society. Furthermore, within each subsystem, role differentiation occurs, with the result that prestige and power go to those positions functionally important to the subsystem. Inevitability and functionality of stratification were supported by Davis and Moore. According to them inequality is general aspect of social structure, and a structural phenomenon which cannot be done away with. These stratification theorists considered stratification as natural or given, and hence something universal in societies assuming impossibility of unstratified society.

For the conflict theory, proposed by Karl Marx, classes have been the basic features of social organisation. In his structural theory of society, Marx equated class stratification with all the other types of stratification systems. He takes power and status stratification as the products of class stratification. To Marx, classes are the product of productive system. For him the basis of stratification lies in economic structure, control over the means of production and human labour and services. Class is a social reality with consciousness regarding position and goal. In this dialectical approach to the study of social stratification, Marx considered economic system as the foundation structure for the superstructure of stratification system involving cultural, political, social dimensions etc.

Keeping economic system at the forefront, Marxians identify two classes namely owners of the means of production (Bourgeoisie) and workers (Proletariat). These two classes are at a clash in terms of their interest, giving rise to class conflict. The surplus value, earned by the bourgeoisie, meets resistance of the proletariat, causing radical or revolutionary transformation of the stratification system of society. Marx, thus, established a correspondence between class as a social category, and as analytical tool to the laws of social motion, giving thereby a scientific theory of social change. Class struggle, which is motor to social change, is the result of changing dynamics of production which cause change in social formations themselves.

According to Marxian concept of class, therefore, the class is inseparately linked to dialectical theory of social change. To Marx, therefore, class is not primarily a category to describe a particular society at a given point of time, but is an analytical tool for extracting sources of structural change in the society, thereby identifying the direction in which the society is heading.

The conflict theory proposes that increases in the productive capacity of a society and in population sizes are associated with an increasing division of labour. The increasing complexity of the division of labour is associated with the rise of industrialisation. Marx clearly suggests that the greater the industrialisation, the greater the inequality. Industrialisation is also associated with formation of a soldiery and cohesive-subordinate class and with a great rate of conflict between dominant and subordinate classes. Further, the more both dominants and subordinates form classes, the more polarised they will be. And the greater the polarisation in a society, the more likely is the conflict to be violent. The greater the inequality in a society, the more subordinates form a soldiery and cohesive class and the greater the polarisation in society, then the greater the rate of conflict and the more likely is revolution to occur.

The requirement of coercion theory is the presupposition of two classes in society. One represents the group which is coercive and the other which is coerced. For Dahrendorf no society is fully coercive or integrated. There are in simultaneous operation processes of change and resistance. The conformists and deviants subscribe to the element of inequality. However, key concept in Dahrendorf's model is coercion. And coercion of authority and power leads to clashes of role and interests. This leads to the organisation of antagonistic groups in society. Dahrendorf and C. Wright Mills tried to reorient social stratification theory by emphasising the importance of coercion, conflict, power and constraint in shaping social relationships.

Dahrendorf argues that we shall have to revise over assumptions radically and move away from the utopian image of society embodied in Parasonian functionalism. He, thus, makes a set of alternative assumptions; society is based upon the coercion of some elements by others; it is continuously subjected to disintegration, conflict and change. He has reiterated these assumptions in a number of places. He argues that they present a more realistic picture of what societies are really like. Dahrendorf believes that the societies are not stable, but in continuous flux.

STRATIFICATION PATTERNS

Since stratification, a specialised aspect of social structure is dealt herewith, we may not stress upon the formats of diverse cultural traits of the tribes in their totality. Even with various manifestations of stratification, as revealed through its patterns, a significant variation is apparent. These are borne of underlying reasons which vary from one situation to the other.

The Northeast Indian tribals show a wide degree of variance in their social organisation and cultural life. Certain types of stratification patterns found among them are discussed here.

Chieftainship system

Among certain tribes of Northeast India, social stratification is exhibited through the system of chieftainship and the social categories which have been created as a consequence of this system. Social division, borne of chiefship custom, has led to the emergence of various social strata. Their interrelationship and interaction of various forms are also defined as per the customarily prescribed norms surviving on the strength of the system of chieftainship.

One of the tribes, where the chieftainship is prominently reported, is the Nocte of Arunachal Pradesh. The Noctes present a distinctly stratified society. They have two distinct categories popularly differentiated as Lowangjat and Samajat. The former is socio-economically higher and represented by the chiefs and their descendents, while the latter by the commoners.

With their social and economic superiority, the Noctes of Lowangjat social division have been ascribed with certain privileges and the people thereof enjoy the same in mundane life. The Lowangjat are the administrators who extract work from Samajat. While the chief's class, called Lowangjat, may take wives from the commoner's class, the commoners may not do so from the chief's class. In social gatherings, like community-feasts, the two classes take different seats. When a whole village goes for hunting and fishing the largest share of meat and fish goes to the chief. The cultivation of the chief's fields are done by commoners. The chief's house is constructed by the village itself. The death of a chief is the concern for the entire village community. Representing Lowangjat social category of the Noctes, the chiefs in villages control the mechanism of social control and thereby manage for law and order in society. The necessary powers for all this are vested in the chiefs who never hail from the Samajat social division of the tribe.

The Lowangjat maintain their distinct identity of a higher order as the chiefship in hereditary and its succession goes by the rule of male primogeniture. For its further consolidation the office of chief has customarily been accorded a sanctity. The Noctes practise shifting (*Jhum*) cultivation. For this they require shifting, at defined intervals of time, from field to field. The Nocte chief are vested with the authority of distributing *Jhum* fields to the villagers. The Samajats have no say in the matter. Recognising the chiefs as supreme, the commoners depend on them in various walks of life. They guide their political life, are expected to provide security in the moments of crisis and help resolve all forms of disputes. Customary laws have protected the interests of the social category of chiefs and their descendents which has perpetuated over the years. The traditional norms-framework has made the commoners so obliged to the administering chiefs that they have been liberally contributing to his granary, consisting such contribution as token of respect.

The traditions pose for other requirements to be met by the members of subordinate group, the Samajat. The death of a chief assumes a festival character as all the subordinate villagers also get enough to eat. A brief formal lament is followed by eating and drinking and dances that continue for several days. A chief is not supposed to do any manual work. A chief enjoys precedence in all matters. Even in walking or marching he must lead, all others follow. A bamboo chair with a bamboo table in front has to be ready where the chief is offered rice beer, meat etc. While visiting other village, he stays in the house of local chief.

The Semas are characterised by the stratification of the nature of chiefly class and the one of commoners. The Semas are migratory in habits and they often set up new villages. The founder of the new village, some wealthy Sema, becomes the chief of the village and is known as father of the villagers and the villagers are known as *Mughemi*, that is, orphan of the chief. The chief is the lord of the village and he is the government.

The Sema chiefs are the administrators which are denied to the commoners or the dependants, popularly termed *Mangheni* or *Churl*. The latter are placed low in local social ladder. On the other hand the chiefs occupy a higher rung in social hierarchy and prefer to maintain marital alliance with the persons of the same status to maintain chiefly prestige. In case of stratified social system of the Semas, the *Kukamis* (rulers or chiefs) occupy the most privileged position followed by *Chochomi* (the ministers selected by the rulers) who advise the chiefs in decision-making.

The hierarchical order has its attending implications in social and material life of the tribe. There are categorically defined procedures meant to protect privileges and position of the people of chiefly class. The land belongs to the chiefs and clans. The allotment of land for cultivation is done every year on a festival day called *Tuluni*. No money is paid for the land for cultivation. The land cultivated by the chief and his followers will belong to the chief. The land for cultivation is distributed by the chief and his deputy to the families. This system still prevails in Sema society and thus the concentration of land is seen with the chief and his deputies in Sema area.

The Semas' principle of social stratification commonly marks the society of Konyak Nagas. In Konyak villages one finds well defined and distinguished social divisions or classes with differing social positions and rights and privileges associated thereof. In order of social hierarchy the top position in Konyak social structure is occupied by the Wangham class or division. The great *Angs* (major chiefs) belong to this class. These Angs mark the hereditary chieftainship. Some great Angs (say of *Mon* and *Chui*) have smaller Angs under them. As in case of Sema chieftainship, the Konyak Angs select ministers from various clans of the village. Among the Konyaks the class of commoners is termed as Ben or Bin. In between are the social categories of Wangsha and Wangshu. Their origin is attributed to particular forms of marital alliance. The Wangsha's origin is attributed to the union of men of Wangham class with the women of lower rank.

Third in hierarchy, that is below the Wangham and Wangsha, is the Wangshu class. Though in certain sense included among the nobility, the Wangshu is just above Ben, the class of commoners. The great Angs from Wangham class seek their principle wives from clans and lineages of equivalent rank to produce sons to succeed them. For procuring secondary wives, sometimes referred to as concubines, the chiefs of Wangham class may approach commoner's clans, though it is not very frequently reported. But the men from Wangsha, a lower division of Ang class, often take their wives from commoners, that is, the Ben. The two categories, falling between the great Angs and the commoners, are not very conspicuously differentiated. Their status attribution and interaction are thinly defined. But the prerogatives and functions of great Angs of Wangham class are vastly differentiated, though the difference in working routine and living, in day-to-day life, of other Angs may not sound that conspicuous.

The daily life of Angs and Ben people does not show any particular difference, the aristocrats do not possess better houses or richer furniture, and except for the village chief himself, the people of Ang class are in no way outwardly conspicuous. The running of the village, however, lies mainly in their hands, the adult men of Ang clan forming the council of the chief, which decides all quarrels and settles disputes over field boundaries and the like. The position of the great Angs is quite different. These powerful village chiefs have the sacred blood of the chiefs, pure and undiluted, in their veins. The great Angs take their wives from their own great Ang clan, and it is only the children of such a union that acquire the father's rank.

Writing on Thadou social classes, Pearson Hungyo asserts that the Thadou chief has the absolute powers over the village land and he distributes the cultivable land to all the villagers at the beginning of every year. In doing so he has to consult his council of ministers called *Semang Pachang* nominated by him from different clans of the village. The villagers give tax to the chief for the cultivation of land. A basket full of paddy equivalent to five tins is given from each household as the tax called *Changsen* on a particular occasion fixed by the chief. On this occasion, the chief gives a feast to the villagers with plenty of meat and drink. *Changsen* is exempted from the widows and new settler of the village who has not established properly. An individual Thadou has no claim over any part of the land. He cannot sell or give it to others as the land belongs entirely to the chief. If he is not satisfied with the distribution of land or displeased in any manner, then he has to leave the village with his belongings leaving behind his house and other property.

More or less on the lines of chieftainship, described above in case of Nocte, Sema, Konyak, Thadou etc., the existence of social stratification is also reported in case of the Singphos. Like the Semas a Singpho becomes the chief of a village he has founded. The position of chief is hereditary. The chiefs exercise a variety of powers and authority. The Singpho society may broadly be divided into three estates; the chiefs, the plebeians and the slaves. The first of these divisions is called *Ddufan* (represented by chiefs) and which is of highest status. The next lower division in hierarchy is called *Mreng-dong* (including the commoners). The lowest in social rank is the division called *Mayam*. The members of the last class are said to be the descendents of those men and women who used to be captured and kidnapped from Assam plains. In course of time they crystalised into separate social entity by adopting Singpho clan names, language and culture.

A village chief is called *Agi* or *Mirang* in whom the social and political control of the village rest. Chieftainship is hereditary. He is not only a clan chief but also a territorial chief. So far his village is concerned, he is the de-jure owner of the village land which he allows to his co-villagers to cultivate. Every Singpho village is an independent unit by itself and is ruled by a chief who holds the legal and administrative power. He directs all village activities concerning the welfare and well-being of the village community. He decides all cases excepting the inter-village disputes and punishes the offender with fine. In case a villager refuses to obey his order, he may even turn the offender out of the village. A Singpho chief normally possesses more than one wife as his social position necessitates him to entertain more guests with food and drink.

Some instance of aristocracy has also been reported from amongst the Sherdukpens. In contrast to the commoners the aristocrats, among the Sherdukpens, represent a distinct class under a separate name of Thongs. No social mobility is permitted from other classes to the Thongs who are traditionally privileged with higher social status. Magnitude of social disparity is marked, among the Sherdukpens, by the fact that the inter-class marriages are usually restrained.

The Sherdukpens are divided into three classes, Thongs, Chhaos and Yanlos. The Thongs form the aristocracy and the Chhaos the middle class. The Yanlos are artisans. Except that there is no inter-marriage amongst these classes, there is no other social disparity. Certain inter-service relationship exists among the classes.

The abolition of chiefship was merely a post-independence phenomenon. But the fact remains that the families of ex-chiefs even today occupy a position of prominence having a status difference with the commoners. This type of intra-tribe stratification based on chieftainship, commoners and the classes in-between continues, by and large, to mark the social systems of the concerned tribes. The chiefs, at times, may not receive the formal recognition from non-tribals but within their own system they continue to carry an image of higher social position and authority.

The substantivism in case of the Nocte, Singpho, Sema, Konyak, Thadou, etc., leads one to certain issues of theoretic concern in respect of stratification. Firstly, these tribal societies are marked by the stratification chiefly borne of descent from noble, royal or aristocratic parentage. Secondly, people from such parentages want to keep up their distinct social division for high prestige and more privileges. Thirdly, they want to control the economic resource which ultimately helps retain the authority of social control and the privileges of various forms already elaborated.

The underlying cause of stratification is materialistic, which is protected through noble descent. However, the materialism, as reported among these tribals, is not of the nature and order reported among the non-tribal feudals. These people hardly accumulate wealth as the surplus is not bothered for. The disparity in terms of rich and poor is insignificant between the chiefs and the commoners, but the position of chief does provide psychic gratification in terms of certain amount of authority and privileges which are associated with this position.

Since the economic disparity between different divisions is not of wide magnitude and since the chiefly classes have extended a variety of concessions, in terms of caring for people in general, the grievances against the system of chieftainship and chiefly classes are of rare occurrence. To some extent the economic egalitarianism is reported among these tribals in spite of the control over resources being concentrated in the hands of chiefly class.

Among other reasons the prominent economic classes could not emerge among these tribals because of the nature of economy being that of subsistence in general. They being predominantly shifting cultivators could not afford to have more of surplus and savings. Profit motives and cash transactions remained, by and large, absent. Any meagre surplus grains, available in chief's granary, was shared with others in the hours of need or through feasts which chief would organise occasionally.

Master-serf system

Among the tribes of Northeast India, another pattern of social stratification reported is based on the criterion different from the one reported among the tribes having chieftainship. Such a stratification sounds intra as well as inter-tribe. It's origin is attributed to master-serf relationship. The system has been in existence for centuries as evident from certain myths explained by the people. Though legally banned since the period needs to be revised to last century, the instances of the serfdom based relationship cannot be ruled out.

The Apatanis are the only people in the Subansiri region who have been practising terraced cultivation from time immemorial, whereas their neighbours the Daflas and Miris are votaries of slash and bum method. No wonder that the Daflas come and consign themselves voluntarily into slavery for they are assured of food, shelter, clothing and security. Thus, slavery, in the ultimate analysis, is in the logic of history. The economic condition of the people necessitated an uninterrupted flow of slaves.

The Apatanis are stratified into two distinct classes known as the *Guth* (patricians) and the *Guchi* (commoners or slaves). The *Guth* is represented by the Apatanis of the village itself, as also by those who have joined the village through marital alliance. The *Guchis* are presented by the descendents or remnants of those who were captured, during wars, from the villages of Nisi and Hill Mini tribes. Over the years these people lost their original clan names and got largely assimilated with the Apatanis in terms of diverse ways of life including food, dress, shelter, behaviour etc. Though formerly treated as slaves these people now live by the side of *Guths* and share many things in common. But still some inequality between the *Guchis* and *Guths* is maintained. The people of *Guchi* class are not allowed to join some religious festivals. The members of two classes, that is the *Guth* and *Guchi* or *Mura*, do not inter-marry and the commensality, specially on ceremonial occasions, is missing.

Generally, a serf depends on his master for basic needs like food, clothing and shelter, and is even permitted to take his master's clan name. While in master's house a serf cannot possess any property. The class of serfs is well identified in terms of local perception of high and low. The supra-ordination and subordination have their implications at operational level of the life-designs. The birth of this kind of stratification is attributed to inter-tribe contact and the ensuing relationship.

The stratification pattern of master-serf relationship is more conspicuously reported from tribes of Arunachal Pradesh. For instance, the Bangnis have been engaging, from the deep past, the Sulungs as their serfs. The Bangnis, recognising themselves as socially superior, belong to the class of *Atto*, the masters. On the other hand the Sulungs, who are socially inferior and who serve the Bangnis, belong to the class of *Bekrau*, the serfs.

Like the Bangnis, the Mijis also engage the Sulung serfs (*Bekrau*). The Miji master's division is termed as *Tau*.

Though not extensively, the serfdom is also reported among the Akas. Their two divisions of Kutsum and Kovatsum are higher than the one of serfs, known as *Khulo*. These instances reveal that the Sulungs have been serving a few neighbouring tribes as serfs for time immemorial. A few families of Sulung, forming a cluster, stay a little away from their master's village and serve them.

The slave system continues among the Bangnis and Mijis of East Kameng District of Arunachal Pradesh. Each Sulung individual is inextricably bound up with a Bangni or Miji. The Bangnis also have slaves from their own community who are known as *Mera* (male slave) and *Paue* (female slave). Even the intra-tribe stratification among the Bangnis; the higher division is represented by the people of *Tau* category and the lower one by those belonging to *Mera* and *Paue*.

The divisions of Akas—the Kutsum and Kovatsum—are two political units under two chiefs. Among Akas the rich men occupy the highest status in the society and slaves occupy the lowest status. The *Khulo* (slaves) usually belong to the Sulung tribe, a hunting and gathering tribe. The Sulung's relationship with the Bangnis is based on *mithun* which is an indispensable item of bride-price. They do not have had *mithuns* of their own. As the myth goes, sons of Jago and Keya borrowed *mithuns* from the Bangnis and could not pay their values and since then they became age-old debtors to the Bangnis for *mithuns*. Thus the Bangnis brought the Sulungs under their full control and became master (*Atto*) over them. The system is still prevailing.

The master and serf stratums are also reported among the Mizos and the Reangs. The feeling of master and the slave that must have existed in the past between the tribes of Kuki-chin group and the Reangs is still evident today wherever these tribes have come in contact. In the Jampui Hills of Tripura the more numerous Reangs are nothing more than serfs of the Mizos a position which the Lushais claim as natural and the Reangs accept as their fate. Though different levels, consisting of masters and their serfs or dependants, are identified, their interaction does not import rigidity of the nature usually prescribed for master-slave relationship. This specially holds true in case of tribes other than the Sulungs.

The pattern of interaction and relationship between the socially superiors and inferiors sounds quite humane. The implications of relationship do not exactly fit in the usual right system of slavery. The arrangement is not based on racial or colour criteria. The treatment meted out to the inferior class is also comparatively relaxed, though the bondage in certain sense is almost permanent. For instance, the relationship between the members of *Guth* and *Guchi* among the Apatanis is not typical of slavery system. The master, among the Apatanis, is addressed as father, if he is elder, by a slave. And the master reciprocates by calling him a son.

In case of Akas, the position of slaves is not extremely bad as we might anticipate under the system. The treatment meted out to them by their masters is not totally devoid of humanitarian considerations; it is on the other hand, often humane and sympathetic. The masters generally do not maintain much difference with them so far as the sharing of field toil is concerned. The slaves may have to work hard, but nevertheless their masters do have to provide for their minimum requirements in turn for their services. The *Khulo* are virtually the menial servants with the further imposition of that the services are compulsory. They are slaves in the sense that they do not have a right of liberation.

The Bangni and Mizi come rather hard on their Sulung slaves. The Sulungs are not allowed by their masters to mix freely with outsiders as they might somehow loose their control over them. Though they do not work in their master's house all the time, they have to render their services whenever required. The female Sulungs are required to prepare yarn from the fibres of wild nettle shrubs, and to collect jungle roots and tubers for their masters.

All major disputes of the Sulungs are decided by their masters in consultation with the elders of their respective villages. The Sulungs cannot take any decision by themselves. The Bangnis of today are more liberal upon the Sulungs than in the past. The Anti Slavery Act has also curtailed the capturing of slaves. But in many cases the psychology of serfs, vis-a-vis their masters, is yet to be radically changed. Many intend keep up the relationship.

In 1960s the government decreed the freeing of slaves and undertook the compensation of slave-owners. But this measure brought about less change than one might have expected. Raiding for the sake of capturing prisoners and selling them as slaves had already largely come to an end and many of the still existing slaves chose to stay with their owners because they considered themselves as member of the family and had nowhere else to go. Since the abolition of slavery people are no more captured with the intention of selling them as slaves, but in disputes arising from cases of adultery or fraud, offenders are sometimes still tied up and kept in stocks until the quarrel has been settled by negotiations. The administration wisely does not interfere with such coercive practices as long as the village elders (*gaonbura*) approve of them and involve themselves in the settlement of the dispute.

The served and the serving classes, that is the master and serfs, explain the origin of their stratified social order on the strength of their myth and supernatural belief. But the economic implications of such stratification pattern cannot be ruled out in mundane life. They are rather deeper under this social arrangement of inequality and hierarchy. More illuminating of these is the non-repayment of dues against *mithuns* which Sulungs take from the Bangnis and Mizis and pledge themselves to their masters. Being the poorest they go in for economic security under this arrangement. The chiefly class controls the economic resource and distributes the same among the commoners. The masters, on the other hand, own the resource and the serfs are usually the landless, or in a few cases the tenants at the mercy of masters. As such the gap in terms of rich and poor is far wider in case of stratified social order of master-slave kind.

In case of the chief-commoner situation, all are allotted *Jhum* land and the product goes to the people themselves. Though the members of chiefly class enjoy certain extra privileges, specially in terms of petty material benefits, the commoners do get a share in the major economic resource, that is, the land and the forest. As a common hypothesis it is assumed that the rich-poor gap should be wider in case of chief-commoner situation, but it is not the case among the majority of Northeast Indian tribes.

On certain occasions, say one marking prestige of chief or in the event of some emergency, the granaries of the chiefs are also shared by the commoners. The element of economic exploitation, especially borne of stratification, too, is not that conspicuously reported in case of chief-commoner pattern. In fact the commoners only render, some labour help on certain occasions, or at times donate a basket or two of the product to the chief's granary or share portion of meat of the game killed in hunting in recognition of chief and his services to the community.

Under the customary law, the chief too is obliged to take care of the commoners. On the other hand, the element of exploitation finds a prominent place in case of the stratified social order borne of master-serf relationship. The serving class of serfs suffers from a variety of complexes, denials and deprivations. They, and at times even their families, are bogged down under compulsions of various forms. High-handedness is also reported in master-serf pattern of stratification, more so in case of Bangni-Sulung and Mizi-Sulung relationship. Most of them do not have right even over the land of their habitation, which usually belongs to the masters. However, they are looked after at the minimal level of human existence. People have been in bondage for generations.

Among the slave class such as Sulungs, Miris, Nishis and Daflas, the state of poverty is comparatively acute. Among the masters the well-off are the Apatanis, followed by the Bangnis and Mizis who are socio-economically far better than the Sulungs. The commoners, though at subsistence level of economy, cannot be equated with the abject poverty marking the class of serfs who attribute it to their poor fate. Master-serf pattern of stratification, thus, caters more to the requirement of conflict model of stratification, though its functional aspect cannot altogether be ignored. In the sense of functional, the pattern of chief-commoner stratification sounds, more so at perception level, comparatively somewhat functional to all categories of stratums, but slightly more to the members of chiefly class who derive psychic gratification in terms of prestige and authority in addition to a few petty material benefits. Both in manifest as well as latent perspectives the master-serf or patrician-serf pattern of stratification appears more conflicting to the serving group of serfs. The material benefit, that they have been deriving, is of extremely a meagre nature.

Structural Analysis

The structural analysis of the social stratification among the tribes of Northeast India, a few models can be conceived as of interpretative relevance in terms of scientific analysis of the social system. Implications of these constructs cannot be ruled out in case of parallel social situations reported elsewhere too.

One of these relates to the very creation or origin of stratification, of the chief-commoner kind, where it can be propounded that social arrangement is to be primarily and essentially attributed to the urge for acquisition of superiority, prestige, authority and power as elements of psychic gratification of humans, economic necessity could not have been the basis of this form of social system. The control over and distribution of economic resource, in this case land and forest, came up later as a consequence and intended follow-up of the above given non-economic content of stratification-base among the Nocte, Konyaks, Semas, Tangkhuls, Thadous etc. Even the rise of noble or aristocrat class, represented by the chiefs and their descendents, can be attributed to the subsequent stage through the process of seeking descent from the chiefs, recognising them carrying pure noble blood. This could be further substantiated and consolidated in the interest of perpetuating the system, through the declaration of chief's position as hereditary. Quite contrary to the paradigm, in the context of chief-commoner pattern, is the one that can be conceived for the system of socially stratified divisions borne of master-serf relationship. In case of the latter it can be interpreted that it was basically the economic requirement that led to the rise of such social stratification. Such an explanation is of relevance to both the social divisions, that is, formed of the masters and the serfs. Hard pressing economic necessity led some to pledge themselves as serfs; and the requirement of additional working hands enthused comparatively big land-holders to acquire serfs through various means. In former category come the Sulungs, Dafla, Nisi, Mizi etc., and in the latter can be included the Apatanis, Bangni, etc.

Under this model of conceiving the origin, rise and sustenance of social stratification, the craze for prestige, authority, superiority etc., grew at a subsequent stage, and that too not in any conspicuously illuminating form. Even in the contemporary social situation, economic requirement, in case of stratification of master-serf nature, forms an element of priority and prominence over the non-economic criteria. This is obvious from the perpetuating social situations too.

The dominant group of the masters or patricians, representing higher order in stratification, has even provided minor concessions to the class of slave in the interest of relating the bondage system. Through these concessions the serfs feel obliged to serve the masters. The members of master's class occasionally extend what they call as human and sympathetic gestures. For instance, the serfs, in some cases, are allowed to call a master by the terms of father, and the master reciprocates it by the term of son. On some occasion the master may depute a serf, especially if the latter is intelligent, as his spokesman to represent on behalf of the master. At times the master may pay for the bride-price or fine penalty on behalf of the serf. Sometimes a piece of land may also be allotted to the serf family for cultivation. They use its produce for themselves though the ownership of land remains with the master. The Apatanis allow their serf class to even borrow their clan names so that they may mentally feel like the freeman. But they never marry with them and restrain their social participation in certain rituals and festivals.

A second model characterised by a few ingredients, is of quite an importance in the context of social stratification reported in the tribal situation of Northeast India. In case of chief-commoner pattern of stratification, a forceful element is that it is, in general intra-tribe. That means the people belonging to different social stratums are of the same tribe, and who share certain common characteristics, other than those barred by the stratification, at equal footing. This includes even their origin in terms of the tribe as a whole. It gives rise to the recognition of certain other common bonds based on obligations borne of common value system and in group feelings. Background of this kind paves way to more humanitarian considerations. Among other factors, involving mutual obligations, the communal ownership of land strongly holds their fraternity and community feelings. Almost a fair distribution of this resource further strengthens the process. The force of communal ownership of land, in terms of many human and societal conditions and reciprocities, is almost as strong as the kinship ties borne of descent and alliance groupings.

Belongingness to the same tribe, and as such sharing of many ideological and actual things in common, have correspondingly reflected in certain areas of stratification. The stratum gap is not that wide in terms of social distance, rights and privileges. At the same time there are no rigidly ascribed deprivations and constraints, though the chiefly clans do enjoy an air of superiority. Then the exploitation of commoners is not of any significant dimension. Petty favours given to the chiefs, who are their own tribesmen, do not exactly support the basis of exploitation as per native perception. The commoners, in general, take it lightly in the background of services rendered by the chiefs, more so in the arenas of social and economic control which they are authorised to exert. It appears that ethnic homogeneity at the level of tribe, and people's recognition of and adherence to the same have contained the stratification pattern only at mild level. The system sounds more voluntary rather than one involving serious elements of compulsion.

In case of stratification based upon master-serf tangle, the picture is altogether different. Here the masters belong to one tribe and the serfs to the other. As such there is no affinity on the ground of belongingness to the same tribe when it comes to different social stratums placed in an hierarchical order. Each stratum is identified with a different tribe. In this background the nature of in-group feeling and obligations differ widely. Against the communal ownership of land, reported in case of chief-commoner pattern of relationship, the ownership in case of master-serf situation is individual. The Apatanis and many others adhere to this form of resource ownership. The slaves are, by and large, landless.

In this context, too, as the norms of the members belonging to two different tribes differ, there is hardly any check on economic exploitation. The dominant masters, representing a common tribe, do come hard on the serving serfs who, in general, belong to another tribe. Under this arrangement the gap marking different rungs of social ladder sounds pretty wide. The wider gap derives its strength from ethnic heterogeneity and an extremely unequal distribution of resource. Since the tribes, under this situation, do seek different origin and descent, their feeling of fraternity lacks to a large extent. Because of differing ethnic background and other associated considerations, say unequal distribution of resource, there is no check on exploitation as the norms differ as per the tribe. Element of force and compulsion appear sharp, more so when we review them from the socio-economically superior to the inferior groups.

In case of intra-tribe stratification, essentially borne of chief-commoner relationship, the trend of change is in terms of substitution of chiefs. The educated elites, more so of younger generation, sometime question the hereditary-based chieftainship. And they care to do so more because the fundamental of such customary system is non-economic, that is, prestige, authority and power etc., based. Many of these emerging elites also express their inclination to such elements of psychic gratification. The secondary base of resource control and its distribution, as managed by the traditional chief, is not difficult to mange even by these elites, as is evinced from their state of mind on the issue. However, in the interest of systemic arrangement, the change trend only suggests for alternative substitutes—say replacement of chiefs by the Gaonburas or by other educated and employed persons in the villages. As such the instance of total revolt against the ongoing traditional system is unheard of. But of late the people are keen to try alternatives challenging thereby the hereditary provision. Further, the total revolt against the chieftainship and their class is not likely to be resorted to as the distribution of economic resources is not usually unfair.

Even the element of economic exploitation is not of any alarming form which could lead to any serious imbalance. As the commoners share and enjoy economic resource, though mainly at the discretion of chief and his assistants, they remain, by and large, quiet and contented. So, even if the hereditary chiefs are replaced, by the educated elites, in near future, the system as such would not collapse. Rather, it is likely to be restructured in the still larger interest of masses. But then the terms of privileges, attached with certain category of people, may not disappear. These would remain in the interest of running the system.

As the pattern of master-serf stratification always and essentially derived strength from the material or economic base, involving denial to fair resource distribution and more exploitation of serfs, some people have been keen to go for total revolt against the customary system. However, a majority of serf did not expose it or made explicit for reasons of economic oppression, obligation and lack of alternative, though it always remained at the back of their mind. Since people from within the system took this social order forced upon them, they waited for some opportunity to do away with the traditional socio-economic arrangement. Here the enthusing change base lies in economic deprivations. The serfs themselves being economically extremely weak could not organise any large scale movement against the tyranny of their masters. But feeling their pulse, the government went for banning the slavery or serfdom. The depressed lot, in general, outrightly supported the move expressing solidarity for total abolition of the system. The change trend, in this case, goes for total abandoning of the traditional system by the new social and economic arrangement proposed by the outside agents of change in consonance with the affected insiders. The latter, in general, opted to support the new systemic arrangement as the customary one was felt as hard and forced upon.

Bibliography

Aggarwal, R.C., *Principles of Political Science*, S. Chand and Company Ltd., New Delhi, 1982.

Aiyappan, A., Development of tribal areas. *Economic Weekly,* 17: 24 (12 June, 1965) 949-50.

Annual Plan for Tribal Development in Rajasthan (1987-88) Vol.1, 1987, *Tribal Areas Development Department*, Government of Rajasthan, Udaipur-313001.

____________ , (1986-87), issued by *T.A.D. Dept.*, Rajasthan, Udaipur.

____________ , (1993-94), issued by *T.A.D. Department*, Rajasthan, Udaipur.

Anthony, William P. and Edward A. Nicholson. *Management of Human Resources: A Systems Approach to Personnel Management.* Ohio: Grid, 1977.

Appleby, Paul M., *Public Administration for a Welfare State*, Asia Publishing House, New Delhi, 1961.

Armstrong, Michael: *A Handbook of Personnel Management Practice*, Kogan Page Ltd., London, 1977.

Arora, Ramesh K. and Sogani, Meena, *State Administration in Rajasthan*, 1989.

Asha, Robert E. and others. *Development of the Emerging Countries: An Agenda for Research.* Washington, D.C.: Brokings Institution, 1962.

Avasthi, A. and R.K. Arora (eds.). *Bureaucracy and Development: Indian Perspective.* New Delhi: Associated, 1978.

____________ and S.K. Verma (eds.). *Aspects of Administration.* New Delhi, Allied, 1964.

____________ , *Revenue Inspection at District Level.* New Delhi: Indian Institute of Public Administration, 1965.

______________ , Amreshwar and Maheshwari, Shri Ram: 'Public Administration', 1986, Laxmi Narain Agrawal, Educational Publishers, Hospital Road, Agra-3.

Bagchi, A.K. 'Some characteristics of industrial growth in India'. *Economic and Political Weekly,* 10:5-7 (February 1975, Annual Number) 157-64.

Bajpai, S.R. 'Methods in Social Survey and Research', Kitabghar, Kanpur, 1960.

Banerjee, M. *Primitive Men in India.* Ambala: Indian Publications, 1963.

Barnabas, A.P. and Donald C. Pelz. *Administering Agricultural Development.* New Delhi: Indian Institute of Public Administration, 1969.

Barnett, H.G. *Anthropology in Administration.* Evanston: Peterson, 1956.

Basu, Ashok Ranjan, 'Tribal Development Programmes and Administration in India', National-Book Organisation, *The Mail,* Shimla-1, 1985.

______________ , "Educational administration in the tribal areas of Chamba District". Presented at University Grants Commission Seminar on Education and Social Change in Himachal Pradesh held at Himachal Pradesh University, November 13-16, 1978.

______________ , *"Goals of tribal development in the pers-pective of national development".* Presented at a Seminar on Integrated Tribal Development Planning held at the National Institute of Community Development, Hyderabad, January 20-22, 1977.

______________ , "Tribal Development: a conceptual frame-work". Presented at 10th International Congress on Anthropological and Ethnological Sciences held at New Delhi, December 10-16, 1978.

______________ , "Tribal development: goals and approaches". Presented at the Conference of Indian Public Administration Association heid at Osmania University, Hyderabad, June 14-16, 1978.

______________ , High passes in Bharmour. *Himavanta,* 3:9 & 10 (1973) 8, 2-3.

______________ , *Integrated Tribal Development Project Report for Bharmour and Pangi Sub-divisions of Chamba District.* Chamba, 1973.

______________ , Mani Mahesh. *Himavanta,* 5:10 (1974) 4-6.

______________ , "Problems of implementing plans in the tribal areas". Presented at a Seminar on Integrated Tribal Development Planning held at the National Institute of Community Development, Hyderabad, January 20-22, 1977.

______________, *Technological Possibilities of Indian Agriculture.* Calcutta: Firma KIM, 1978.

Beri, B.P. (C.J.) 'Report of the Rajasthan Pay Commission' (1979-81), Government Central Press, Rajasthan, Jaipur, 1981.

Berreman, Gerald D. *Hindus of the Himalayas.* Berkeley: University of California Press, 1963.

Beteille, Andre: Tribe, Caste and Religion, Mac Milian, India.

Bhalerao, C.N., 'Administration, Politics and Development in India'; Lalvani Publishing House, 210, Dr. D.N. Road, Bombay-1, 1972.

Bhambhri, C.P., 'Administrators in a Changing Society', National Publishing House, New Delhi, 1972.

______________, 'Public Administration', Jai Prakash Nath and Company; Educational Publishers, Meerut City, 1984.

Bjorkhan, James Warner. 'The politics of administrative alienation: relation among civil servants and political leaders in rural India's development programmes' (Ph.D. Thesis, VALE University, 1976).

Bose, N.K. "Tribal welfare in India". *Africa Quarterly, 9:1* (April-June, 1961) 58-63.

______________, Nirmal Kumar. *Some Indian Tribes.* New Delhi: National Book Trust, 1973.

Bose, S. "The Gaddi of Chamba". *Man in India,* 43:3 (1963) 191-213.

Braibanti, Ralph and Joseph J. Spengler (eds.). *Administration and Economic Development in India.* Durham (N.C.): Duke University Press, 1963.

______________, (eds.). *Tradition, Values and Socio-Economic Development.* Durham (N.C.): Duke University Press, 1961.

Brunhes, *J. Human Geography.* London: George G. Harrap, 1952.

Caiden, Gerald E. *Administrative Reforms.* London: Allen & Unwin, 1970.

Capoor, H.K.L. "Development administration". *Journal of the National Academy of Administration, 12* (July, 1967) 1-17.

Cernea, Michael M. and B.T. Tepping. *A System for the Monitoring and Evaluating Agricultural Extension Projects.* Washington, D.C.: International Bank for Reconstruction and Development, 1977.

Chattopadhyaya, Kamladevi. *Tribalism in India,* New Delhi: Vikas, 1978.

Chaturvedi, T.N. (ed), 'Development Administration', Indian Institute of Public Administration, New Delhi, 1984.

______________, (ed), 'The Indian Journal of Public Administration', Vol. XXV, 1979, Navchetan Press Pvt. Ltd., 1-E/2, Jhandewalan Extn., New Delhi-110055.

______________, and Handa, K.L.: Financial Administration, Indian Institute of Public Administration, New Delhi.

Cohen, R.L. *The Economics of Agriculture,* London: Nibet, 1948.

Collins, Paul. "Theories of the popular participation in development administration: an empirical comment. *Planning and Administration,* 2:2 (Autumn 1975) 58-59.

Credric Robinson, "Indiana Jones, The Third World and American Foreign Policy: A Review Article", *Race and Class,* 26(2) (Autumn 1984), p. 87.

Davar, G.R. "The energy crisis and its impact on planning and administration". *Indian Journal of Public Administration, 21: 4* (October-December *1975) 762-87.*

Davis, Kingsley. *Human Society.* London: Macmillan, 1960.

Dayal, Ishwar and Dayal, Amrit Kala : Organisation for Management in Developing Countries, Concept Publishing Company, New Delhi, 1983.

Development Administration. New Delhi: Centre for Policy Research, 1978.

Dey, B.K. Bureaucracy and development—some reflections. *Indian Journal of Public Administration,* 15:2 (April-June 1969) 228-48.

______________, *Bureaucracy, Development and Public Management in India.* New Delhi: Uppal, 1978.

Draft Eighth Five Year Plan for Tribal Development in Rajasthan (1992-97), including Annual Plan for 1992-93 Vols. I & 11, 1991 Issued by T.A.D. Dept., Rajasthan, Udaipur-313001.

Dube, S.C. (ed.). *Public Services and Social Responsibility.* New Delhi: Vikas, 1979.

Dubey, S.N. and Ratna Murdia. *Administration of Policy and Programmes for Backward Classes in India.* Bombay. Somaiya, 1976.

______________, "Tribal welfare programmes: an analysis of their organisation and administration". *Indian Journal of social work,* 32:3 (October 1971) 207-20.

Dubhashi, P.R., 'Rural Development Administration in India', Bombay, Popular Prakashan, 1970.

Elwin, Verrier. *A Philosophy for NEFA.* 2nd ed. Shillong: NEFA Administration, 1959.

_____________ , *New Deal for Tribal India.* New Delhi: Ministry of Home Affairs, 1963.

Ghurye, G.S. *The Scheduled Tribes.* Bombay: Popular Prakashan, 1964.

Gisbert, P. *Tribal India: A Synthetic View of Primitive Man* Jaipur: Rawat Publications, 1978.

Golembienski, Robert *T.: Public Administration as a Developing Discipline.* New York: Marcel Dekker, 1977.

Goodenough, W.H. *Cooperation in Change: An Anthropological Approach to Community Development.* New York: Russel Sage Foundation, 1963.

Gupta, B.N. *An Introduction to Modern Statistics.* Calcutta: Bookland, 1973.

_____________ , Ranjit (ed.): *Planning for Tribal Development.* New Delhi: Ankur, 1977.

Hagen, Everett *E. On the Theory of Social Change: How Economic Growth Begins.* Homewood (111.): Dorsey Press, 1963.

Hanson, A.H. *The Process of Planning: A Study of India's Five Year Plans* 1950-1964. London: Allen & Unwin, 1966.

Heady, Ferrel and Sybil L. Stokes (eds.). *Papers in Comparative Public Administration.* Michigan: Michigan University Press, 1962.

Heaphey, James *J. Spatial Dimensions of Development Administration.* Durham (N.C.): Duke University Press, 1971.

Higgins, B. *Economic Development: Principles, Problems and Policies.* New York: McGraw-Hill, 1958.

Himachal Pradesh Revenue Department. *The Himachal Pradesh Relief of Agriculture Indebtedness Act.* Simla, 1976.

Himachal Pradesh, Department of Agriculture. *Report on Agriculture Census,* 1970-71. Simla, 1972.

_____________ , Department of Horticulture. *A Glimpse of Himachal Horticulture,* Simla, 1974.

_____________ , Department of Horticulture. *Annual Administration Report.* Simla, 1983.

_____________ , Department of Personnel. *Himachal Pradesh Administrative Service Rules.* Simla, 1973.

_____________ , Directorate of Economics and Statistics *An Evaluation Study of Bharmour.* Simla 1964.

_____________ , Directorate of Economics and Statistics *Economic Review of Himachal Pradesh.* Simla, 1975.

_____________ , Directorate of Economics and Statistics. *Economic Review of Himachal Pradesh.* Simla, 1978.

_____________ , Directorate of Economics and Statistics. Pangi

Valley: *An Evaluation and Socio-Economic Study*. Simla, 1966.

_______________, Directorate of Economics and Statistics. *Report of the Indebtedness Survey among Scheduled Tribe Population of Himachal Pradesh*. Simla, 1978.

_______________, Directorate of Economics and Statistics. *Statistical Outline of Himachal Pradesh* 1983. Simla, 1984.

_______________, Directorate of Economics and Statistics. *Symposium on Social and Economic Problems of Hilly Areas*. Simla, 1973.

_______________, *District State Gazetteers, Himachal Pradesh, Chamba*, edited by T.S. Negi, Simla, 1963.

_______________, *First National Seminar on Problems and Potentials of the Hill Areas of India*. New Delhi, 1975.

_______________, Planning Department. *Draft Five Year Plan and Draft Tribal Sub-Plan*, 1978-83, Himachal Pradesh. Simla, 1978.

_______________, Planning Department. *Migrating Gaddis and the Problems of Education*. Simla, 1977.

_______________, Planning Department. *Revised Tribal Sub-Plan*. Simla, 1976.

_______________, Planning Department. *Sub-Plan for Tribal Belt* (1974-79): *A Draft Outline*, Simla, 1974.

_______________, Rajpatra, Simla, *1977*.

_______________, Revenue Department. *Settlement Report of Chamba District* (1951-58), by T.S. Negi, Simla, 1966.

_______________, Revenue Department. *The Himachal Pradesh Registration of Money Lenders Act*. Simla, 1976.

_______________, State Electricity Board. *Administration Report*, 1984-85. Simla, 1985.

_______________, State Electricity Board. *Exploitation of Hydel. Potential of Himachal Pradesh for Northern Region*. Simla, 1974.

Hobson, W. (ed.). *The Theory and Practice of Public Health*. London: Oxford University Press, 1965.

Honewell, Roy J. *The Educational Work of Thomas Jefferson*. Cambridge (Mass.): Harvard University Press, 1931.

Hudson, C. Saikler: Organisation and Management—Theory and Practice, The American University Press, Washington, D.C., 1954.

Iglesias, G.V. (ed.) *Implementation, the Problem of Achieving Results: A Case Book or, Asian Experience*. Manila: Eastern Regional Organisation for Public Administration, 1976.

India, Planning Commission. *Report of the Study Team on Tribal Development Programmes: Himachal Pradesh* (Chairman: P. Shilu Ao) New Delhi, 1969.

_____________ , *Administrative Reforms Commission. Report on Personnel Administration.* New Delhi, 1969.

_____________ , *Expert Committee on Tribal Department. Report.* New Delhi, 1970 (Chairman: S.C. Dube).

_____________ , *Health Survey and Department Committee. Report.* New Delhi, 1946. (Chairman: Joseph Bhore).

_____________ , Ministry of Home Affairs. *Approach to Tribal Development in the Sixth Plan: A Preliminary Perspective.* New Delhi, 1977.

_____________ , Ministry of Home Affairs. *Proceedings of Conference of Tribal Commissioners,* July 14-15, 1977. New Delhi. 1977. (Occasional Papers on Tribal Development).

_____________ , Ministry of Home Affairs. *Report of the Committee on Special Multipurpose Tribal Blocks* (1959), New Delhi, 1960.

_____________ , Ministry of Home Affairs. *The State of Himachal Pradesh Act.* New Delhi, 1970.

_____________ , Ministry of Home Affairs. *Tribal Development in the Fifth Plan: Some Basic Policy Papers.* New Delhi, *1975.*

_____________ , *National Commission on Agriculture. Report.* New Delhi, 1976.

_____________ , Planning Commission. *Formulation of Area Development* Plan. New Delhi, 1966.

_____________ , Planning Commission. *Identification of Backward Area. Report of the Working Group* (Leader: B.D. Pande) New Delhi, 1969.

_____________ , Planning Commission. *Report of the Working Group on Personnel Policy for Tribal Areas.* (Chairman: R.N. Haldipur, New Delhi, 1973).

_____________ , Register-General. *Census of India. Vol. 20, pt. 6. no, 5; A Village Survey of Bharmour,* Delhi, 1963.

_____________ , Registrar-General. *Census of India. Vol. 20, pt. 6 no. 7; A Village Survey, Kupha, Parmas, Thamoh and Malet,* Delhi, 1964.

_____________ , *Schedule Tribes Commission. Report,* New Delhi, 1961.

_____________ , *Study Group on Relief on Indebtedness, Land Alienation and Restoration in Tribal Development Agency Areas. Report.* New Delhi, 1974.

_____________ , *Task Force on Development of Tribal Areas. Report.* New Delhi, 1973.

Indian Institute of Public Administration. *New Challenges in Administration.* New Delhi: Indian Institute of Public Administration, 1972.

____________ , *Study of Committees and Commissions Appointed by the Government of India for Tribal Welfare in Post-Independent India.* New Delhi: Indian Institute of Public Administration, 1979.

Indian Journal of Public Administration—Special Number—State Administration in India, July-Sept., 1976, Vol. XXII, No.3, New Delhi.

____________ , Special Number-Development of Backward Area, July-Sept., 1988, Vol. XXIII, No.3, New Delhi.

International Bank for reconstruction and development. *Report of the World Bank in Aid India Consortium.* Paris, 1971.

Jacob, K.K. Personnel Management in India, S.J.C. Publications, P.O. Box 60, Udaipur-313001, 1973.

Jahoda, Marie. Morton Deutsch and Surat W. Cook. *Research Methods in Social Relations.* New York: Dryden Press, 1951.

Jain, C.M. *Dynamics of Development Administration: An Enquiry into the Office of Vikas Adhikari.* Delhi: Research Publications, 1978.

Jain, S.C. *Agricultural Planning in India.* Delhi: Metropolitan, 1964.

Jaiswal, N.K. *Problems of Agricultural Extension among the Sauria Paharias of the Rajmahal Hills,* Sabour: Bihar Agricultural College, 1957.

Jones, P.E.R. The administration of development planning in traditional societies: three basic concepts. *New Zealand Journal of Public Administration, 33:2* (March, 1971) 66-74.

Kabra, Kamal Narayan. *Land Reforms and Industrialisation: Some Institutional Linkages and their Implications.* New Delhi: Indian Institute of Public Administration, 1978.

Kamat, G.S.: New Dimensions of Cooperative Movement, 1978-Himalaya Publishing House, Bombay.

Kamra, Pawan K. Cooperative Management, Practices, Problems and Prospects, Deep and Deep Publications, New Delhi, 1987.

Katz D. and Kalm, R.L., The Social Psychology of Organisation, Willy Eastern Private Ltd., New Delhi, 1970.

Kautilya, Arthashastra (Translated by R., Shamasastry), 1956, Raghuveer Printing Press, Mysore.

Kayastha, S.L. *The Himalayan Beas Basin: A Study in Habitat, Economy and Society.* Varanasi: Banaras Hindu University, 1964.

______________ , Gaddis of Dhauladhar—A study in human ecology. *National Geographical Journal of India,* 3:2 (1957).

Khan, Ziauddin; Sinha, V.M. and Trivedi, K.D., State Administration in Rajasthan, Asia Publishing House, Jaipur, 1973.

Khosla, J.N. Development administration—new dimensions. *Indian Journal of Public Administration, 13:1* (January-March, 1967) 16-31.

Kindleberger, Charles P. *Economic Development.* New York: McGraw-Hill, 1965.

Krishnamachari, V.T., 'Problems of District Administration' (Part II), 1962.

Kulkarni, M.G., 'Problems of Tribal Development', Parimal Prakashan, Aurangabad, 1974.

Kumbhar, B.L. 'Transforming tribal agriculture'. *Yojana,* 22:17 (16 September, 1978) 5-8.

La Palombra. Joseph (ed.). *Bureaucracy and Political Development.* Princeton (N.J.), Princeton University Press, 1973.

Lal, Shyam, 'Education among Tribals', Printwell Publishers, Jaipur, 1987.

Latif, J.A.A., Training for Management, Sterling Publishers Pvt. Ltd., New Delhi-110 016, 1977.

Lee, Hann-Been and Abelaroog Samonte. *Administrative Reforms in Asia.* Manila: Eastern Regional Organisation for Public Administration, 1970.

Lekha Vig., July, 1985—Published by Lekha Vig Sahayak Sansthan, Jaipur.

Lyotard J.F., *The Postmodern Condition,* trans., G. Bennington and B. Massumi (Manchester, 1994), p. XXV.

Maciver R.M. *Society: A Textbook of Sociology.* New York: Macmillan, 1950.

Maheshwari, Dr. S.R., The Administrative Reforms Commission, Laxmi Narian Agrawal, Agra, 1972.

______________ , Indian Administration, Orient Longmans Ltd., 3/5 Asaf Ali Road, New Delhi- 110001, 1974.

Majumdar, D.N. *Himalayan Polyandry: Structure, Functioning and Cultural Change: A Field Study of Jaunsar-Bawar* Bombay: Asia, 1962.

Malhotra, I.D. A tribe of the Western Himalayas: the semi-nomadic gaddis of Dhauladhar. *Scottish Geographical Magazine, 1935.*

Mamoria, C.B., Personnel Management, Himalaya Publishing House, Bombay-400004, 1980.

Mandelbaum, David G. "Anthropology and the Challenges of

development". Presented in the plenary session of 10th International Congress on Anthropological and Ethnological Sciences held at New Delhi, December 10-16, 1978.

Marglin, S. *Public Investment Criteria: Benefit-Cost Analysis for Planned Economic Growth.* London: Allen & Unwin 1967.

Matheson, Ross. *People Development and Developing Countries.* London: Associated Business Programmes, 1978.

Mathur, Hari Mohan (Ed.) Development Administration in Tribal Areas—The H.C.M. State Institute of Public Administration, Jaipur, 1976.

________________ , (ed.). *Development Administration in Tribal Areas.* Jaipur: HCM State institute of Public Administration, 1976.

Mathur, J.S. : Tribal Development Administration; Perspective on Tribal Development and Administration, Hyderabad, 1976.

Mathur, Kuldip. 'Policies and implementation of land reforms in India'. Paper presented at the Seminar on Policies and Implementation of Land Reforms Organised by the Asian and Pacific Development Administration Centre, Kuala Lumpur. Malaysia, September 11-20, 1978.

McCurdy, Howard E. *Public Administration: A Synthesis.* Mexio Park, Clifo: Cummings, 1977.

Megginson, Leon C. *Personnel and Human Resources Administration.* Homewood: Richard D. Irwin, 1977.

Mehta, Om. *Education for Scheduled Castes and Scheduled Tribes.* New Delhi. Ministry of Home Affairs, 1976.

Misra, Dr. N.L., Responsive Administration, Amar Jyoti Publications, Jaipur, 1989.

Montgomery, John D. and Stiffen, Wiliam J. (Eds): 'Approaches to Development: Politics, Administration and Change', New York, 1966.

________________ , (eds.). *Approaches to Development, Politics, Administration and Change.* New York: McGraw-Hill, 1966.

Mundle, Sudipto. Developing backward areas: Some questions concerning strategy. *Indian Journal of Public Administration,* 23:3 (July-September 1977) 470-9.

Mushkin, S. Health programming in developing nations. *International Development Review,* 6:1 (March 1964) 7-12.

Muthayya, B.C. and I. Gnanakannan. *Development Personnel: a Psycho-Social Study Across Three States in India.* Hyderabad: National Institute of Community Development, 1973.

Muttalib, M.A. *Development Administration in Rural Government for Agricultural Production.* Hyderabad: Osmania University, 1973.

______________ , The mileu of rural bureaucracy. *Journal of the Society for Study of State Governments,* 6:4 (October-December 1973) 199-209.

Myrdal, Gunnar. *Asian Drama: An Enquiry into the Poverty of Nations.* London: Lane, 1968.

National Institute of Community Development. *Integrated Tribal Development Planning: Papers and Proceedings of Seminar held at the NICD, Hyderabad. May* 2-4, 1965. Hyderabad: National Institute of Community Development, 1975.

______________ , *Perspective on Tribal Development and Administration: Proceedings of the Workshop held at the NICD.* 18-20 April 1974. Hyderabad: National Institute for Community Development, 1975.

Negi, T.S. *Scheduled Tribes of Himachal Pradesh: A Profile.* Simla: the author, 1976.

Nurkse, R. *Problems of Capital Formulation in Underdeveloped Countries.* London: Oxford University Press, 1953.

Pai Panandiker, V.A. *Personnel System for Development Administration.* Bombay: Popular Prakashan, 1966.

Pamecha, Dr. (Mrs.) Renuka: Elite in a Tribal Society, 1985, Printwell Publishers, Jaipur.

Panandiker, Dr. V.A. Pai (Programme Director): Personnel Administration, Report of Conference on A.R.C. recommendations—The Indian Institute of Public Administration, New Delhi, 1970.

______________ , Pai: Development Administration in India, Mac-Millan Company of India, Madras, 1974.

Pande, Ram: *Tribals Movement*, Shodak, Jaipur, 1984

Pandit, C.S. Himachal Pradesh. *Illustrated Weekly of India,* (1973 Annual Number) 132-5.

Panse, V.G. and P.V. Sukhtame. *Statistical Methods for Agricultural Workers.* New Delhi: Indian Council of Agricultural Research, 1954.

Parmar, Y.S. *Polyandry in the Himalayas.* Delhi: Vikas, 1975.

Parsons, Earnest C. Administration and development: new tasks in the new age. *Enterprise, 6* (February 1972).

Patel, M.L. Land problems of scheduled tribes in India. *Economic Studies,* 16:3 (September-October 1975) 162-4.

Patnaik, N. and S. Bose. *An Integrated Tribal Development Plan for Keonjhar District, Orissa.* Hyderabad: National Institute of Community Development, 1976.

Pfiffner, J.M. and F.P. Sherwood, *Administrative Organisation.* Englewood Cliffs (N.J.) Prentice Hall, 1960.

Pigors, Paul and Charles A. Myers. *Personnel Administration: A Point of View and a Method.* New York: McGraw-Hill, 1973.

Pragati Prativedan of R.T.A.D.C.F. for the year 1986-87 (Up to April, 87) Rajasthan Tribal Areas Development Cooperative Federation Ltd., Udaipur, May, 1987.

____________ 1985-86 R.T.A.D.C.F. Ltd., Udaipur, 1987.

Punjab. Hutchinson J. *et al. Chamba State Gazetteers,* 1909-13, 22. Lahore, 1910.

____________, Revenue Department. *The Punjab Land Administration Manual,* compiled by James Mc Douie. Dhandigarh 1972.

Quraishi, M.A. Tribal development in the Fifth Plan. *Kurukshetra,* 23:1 (10 October, 1974) 13-15.

Rai, K.N. Growth and stagnation of Indian industrial development. *Economic and Political Weekly,* 1976, Annual Number)

Ramchandran, Padma (Ed.) Issues in Public Administration, Oxford and IBH Publishing Co., New Delhi, 1986.

Report of the Working Group on Development of Scheduled Tribes During Seventh Five Year Plan (1985-90), Government of India Press, Ring Road, New Delhi-110064.

Riggs, Fred W. (ed.). *Frontiers of Development Administration.* Durham: Duke University Press, 1970.

____________, *The Ecology of Public Administration.* Bombay-Asia, 1961.

____________, *Administration in Developing Countries: The Theory of Prismatic Society.* Boston: Houghton Mifflin, 1964.

Roat, Harish Chandra: Tribal Settlement System and Development Strategy, Himanshu Publications, Udaipur and New Delhi, 1987.

Rowat, D.C. (ed.). *Basic Issues in Public Administration.* New York: Macmillan, 1961.

Sachdeva, Dr. D.R.: Social Welfare Administration in India U.G.C. Sponsored Project, Kitab Mahal, 22-A, Sarojini Naidu Marg, Allahabad, 1992 (First Edition).

Sahay, B.N. *Pragmatism in Development: Application of Anthropology.* New Delhi: Bookhive, 1969.

Saptarn Varshik Prativedan and Accounts for the years 1983-84 and 1984-85 R.T.A.D.C.F. Ltd., Udaipur, 1987.

Saxena, Pradeep: Personnel Administration and Management, Rupa Printers, Jaipur-302003, 1987.

Schedule of Delegation of Powers to Officers in RTADCF Ltd., Udaipur, 1976.

Schneier, Craig Eric and Richard W. Beatty. *Personnel Administration Today: Readings and Commentary.* Reading (Mass.): Addison-Wesley, 1978.

Schultz, Theodre O. *The Economic Value of Education.* New York: Columbia University Press, 1963.

Sen, A.K. *Choice of Techniques: An Aspect of the Theory of Planned Economic Development.* Bombay: Oxford University Press, *1962.*

Sen, L. K., *Planning Rural Growth Centres for Integrated Area Development: A Study in Miryalguda Taluka.* Hyderabad: National Institute of Community Development, 1971.

____________, The role of Rural Electrification Corporation in the development of backward Areas. *Indian Journal Of Public Administration,* 23:3 (July-September, 1977) 570-8

Sengupta. A.K. Tribal welfare in India: a need for correct approaches. *Social Welfare,* 9:2 (May 1962) 81-2.

Seshadri, K. Co-ordination of development programmes at block level. *Indian Journal of Public Administration,* 12:1 (January-March 1966) 60-67.

____________, Functioning of the block development in relation to agriculture. *Indian Journal of Public Administration,* 13:1 (January-March 1967) 65-99.

____________, *Political Linkage and Rural Development.* New Delhi: National, 1976.

Seventh Five Year Plan (1985-90) Vol. 1-Govt. of India, Planning Commission, New Delhi, 1985.

Seventh Five Year Plan for Tribal Development in Rajasthan (1985-90) including Annual Plan for 1985-86, Vol.1, Tribal Areas Development Department, Government of Rajasthan, Udaipur, 1985.

Shafritz, Jay M. *et. al. Personnel Management in Government: Politics and Process.* New York: Marcel Dekker, 1978.

Sharkansky, Ira, Public *Administration: Policy Making in Government Agencies.* Chicago: Rand McNally, 1978.

Sharma, B.D. Administration for tribal development. *Indian Journal of Public Administration,* 23:3 (July-September 1977) 515-39.

____________, Economic development of extremely backward tribal regions. *Indian Anthropologist,* 3 (1973).

____________, Environmental context and its implications on the personnel policies. *Indian Journal of Public Administration,* 22:1 (January-March 1976) 24-47.

__________, *Legislative Powers about Tribal Areas.* New Delhi: Ministry of Home Affairs, 1978 (Occasional Papers On Tribal Development, on. 25).

__________, *Micro-level Planning for Full Employment in Tribal Areas.* New Delhi: Ministry of Home Affairs, 1979 (Occasional Papers on Tribal Development).

__________, *Planning for Educational Development in Tribal Areas.* New Delhi: Ministry of Home Affairs, 1976 (Occasional Papers on Tribal Development).

__________, Planning from below, with special reference to tribal areas. *Community Development and Panchayati Raj Digest,* 8:1 (July 1976) 19-29.

__________, *Tribal Development: A Brief Review.* Bhopal: Tribal Development and Research Institute, 1978.

__________, Administration for Tribal Development, 1977, Government of India Press, Ring Road, New Delhi-110 064.

__________, Administration for Tribal Development, The Indian Journal of Public Administration-Special Number-Development of Backward Areas-July-September, 1977, Vol. XXIII, No.3, New Delhi.

Sharma, L.R. Development problems of a hill region, with special reference to Himachal Pradesh *AICC Economic Review,* 18:5 (15 September 1966) 33-5.

Sharma, M.P., Public Administration in Theory and Practice (4th Edn.), Kitab Mahal Pvt. Ltd., Zero Road, Allahabad, 1963

Sharma, R.D. (Ed.), Development Administration in a Changing Society, National Book Organisation, New Delhi, 1987.

Sharma, R.N. and Bakshi, Santosh: Tribes and Tribal Movement, Uppal Publishing House, New Delhi, 1984.

Sharma, S.K., Development Administration in India; Theory and Practice, Jullunder, 1971.

Sharma, Sudesh Kumar (ed.). *Dynamics of Development: An International Perspective.* Delhi: Concept, 1978.

__________, *Deputy Commissioner in Punjab.* New Delhi: Indian Institute of Public Administration, 1971.

__________, *Development Administration: Theory and Practice.* Jullundur: International Book Company, 1971.

Sharp, Walter R., Field Administration in the United Nations System, London, 1961.

Shashi, S.S. *Himachal-Nature's Peaceful Paradise.* Delhi: Indian, School Supply Depot, 1971.

Sikula, Andrew F. *Personnel Administration and Human Resources Management.* New York: John Wiley, 1976.

Singh, B.P. and Chhabra, J.N., Essentials of Management, Kitab Mahal, 15, Thornhill Road, Allahabad, 1979.

Singh, Charan. Notes on Indian economy. Seminar on Economic Policy Options held at the Indian Institute of Public Administration, New Delhi, September 24-25, 1977.

Singh, J.P. and Was, N.N., Tribal Development: Past Efforts and New Challenges: M.L.V. Tribal Research and Training Institute; Tribal Areas Development Department, Rajasthan, Udaipur, 1987.

Singh, K. Suresh (ed.). *Tribal Situation in India: proceedings of a seminar,* Simla: Indian Institute of Advanced Study, 1974.

Singh, N.K. *Dimensions of Personnel Management.* New Delhi: Samkallen Prakashan, 1973.

Singh, Sundra Rani : Urban Planning in India—A Case Study of Urban Improvement Trusts, Ashish Publishing House, H-12, Rajouri Garden, New Delhi-1 10027, 1979.

Singh, Tarlok, *India's Development Experience.* New Delhi: Macmillan, 1972.

Singh, Y.P. *Peoples Response to Soil Conservation in two Damodar Valley Villages.* Sabour: Bihar Agricultural College, 1960.

Sinha, V.M., Personnel Administration, Concepts and Comparative Perspective, R.B.S.A. Publishers, Jaipur-302003, 1986.

Sixth Annual General Body Meeting Proceedings (5.12.86) of R.T.A.D.C.F.—R.T.A.D.C.F. Ltd., Udaipur, 1986.

Sixth Varshik Prativedan and Accounts for the year 1981-82 and 1982-83—R.T.A.D.C.F. Ltd., Udaipur, 1985.

Srikant, L.M. Tribal welfare. *Indian* 14:4 (March-May 1954) 360-87.

Stahl, O. Glenn. *Public Personnel Administration.* New York: Harper & Row, 1962.

Stiliman, Richard J. *Public Administration, Concepts and Cases.* Boston: Houghton-Mifflin, 1976.

Stone, Donald C. Tasks. Precedents and approaches to education for development administration. In International Institute of Administrative Sciences, Education for Development Administration: a symposium. Brussels, HAS, 1966, 19-41.

Swerdlow, Irving. *Development Administration: Concepts and Problems.* Syracuse University Press, 1963.

Thavaraj, M.J.K., Financing Management of Government, Sultan Chand and Sons, New Delhi, 1978.

The Collector in the nineteen sixties. *Indian Journal of Public Administration, 11:3* (July-September *1965,* Special Number) 345-668.

The Constitution of India—Publication by Ministry of Law and Justice, Govt. of India, New Delhi, 1986.

Toppo, Sita. *Dynamics of Educational Development in Tribal India.* New Delhi: Classical Publications, 1979.

Tribal Area Sub-Plan Annual Development Programme, 1987-88 of Gujarat State, 1987—Issued by Tribal Development Department, Govt. of Gujarat, Gandhinagar.

Tripathi, P.C., Personnel Management, Sultan Chand and Sons, New Delhi-110002, 1983.

Trivedi, Harshad R. Salient features of tribal administration in states. *Indian Journal of Public Administration,* 22:3 (July-September, 1977) 430-8.

Tyagi, A.R., Public Administration, Atma Ram and Sons, Educational Publishers and Book Sellers, Kashmiri Gate, Delhi-6, 1983.

United Nations, *Report of the Conference on the Application of Science and Technology for the Benefit of the Less Developed Areas.* New York, 1963.

______________, *Development Administration: Current Approaches and Trends in Public Administration in National Development.* New York, 1975.

Uphoff, Norman. An analytical model of process and performance for developing indicators of administrative capability. *Philippine Journal of Public Administration,* 17:3 (1973).

Vajpey, S.C. Industrial promotion in backward areas: role of specialised financial institutions. *Indian Journal of Public Administration,* 23:3 (July-September, 1977) 629-52.

Varshik Prashasnik Prativedan, 1986-87—Tribal Areas Development Department, Rajasthan, Udaipur, 1987.

______________, 1987-88—T.A.D. Dept., Rajasthan, Udaipur (1988)

______________, 1988-89 T.A.D. Dept., Rajasthan, Udaipur (1989)

______________, 1989-90 T.A.D. Dept., Rajasthan, Udaipur (1990)

______________, 1990-91 T.A.D. Dept., Rajasthan, Udaipur (1991)

______________, 1991-92 T.A.D. Dept., Rajasthan, Udaipur (1992)

Vasudevan, R. Hill area development: problems and strategies. *Kurukshetra,* 23:1 (1 October, 1974) 11-12.

Vepa, Ram K. Implementing development programmes. *Indian Journal of Public Administration,* 20:1 (January-March, 1974) 257-92.

Verma, S.P. and Sharma, S.K. (Volume Editors): Development Administration., Indian Institute of Public Administration, Indraprastha Estate, Ring Road, New Delhi, 1984.

Vidyarthi, L.P. (ed.). *Anthropology and Tribal Welfare in India.* Ranchi: Bihar University, 1959.

_______________, Tribal Development and its Administration, Concept Publishing Company, New Delhi, 1986.

_______________, and B.K. Rai. *The Tribal Culture of India.* Delhi: Concept, 1977.

_______________, Problems and Prospects of tribal development in India. *Indian Anthropologist,* 2:2 (1973).

_______________, Tribal development in independent India and its future. *Man in India,* 54:1 (January-March, 1974) 45-72.

Wimmick, Charles: Dictionary of Anthropology, London, 1957.

Wood, W. Development administration: an objection. *Indian Journal of Public Administration,* 13:4 (October-December, 1967) 702-15.

Wright, Waldo D.: The Study of Public Administration, New York, Random House, 1961.

Index